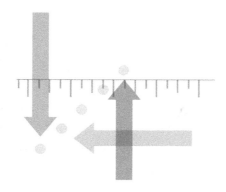

A Guide to
Assessing
Needs

A Guide to Assessing Needs

Essential Tools for Collecting
Information, Making Decisions,
and Achieving Development Results

Ryan Watkins
Maurya West Meiers
Yusra Laila Visser

 THE WORLD BANK

1 2 3 4 14 13 12 11

This volume is a product of the staff of The World Bank with external contributions. The findings, interpretations, and conclusions expressed in this volume do not necessarily reflect the views of The World Bank, its Board of Executive Directors, or the governments they represent.

The World Bank does not guarantee the accuracy of the data included in this work. The boundaries, colors, denominations, and other information shown on any map in this work do not imply any judgment on the part of The World Bank concerning the legal status of any territory or the endorsement or acceptance of such boundaries.

ISBN (paper): 978-0-8213-8868-6
ISBN (electronic): 978-0-8213-8901-0
DOI: 10.1596/978-0-8213-8868-6

Library of Congress Cataloging-in-Publication Data

Watkins, Ryan.
    A guide to assessing needs : essential tools for collecting information, making decisions, and achieving development results / by Ryan Watkins, Maurya West Meiers, Yusra Visser.
        p. cm.
    Includes bibliographical references and index.
    ISBN 978-0-8213-8868-6 (alk. paper) — ISBN 978-0-8213-8901-0
(electronic : alk. paper)
    1. Economic development projects—Evaluation.   2. Economic development projects—Planning.   3. Organizational effectiveness—Evaluation.
4. Employees—Training of—Evaluation.   I. West Meiers, Maurya, 1967–
II. Visser, Yusra Laila.   III. Title.
    HD75.9.W38 2011
    338.91068′4—dc23
                                                                                2011039603

Cover design: Naylor Design

CONTENTS

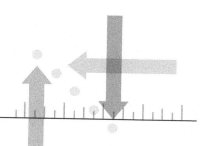

Figures

Tables

A Guide to Assessing Needs

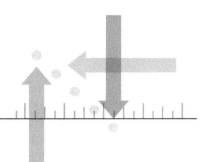

PREFACE. OUR VALUE PROPOSITION

The earliest decisions that lead to development projects (or programs) are among the most critical in determining long-term success. This phase of project development transforms exciting ideas into project proposals, thereby setting the stage for a variety of actions that will eventually lead (if all goes well) to desirable results. From deciding to propose a sanitation project in South Asia to selecting approaches that strengthen school management in South America, those early decisions are the starting place of development results.

Needs assessments support this earliest phase of project development with proven approaches to gathering information and making justifiable decisions. This book, in turn, is your guide to assessing needs and then making essential decisions about what to do next. You will find that this book—filled with practical strategies, tools, and guides—covers both large-scale, formal needs assessments and less-formal assessments that guide daily decisions. Included in the book is a blend of rigorous methods and realistic tools that can help you make informed and reasoned decisions. Together, these methods and tools offer a comprehensive, yet realistic, approach to identifying needs and selecting among alternative ways as you go forward.

The early phase of project or program development is challenging, even for the most seasoned professionals. The phase sometimes begins with a noteworthy change (such as a natural disaster or the ambitions of a new government) or a request (such as when a ministry official asks for help to achieve mandated results). But more often than not, the concepts that lead to significant accomplishments come out of simple conversations (such as those that take place almost every day in the offices of government or development agencies). The concept—sometimes a question, sometimes an identified need, and sometimes a potential solution—is thereby the precursor to decisions that lead to actions and activities that, we hope, lead to results.

Among the critical early decisions of development projects are considerations of establishing essential partnerships, funding opportunities, being aware of potential unintended consequences, and building capacity to achieve results. Aligning these early decisions with the results to be accomplished often sets the stage for future success. Needs assessments provide the structure and tools to collect information and to guide these (and other) important decisions.

Written in what we believe to be a sensible format, this book makes it easy for you to quickly refer to the essential tools that you want while planning and conducting your next needs assessment—or while making your next decision. The book has no long chapters or complex formulas—just adaptive resources that give you the flexibility to use them to accomplish results within your context.

Sections 1 and 2 offer quick, yet full, answers to many frequently asked questions regarding how to make justifiable decisions. Next, section 3 examines a variety of tools and techniques that can be used for both collecting information and making decisions. Appendix A then offers a number of checklists and guides for managing the systematic assessment processes that lead to quality decisions. Finally, the reference list at the end of the book is a valuable resource to research, tools, and discussions of needs assessment.

Collectively, the book represents a unique—and useful—resource for development professionals. The book is intended to be a user's guide, leading you from an initial concept to a decision about what to do next. Whether you are making decisions about how to improve the capacity of ministry employees or choosing which infrastructure project will best achieve desired development goals, conducting needs assessments can lead to better and more informed decisions. This book offers a variety of needs assessment tools that can strengthen your decisions across numerous contexts.

Note: For the convenience of our readers, copies of the individual tools are available and can be downloaded as single PDF files at http://www.needs assessment.org.

ACKNOWLEDGMENTS

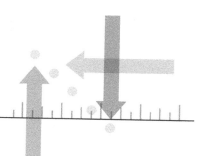

We would like to express our appreciation and gratitude for the encouragement, contributions, and patience that we have received from our spouses and families throughout the development of this book. We would especially like to thank the following for their support: Christina Gee, Jordan Gee, Ryder Gee, Don Meiers, and Ray Amirault.

We would also like to thank our colleagues who have contributed ideas that became part of this book, including Roger Kaufman, James Altschuld, Patrick Grasso, Michael Bamberger, Samuel Otoo, Joy Behrens, and Violaine Le Rouzic. For their excellent work on the production and editing of this book, we thank Stephen McGroarty, Cindy Fisher, and Nora Ridolfi of the World Bank Office of the Publisher and Barbara Hart of Publications Professionals.

Finally, we would like to thank the many participants in our courses and workshops who have, over the years, helped us develop our ideas and have provided the real world challenges that pushed us to further refine our thinking.

About the World Bank Institute Capacity Development and Results Practice (WBICR)

WBICR provides advisory services, knowledge products, action research, and knowledge sharing that inform and support the design and management of results-focused capacity development strategies, policies, and programs. For more information, email capacity4change@worldbank.org.

ABOUT THE AUTHORS

Ryan Watkins, Ph.D., is an associate professor at the George Washington University in Washington, DC. He is an author of several books, including the *Handbook for Improving Performance in the Workplace*, Vol. 2: *Selecting and Implementing Performance Interventions*, co-edited with Doug Leigh (2010); *Performance by Design: The Systematic Selection, Design, and Development of Performance Technologies That Produce Useful Results* (2007); *75 e-Learning Activities: Making Online Learning Interactive* (2005); and the best-selling *e-Learning Companion: A Student's Guide to Online Success*, co-authored with Mike Corry (2010).

In addition, he has co-authored two other books on planning and more than 90 articles on instructional design, strategic planning, needs assessment, distance education, and performance technology. In 2005, Watkins was a visiting scientist with the National Science Foundation. He has consulted with the World Bank since 2003, including work in China and the Lao People's Democratic Republic. For more information, please visit http://www.ryanrwatkins.com or http://www.needsassessment.org.

Maurya West Meiers is an evaluation officer with the World Bank Institute (WBI). She has been a team leader of a monitoring and evaluation (M&E) training program at WBI and has trained government professionals in Europe, Asia, and Latin America about M&E and needs assessment topics. As a World Bank employee, she has provided M&E and needs assessment advisory services to government agency employees across a range of areas and sectors, including municipal services, infrastructure projects, primary and secondary education, social protection, and health. Most recently, she has provided needs assessment training and advisory services for government ministries in China and the Lao People's Democratic Republic. She holds a master's degree in international affairs (specializing in economics) and a second master's degree in education, both from the George Washington University.

Yusra Laila Visser, Ph.D., is a faculty member at Florida Atlantic University and coordinates the Digital Education Teacher's Academy. The academy is a K-20 collaboration between Florida Atlantic University and Broward County, one of the largest school districts in the United States. Previously, Visser held positions as assistant professor in instructional technology at Florida Atlantic University and at Wayne State University. She was project manager for a major distance learning initiative at Florida State University and program associate for International Programs at Education Development Center.

As a consultant, Visser has served clients including the U.S. Department of Homeland Security, the Netherlands Ministry of Foreign Affairs, the U.S. Navy, the World Bank, and the United Nations. Her doctorate degree is in instructional systems from Florida State University.

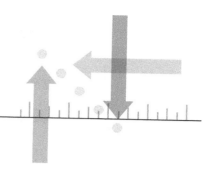

Introduction

What Is This Book About?

In short, this book is about making informed and justifiable decisions—decisions that achieve development results. More specifically, they are decisions that move you, your agency or institution, or entire nations from achieving current results to accomplishing desired results.

From deciding which computer to buy, to determining how to improve the performance capacity of a government ministry, numerous decisions must be made every day. Many are routine; others are extraordinary. Some are complex; some are rather straightforward. At times, the decision is yours alone, or it may require collaboration with partners or clients. Some decisions are guided by policies, others by laws, others by traditions, and still others are unique to the situation. Regardless of the characteristics, all of us make decisions that sometimes lead to useful results. At other times—well, most of us would rather not talk about those other times when our decisions led to less-than-desirable results.

Making good decisions about what to do is not easy, nor should it be taken for granted. All of us must continually work on improving our ability to make quality decisions as we study and reflect on what leads up to our making a decision and taking action. The change may come through coaching by a mentor or attending a training course. You may improve your decisions after listening to an audiobook or observing the decisions of a colleague. The management section of any bookstore is filled with books on how to improve decisions in the workplace just as the self-help section is filled with volumes on how to improve decisions in your personal life.

Yet, no matter what we are doing to improve our decisions, we make decisions each day. Most of us are already using a variety of activities to inform our decisions before we jump into action. Leading up to the actual decision and the resulting action, such activities are the precursors that typically define the quality of the decision-making process, as well as the decision itself. From our reviewing lessons learned in previous projects to interviewing community members, numerous techniques can be used in the hours, days, or months leading up to a decision. Likewise, you can use numerous tools to facilitate the actual making of a decision—either an individual or a group decision.

No ideal and widely accepted term captures the breadth and depth of the activities leading to a decision, though much of the academic literature refers to them as "needs assessments" (a term that we will also use in this book to describe the group of activities that lead up to decisions that result in actions). Do not get hung up on the specifics of the term, however. The concepts behind needs assessment are far more important to improving the quality of decisions than the possible carry-over conceptions (or misconceptions) that you may have from previous encounters with the term.

As precursors to taking action, needs assessment concepts are likely already familiar to almost everyone. At the shopping mall or hardware store, for instance, informal needs assessments guide our comparisons, thus leading us to select the products and brands that will best help us achieve our desired results. Likewise, a more formal needs assessment will guide our decision in the workplace, thereby helping us manage complex choices about what actions should be taken to accomplish results.

From the mundane, such as selecting a new coffee vendor, to the imperative, such as prioritizing the needs of indigenous people affected by a dam-building project, informed and justifiable decisions rely on the results of formal and informal needs assessments. Those assessments are actually so integrated into our daily lives that we frequently fail to recognize them as part of our decision-making process. In addition, we often forget that numerous tools, techniques, and guides are available to help us collect information—and then make informed decisions based on that information.

Needs assessments offer value by providing logical and disciplined methods for collecting useful information and making decisions based on that information. Needs assessments are often done before any action has been taken (as with an assessment to define the needs of a community before a development loan is requested), although at other times a needs assessment is done to provide strategic direction to activities that are already planned (as with an assessment to define the desired outcomes and objectives of an infrastructure development grant). At still other times, needs assessments are done to inform decisions within the context of larger projects (as with an assessment to identify the results required in local jurisdictions to achieve the objectives of an ongoing national initiative). In all cases, the needs assessment offers a careful process for assessing gaps between current results and desired results (that is, needs) and then for applying that information to identify the available options so that decisions can be made.

As a precursor to decision making, needs assessments are unlike many other strategic processes. They require a performance perspective that focuses on the results to be accomplished—unlike the more common (and flawed) decision-making processes that focus on solutions or activities to be undertaken (see box I.1). Selecting solutions or activities is obviously part of making decisions, but the decisions should be based on a clear definition of the performance gap and should be chosen on the basis of criteria rather than assumptions.

Processes such as building roads, outsourcing, training teachers, reforming policies, taking loans, or using community participation and thousands of others are activities or solutions (often, solutions in search of problems). Many times initially preferred activities will contribute to solving, or indeed will solve, our problems, but we have insufficient basis for knowing this or for justifying our decisions without some form of predecison assessment. A needs assessment is, in response, a process for clarifying what results must be accomplished and then assessing the potential value of numerous alternative solutions to make an informed and reasonable decision.

Who Can Benefit from This Book?

This book will benefit people and teams involved in planning and decision making. On the basis of their pragmatic value in guiding decisions, needs assessments are used in various professions and settings—from emergency rooms to corporate boardrooms—to guide decision making. Nonetheless, although needs assessments have many different applications, we focus in this book on needs assessments as they are applied in organizations to accomplish results, as opposed to their use in personal decisions or medical triage.

Needs assessments are conducted in many diverse organizations, from steel mills to financial services firms, and their tools can be applied in private sector businesses, government ministries, municipality agencies, local nonprofit institutions, and organizations of all varieties. However, through discussion and examples, this book more specifically focuses on how needs assessments are applied in relation to international development efforts in the public sector (for instance, reducing poverty, improving access to clean water, or addressing gender inequality). This context offers many realistic and pragmatic opportunities to illustrate how various needs assessment steps, tools, techniques, and guides can be used to collect valuable information, to make informed decisions, to achieve results, and to have a positive influence on the lives of people around the world.

People who can benefit from needs assessments could be community leaders and policy makers who oversee decision-making processes and implementation. Agency employees or contractors who design and implement projects can also benefit from building needs assessments into their routine planning processes. Monitoring and evaluation practitioners or auditors can use needs assessments to measure and track results. Community members and other project stakeholders can and should also be involved in needs assessment processes—typically as informants, but increasingly as joint decision makers with policy makers.

To illustrate, when initiating plans to address education improvement issues in a community, policy makers and education system leaders should not limit decision making to their own internal committees. Instead, they should encourage the use of needs assessment processes to gather and gain information about prioritized areas for improvement (and a range of other decision topics) from a host of individuals and groups: parent-teacher committees, individual parents from different socioeconomic or ethnic backgrounds, principals, teachers, education researchers, students, businesspeople, and others. Having a participatory approach to data gathering and decision making—although not trouble-free—can contribute to more informed and better decisions for the community and to increased acceptance of final decisions by stakeholders.

There are, of course, many interesting theories that inform the needs assessment literature and many models that try to link individual decisions to international development outcomes. To us, as authors of this book, such theories and models are both exciting and interesting. But we recognize that most readers want us to synthesize all of that information into practical tools that can be used to achieve results. Therefore, what you will find abundant in our book are the steps, tools, techniques, guides, and checklists that you can apply. In sections 1 and 2, we answer general questions you may have about needs assessments with short, straightforward responses. Then in section 3 and appendix A, we equip you with the tools to make informed decisions and to manage the process.

This book is about accomplishing results—focusing on the practical use of needs assessments as the starting place for making knowledgeable and justifiable decisions. Our goal is not to make you an expert in the application of any particular tool or technique; rather, we introduce each approach, describe its strengths and weaknesses in terms of needs assessment applications, provide an overview of what the process could look like in your organization, and then offer a variety of resources where you can learn more.

It should be noted that, although we refer to "you" throughout this book, most needs assessments are actually conducted as a team effort. James Altschuld has written extensively about this collaboration in his *Needs Assessment Kit*, a series of five books on how to organize, develop, and manage "needs assessment committees." You may be the leader of such a team or committee, or you may be a contributing member. In either case, your participation in the needs assessment can be guided by the tools found throughout our book.

Why Should I Care about Needs Assessments?

You must make decisions. Needs assessments can help improve the quality of those decisions—thus leading to improvements in performance and the accomplishment of desired results.

Improving results—that is, moving from current to desired performance—is typically a worthwhile and valuable (and often valiant) effort. Improvement efforts routinely bring about benefits for your organization, and they likewise change lives. After all, improving performance isn't just about improving productivity; it can also lead to increased job satisfaction, longer retention, improved quality of life for employees and others, reduced

Figure I.1   General Performance Improvement Framework

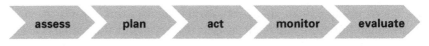

Source: Authors.

stress, new social networks, retained knowledge, creative and innovative thinking, and numerous other benefits that influence the individuals who make up an organization. And the value of improving our ability to achieve results does not end with the organization. Our clients, partners, and society at large can all benefit when we accomplish desired results.

Those beneficial results, however, rarely happen by chance alone. Systematic and continual efforts to improve performance (that is, *results*) are required to ensure success. This book focuses on one critical and foundational process in any performance improvement effort: the needs assessment. The results of your assessment will then guide your subsequent decisions—including the design, implementation, and evaluation of projects and programs that will lead to achieving desired results (see figure I.1).

Throughout this book, you will find guides, tools, and techniques for your needs assessment—no matter how formal or informal your assessment efforts. Section 3 provides two categories of tools and techniques: those used mainly for data collection and those used primarily for decision making. There is no single best way to use the tools or preferred combination of tools, nor should there be. Needs assessments—and the associated tools— are meant to be adaptive, thereby giving you the flexibility to use them to accomplish results within your context.

Many diverse tools may be used to guide your decisions and performance improvement efforts. Use those resources to inform your daily decisions. Use them to weigh your options. Use them to justify complex choices. Use them to *improve performance.*

Improving performance, as we use the term in this book, is the move from achieving current results to accomplishing desired results. Thus, *improving* refers to the measured progress from a less-than-desirable state to a desirable state, whereas *performance* refers to the results—no matter if your organization classifies them as products, outputs, outcomes, impacts, or some combination of these titles. This focus on achieving desirable results guides our approach to needs assessment and its tools. Thus, rather than asking people what they "need," needs assessments more importantly define gaps in results and highlight opportunities to improve performance.

A Guide to Assessing Needs

Figure I.2   Needs Assessment within a Performance Improvement Framework

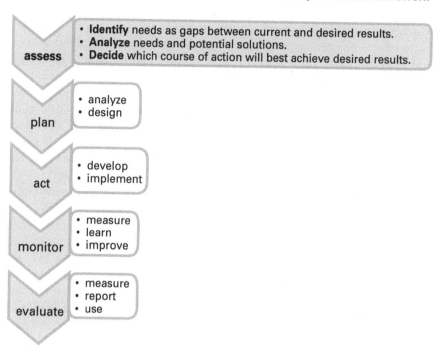

Source: Authors.

Within a performance improvement framework, needs assessments play a critical role in starting the improvement process (see figure I.2). Assessments inform future decisions; at the same time, they are informed by the results of past decisions. Needs assessments thereby link together past and future performance, guiding decisions throughout the improvement effort.

To guide your improvement efforts, we wrote this book in a format that will make it easy for you to quickly refer to the tools that you want while planning and conducting your next needs assessment—or making your next decision. There are no long chapters or complex formulas. With this book, we have tried to create a reference resource for the next time you want to collect and use information to enhance your decisions. Ideally, you will read this book once and then keep it on your shelf for the next time you have an opportunity to complete a needs assessment, to collect information, to make a decision, and to accomplish results. Individual tools are available as single PDF files at http://www.needsassessment.org.

How Will This Book Help Me Collect Information?

Making quality decisions has become a complex, yet daily, task for most of us. In most organizations today, rarely will your decisions be straightforward and clear-cut, or focused solely on short-term, localized results. Complex organizational structures and processes have become mainstream characteristics of businesses and international development organizations alike, from large multinational companies that supply products to worldwide markets to local nongovernmental organization (NGO) offices. At the same time, organizations now rely on employees—at all levels and in all positions—to make quality decisions on a daily (if not hourly) basis, and they no longer leave all of the "important decisions" to senior management.

What started with companies like Nordstrom, a department store chain that empowered front-line employees to make essential business decisions, has now expanded to other organizations as people in all positions are being asked to make difficult choices and challenging decisions. Similar approaches to improving performance have been embraced in the public sector, in both developed and developing countries. Performance matters and is increasingly measured in all sectors. As a consequence, employees throughout the hierarchies of public sector organizations are being asked to make challenging decisions and to perform at certain levels on which they are judged. Hence, as a precursor to high-quality and justifiable decisions intended to accomplish results, the gathering of useful—as well as valid—information is essential for professionals in almost any role, at almost any level, and within all organizations.

Sometimes collecting the useful information for making a quality decision requires only a few informal conversations with your colleagues. But more often than not, the potential long- and short-term consequences of your decisions require that considerable attention be paid to gathering valuable facts, trend data, differing perspectives, and general advice before making an important choice or selection. Whether your decision is related to building infrastructure (such as roads, wells, or information technologies) or to choosing how to best develop the skills of employees on your project team, you make your best decisions when you have practical information.

Accordingly, you should use a diverse range of information-gathering tools and techniques to ensure that you have the essential details for making sound decisions (see boxes I.2 and I.3). Using tools—such as nominal group technique, fishbone diagrams, and guided expert reviews—that are systematic and replicable from one decision to the next provides information that guides, as well as justifies, the complex decisions you routinely make.

Box. I.2 Information-Gathering Tools in Part 3.A

Box I.3 Decision-Making Tools in Part 3.B

How Will This Book Help Me Make Decisions?

In the end, making informed and justifiable decisions about what to do next is the goal of any formal or informal needs assessment. Whether you are deciding on your own or with others, you should apply systematic tools and techniques to analyze, synthesize, and then use valid information in all steps of your decision making (see box I.3).

We provide many tools—such as root cause analysis, fault tree diagrams, and pair-wise comparisons—as resources to ensure that the information you have collected is used to support your decision making. When completing a needs assessment or, for that matter, making almost any decision, you should use information that is from multiple sources and is often collected through a range of techniques and tools, so you can represent varied perspectives. Doing so will ensure that you make the most informed decision possible.

All informed decisions are, of course, not necessarily the "right" decisions, because only time can distinguish the true value of a decision. But more often than not, the results of a decision informed by quality facts will outperform results derived from instinct, political expediency, matters of convenience, or other reasons not always based on evidence.[1]

How Will This Book Help Me Accomplish Results?

Sustainable results are the consequence of organized efforts to make quality decisions, thereby leading to the development of systemic activities that improve accomplishments. Just as you would not benefit from seeing *only* a podiatrist after a heart attack—focusing solely on your feet with no regard for the rest of your body—neither does your organization benefit when single interventions are used to address complex issues. Although you may specialize in providing a particular solution (ranging from irrigation or microfinance to training or economic policy), it is rarely the case that any of those solutions alone will accomplish sustainable improvements in results.

Improving results requires a long-term, systemic perspective. By undertaking this more durable approach, we avoid quick fixes or one-size-fits-all solutions that may not lead us to our desired results. Additionally, this approach shields us from the latest fads, marketing brochures, or new gadgets. Ultimately, we avoid implementing "solutions" in search of problems.

Solutions, interventions, and activities are obviously important so we can accomplish desired results. Strategic plans will not reduce poverty, nor will good ideas feed the hungry. At the same time, building schools, for example, without regard for training teachers, providing meals, building access roads, finding books, and addressing other systemic issues of education also will not achieve sustainable results. Thus, your transition to achieving desired results, not just current ones, requires a holistic approach; and a needs assessment becomes your essential tool for determining what activities should take place within the context of those complex systems.

Too often, especially in relation to international development assistance projects, activities that worked in one country are viewed as solutions to the challenges being faced by other countries half a world away. From freshwater wells to HIV/AIDS interventions, the complex challenges that face developing countries are rarely the same. As a consequence, a needs assessment can help you determine what activities are most appropriate to address the problems in different contexts.

It is important to keep all of your options on the table. Conduct your needs assessments without any preconceived notions about which improvement activities will be most valuable to your organization or your clients. Listen to others inside and outside your institution, maintain an open perspective to creative ideas, and collect information that will justify your recommendations or decisions in the end.[2]

Use the steps of a needs assessment to identify needs and opportunities that are based on facts and information rather than on assumptions. Analyze your needs, weigh the benefits and risks of alternative activities, and then make decisions about what to do next. In other words, decide what results should be accomplished before you determine what processes (building dams, developing local training programs, buying computers, offering microloans, and so on) or combinations of activities will best achieve those results.

This results-focused, systemic approach also helps you distinguish between people's *wants* and *needs*. Both are important, but each offers different information to inform your decisions. Information about *needs* (gaps between current and desired results) is essential for improving performance; after all, you are unlikely to accomplish desired results if you do not know what they are or where your current results stand in relation. At the same time, *wants* typically describe the resources, activities, methods, or solutions that people prefer—or that they perceive as the only option for moving ahead.

The systematic processes of a needs assessment will help guide you through the steps and challenging decisions while (a) balancing *needs* and *wants* and (b) putting results before solutions. The products of your needs assessment are justifications for the many choices you will make along the way, as well as for your decisions on how to proceed in accomplishing desired results.

Why Does This Book Focus on Tools, Techniques, Guides, and Checklists?

Why reinvent the wheel? With little effort, you can find many websites, books, and articles that provide detailed theories, models, and approaches for how a needs assessment can be applied in various professional fields (for examples, see http://www.needsassessment.org). Our goal for this book is, we believe, more practical: provide diverse tools that you can use next week, next month, and next year to achieve results.

Commonly applied needs assessment tools, such as focus groups and web-based surveys, are useful. But they merely scratch the surface of the many tools and techniques that can be used to collect important information to use while making quality decisions. This book is intended to expand our perspectives on what we can do to improve our decisions.

We, the authors, did not invent needs assessment nor did we invent the tools and techniques described in this book. For instance, we did not discover interviews as a technique for gathering information—rather we have translated interview techniques from numerous disciplines into a practical tool for needs assessments.

Likewise, throughout the book, we interpret many theories and models to provide sensible steps, guides, and checklists for conducting a needs assessment—no matter how formal or informal. Although conceptual frameworks and models provide a valuable structure to your needs assessments, assessment planners often feel ill equipped to select among the available tools and then implement the tools successfully. In response, we have "boiled down" the tools to their basics and then have applied them to the numerous and diverse resources available herein. The book will serve (a) as a useful guide for scanning your options when designing a needs assessment and (b) as an introduction to a range of data collection and decision-making tools and resources. To use some of the techniques that we introduce—such as focus groups, which are more difficult to conduct well than many people realize—you should also consult other books that provide more details about such techniques.

The book's introductory sections are a primer on needs assessment, thus answering many of the most frequently asked questions that we hear from clients, colleagues, students, and others. These sections answer questions about when, where, why, and how. Also included is an underlying framework for conducting a successful needs assessment that is based on the theories, models, and frameworks of many leading authors and researchers.[3] With this framework as its foundation, the remainder of the book gives you the practical tools, techniques, and guides to successfully conduct formal or informal needs assessments.

Together, this book's resources help you collect valuable information, guide your decision making, and allow you to accomplish useful results.

Notes

1. Based on Nutt (2008).
2. Research by Nutt (2008) illustrates that the systematic "discovery" decision-making process (that is, needs assessment-based) has significant benefits over (a) the more common "idea-imposition" decision-making process, where predetermined solutions are applied to problems, or (b) the "emerging opportunities" decision-making process, where the first plausible solution is selected and where remaining efforts are used to justify that decision.
3. Including James Altschuld, Thomas Gilbert, Kavita Gupta, Roger Kaufman, Donald Kirkpatrick, Robert Mager, Allison Rossett, Gary Rummler, Catherine M. Sleezer, Belle Ruth Witkin, and many others.

References

Altschuld, James W., ed. 2010. *The Needs Assessment Kit.* Thousand Oaks, CA: Sage Publications.

Nutt, Paul. 2008. "Investigating the Success of Decision-Making Processes." *Journal of Management Studies* 45: 2.

Needs Assessment: Frequently Asked Questions

Introduction

Since the 1960s, needs assessments have become a fairly common business practice. Consequently, the term *needs assessment* has taken on several definitions and has led to a number of related process models or approaches. Gap analysis, needs analysis, and performance analysis are occasionally used as synonyms for *needs assessment*, yet they are more frequently (and more accurately) defined as needs assessment tools.

Other tools—such as strategic planning, focus groups, and multicriteria analysis—have also been borrowed and customized from other disciplines to improve our ability to inform decisions. By applying these (and other) tools, needs assessments have arguably become part of the *science* in the *art and science* of many business decisions.

You have, therefore, probably read needs assessment reports (though potentially not given that title) or even participated in related processes—such as a survey or interview—used to inform a pending decision. Although such reports can provide valuable contexts for understanding the topic, there are a number of foundational constructs and relationships that can help you better use needs assessments to achieve desired results. In this section, we offer an introduction to needs assessments as we present many of the most frequently asked questions that we get from colleagues, students, clients, and others. Responses to the questions then provide the basis for how needs assessments are conducted (see section 2), how tools and techniques are applied (see section 3), and how you can manage an assessment project (see appendix A).

Mind the Gaps

Gaps, either as opportunities or problems, are common instigators of action. Gaps lead to projects or programs, thereby steering us to change the status quo. They highlight—often in concrete terms—issues that would otherwise be obscured. Gaps also challenge us to find ways to improve personal and institutional performance. Gaps do not tell us what to do, but rather they characterize the measures we use to define success.

At the beginning of any project or program, there are gaps: gaps between the way things are and the way things could be. Terry Williams and Knut Samset (2010, 39) describe this as the time when a project "exists only conceptually, and before it is planned and implemented." In this period, ideas are being generated, needs are being defined, options are being considered, relationships are being nurtured, and partners are weighing each other's strengths and weaknesses. It is a dynamic period, leading up to a decision that will either lead to an action or not.

Because we live in an imperfect world, gaps exist—they guide our decisions; they define our goals. At their best, gaps determine what results should be achieved before actions are taken. Those gaps are the *needs* of needs assessments, and they help us make justifiable and informed decisions.

Ignoring gaps can be dangerous. When you make decisions about what to do (such as build a dam, start a new HIV/AIDS education program, offer training to a ministry's staff) without a clear distinction between where you are and where you want to be, then the odds of achieving desired results are greatly diminished, and resources are lost. You have also missed the opportunity to compare alternatives. Likewise, it may be that the solution you propose is useful but that it is even more effective when paired with another activity. Each of these concepts is an important consideration that you miss when you ignore needs (gaps).

You should, therefore, pay attention to gaps in results. Let the gaps guide your decisions. Use the gaps to monitor your progress. View the gaps as opportunities rather than problems. Lead projects to close gaps.

Gaps in results (or needs) can then be compared, prioritized, and balanced. Ideas for achieving desired results can be generated. Solutions can be evaluated in differing combinations, thus using their ability to close gaps as one of the main criteria by which alternative activities are compared.

When you make decisions about what to do, it is essential to know the results you are trying to accomplish before trying to determine what actions might work best. Nevertheless, in our rush to get moving, we frequently lose sight of (or fail to ever identify) the desired results, which leaves us without a clear definition of where we are and where we want to go. In those situations, we often must rationalize decisions we have already made (which can lead to trouble), or we move ahead with implementing a solution for which there is no known problem (box 1.1). When this haste happens, we choose our next steps (whether writing a proposal to start a new project or deciding on a capacity development strategy) without the opportunity (a) to verify that they are capable of achieving desired results, (b) to compare among alternatives, (c) to combine a number of solutions to maximize overall effects, or (d) to prioritize the needs to most efficiently use resources.

Gaps in results are both opportunities and problems, depending on your perspective. In either case, they are the foundation that guides justifiable decisions. For instance, when a provincial ministry of education desires improved public education for its schoolchildren in a low-performing school system, it is pointless to choose between building schools or hiring more teachers without first having clear measures of the results that stakeholders want accomplished in comparison to current achievements. Often, development projects proceed with just a vague notion of what should be

Box 1.1 Activities, Not Needs

Often, we begin decisions with solutions already in mind, such as when we say,

- "What we really *need* is to hire more staff members."
- "I *need* more resources."
- "They *need* more training."
- "They *need* new quality assurance practices."
- "You should do a training needs assessment."

Each of these statements begins with a solution before we understand the performance need or gaps in results to be addressed.

achieved—such as improving student performance or increasing educational access—yet this guesswork is not enough to justify significant investments of time and money.

Justifiable decisions are, therefore, best made when considering and comparing a number of alternatives and when assessing combinations of activities for their ability to accomplish desired results. This endeavor, of course, depends on having defined the gaps in results.

Why Call It Needs Assessment?

There are many aspects to the "front end" of any project or program, leading from concept to decision. The associated activities fill the space between strategic planning and project initiation, lead from crisis to the first response, and close the gap between what your boss asks for and the actions you take to meet that request. As such, no widely accepted and appropriate term links together all activities that might take place as precursors to action.

Although *strategic planning* plays a significant role in supporting many decisions, it is only part of the puzzle. Likewise, processes for making decisions, such as pair-wise comparisons (see page 187), are frequently included in the front end, though they are neither necessary nor sufficient by themselves. *Capacity development* is also related to the context in which decisions are frequently made in development projects, but the early front-end decisions we are focusing on in this book are the precursors to capacity development activities, rather than the activities themselves.

Nevertheless, for convenience, we want to use a term throughout this book that will represent the broad concept of the activities and actions that lead up to the point of making a decision. From the academic literature, we find that *needs assessment* is the best option—noting, however, that given its history, the term and related processes may have unwanted baggage derived from other applications. But what term or phrase doesn't?

Allison Rossett (1987, 3), professor emeritus at San Diego State University, defines needs assessment as "The systematic study of a problem or innovation, incorporating data and opinions from varied sources, in order to make effective decisions or recommendations about what should happen next." For our purposes, this is a sensible definition of the desired activities leading to a decision. After all, the earliest decisions of a development project should be guided by systematic steps that inform our decisions to take action (or, in some instances, decisions not to take action).

Because *needs assessment* is, however, a term that you may be familiar with from other applications (such as training needs assessment), we ask that you try to suspend any conceptions (or misconceptions) you may have regarding what a needs assessment is and the results that it can achieve.

What Is a Needs Assessment?

A *needs assessment* is simply a tool for making better decisions. From choosing a new car or finding a house to call home, to selecting an appropriate HIV/AIDS intervention or determining when training will build institutional capacity, needs assessments are used to make informed personal and professional decisions. You may not necessarily refer to the steps you take to inform your decisions as a needs assessment, but whenever you start your decision making by examining what results you are achieving today and what results you want to accomplish tomorrow, you are conducting a needs assessment.

Physicians, for instance, use needs assessments to define and prioritize the critical injuries of people as they enter the emergency room. Plumbers use needs assessments to identify problems, weigh alternative solutions, and make decisions about which parts must be replaced first. Likewise, organizational managers and leaders use needs assessments to define those areas where performance can be improved in the near term and long term.

Roger Kaufman, professor emeritus at Florida State University, defines a *needs assessment* in terms of *gaps in results* (Kaufman, Oakley-Brown, Watkins, and Leigh 2003). From a performance perspective, this definition offers two useful formulas for assessing needs. In the first formula, needs are gaps between current results and desired results. The size and importance of the gaps can then be compared to inform your decisions. For instance, your desired result is perhaps to be in Point B, but your current results have left you in Point A. Therefore, your *need* is the gap between results at Point A and results at Point B.

As an example, your department is responsible for processing all travel reimbursements within 10 days of their arrival from field staff members; yet, current results within your department indicate that it takes 14 days, on average, for staff members to receive their reimbursements. The need, in this example, is then defined as the gap between the objective of a 10-day reimbursement cycle and the current performance of 14 days.

Kaufman's definition also provides a second formula for prioritizing needs. According to the definition, needs are prioritized through the comparison of (a) costs associated with addressing the needs (or closing the gap) and (b) costs associated with not addressing the needs (or leaving the gap). This comparison is the foundation for moving beyond merely identifying problems or opportunities, thereby offering an approach for using information about the needs so you make decisions about what to do next.

As you see, needs assessments are very familiar processes. You are likely most familiar with less-formal, nonsystematic needs assessments that are heuristics within many decision-making models. Although potentially less familiar, the more formalized and systematic needs assessments are also, however, common in most organizations.

What differentiates the needs assessments approach described in this book from the approach you likely already know is the focus on improving performance. This book's approach involves moving the achievement of current results to the accomplishment of desired results. According to Kaufman's definition of needs, this approach focuses each of the steps, tools, techniques, guides, and other resources on first defining what results to achieve before then determining what activities or solutions will best accomplish those results.

Then, What Is a Need?

Needs are simply the differences between your current achievements and your desired accomplishments (see figure 1.1). Thus, needs most commonly represent discrepancies—often deficits—between your ambitions and the

Figure 1.1   Relating Needs to Discrepancies between What Is (Current Results) and What Should Be (Desired Results)

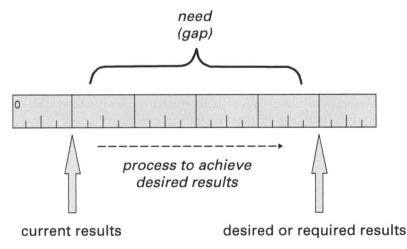

Source: Based on Kaufman, Oakley-Brown, Watkins, and Leigh (2003) and Watkins (2007).

A Guide to Assessing Needs

results of your current performance. In the same way, needs can signify an overabundance of success when your current achievements surpass your desired accomplishments, thereby possibly suggesting an excess of resources going toward the results.

Needs do not, however, include any mention or discussion of computers, budgets, training courses, irrigation systems, HIV/AIDS programs, urban development, executive coaching, leadership, incentives, policy analysis, microfinance strategies, holiday bonuses, reengineering, or any other techniques used to achieve results. Rather, your needs are the basic gaps between current and desired performance (see box 1.2).

When you have defined a need, and have determined that it is a priority for you and your organization, then you will want to look at all of the possible activities that could be done to improve performance and reach your goal (see box 1.3). You can systematically examine alternatives for improving performance and justify your decisions based on criteria related to the results to be achieved. This process ensures that you do not put the proverbial cart before the horse.

When the need is defined in terms of gaps in results, you can then look at the ideas offered by managers and others (such as hiring, building roads, training employees, or establishing new policies) to determine which idea(s) will best achieve the desired results. The suggestions of managers may end up being desirable activities to improve performance, but they are not needs.[1]

When completing a needs assessment, you may find, for instance, that reducing poverty among rural farmers to your desired level requires a combination of direct financial assistance, updates to national agriculture poli-

---

Box 1.2 Needs (Example 1)

In 2009, the Ministry of Public Education in Lao People's Democratic Republic (with its development partners) established a five-year strategic plan to guide its educational programming: the Education Sector Development Framework (ESDF). The ESDF goals are directly linked to the government's long-term plans to exit from least-developed country economic status.

Goals from this report include, for example, 98 percent primary school gross intake rate by 2011 on the basis of completing incomplete schools. This rate is in contrast to a 2008 gross intake rate of 69 percent. The gap of nearly 30 percent is a need that can and should be addressed by a variety of coordinated activities.

Sources: Based on information available at http://www.educationfasttrack.org/media/library/Final_ESDF_19_January_Ready_for_FTI.pdf and http://www.nationsencyclopedia.com/WorldStats/Edu-primary-net-intake-rate-grade-1.html.

Box 1.3 Needs (Example 2)

In 2004, the United Nations Development Group completed a series of needs assessment case studies related to the Millennium Development Goals. The cases included sample needs from Bangladesh, Cambodia, Ghana, Tanzania, and Uganda. For example, in Bangladesh, 50 percent of the population was living in poverty in 2000, and the goal is to lower the poverty rate to 30 percent by 2015.

This gap of 20 percent provides a clear performance need to be addressed. Many other needs are identified in these case studies, along with alternative solutions (and combinations of solutions) that could be considered.

Source: Based on information available at http://www.unmillenniumproject.org/documents/mp_ccspaper_jan1704.pdf.

cies, training in irrigation techniques, partnerships with local shipping companies, and other activities. With your need defined in terms of results to be accomplished, you can now compare differing combinations of these activities to determine where the knowledge, skills, and resources of your organization can best be applied and can partner with other organizations to fill in the remaining cracks. You cannot do this, however, if you defined your need as a solution (such as "we need policy reforms" or "we need high-speed rail").

What Is Meant by Improving Performance?

The efforts of organizations vary widely—from producing farm equipment to making loans to low-income countries—and thus it is next to impossible to adequately describe the desirable results of all organizations with a universal term or phrase. Adding to the challenge, many development institutions apply unique definitions to the typical terms you may use to refer to results (including results, product, outputs, outcomes, or impacts); then the institutions create new ways to describe the relationships among the results.

Yet, for ease of discussing needs assessments in a manner that can communicate with readers from varied organizations, in this book we have settled on the phrase *improving performance* to represent the results that are the focus of a needs assessment. The phrase is not ideal in all contexts, but we hope it works for most readers.

Improving performance, as we use it here, is the move from achieving current results to accomplishing desired results. Thus, *improving* refers to the measured progress from a less-than-desirable state to a desirable state, whereas *performance* refers to the results—no matter if your organization classifies them as products, outputs, outcomes, impacts, or some combination of these. Results are interrelated and interdependent; impacts depend on products, for instance, just as outputs should contribute to outcomes. Without the products of individual staff members, organizations would not have deliverables to provide to clients nor would communities benefit from the outcomes or effects of those deliverables. Therefore, alignment of results is critical to success, much more so than the titles we give those results.

Embedded in the phrase *improving performance* is the notion that improving how people perform is also essential to accomplishing results, although *performing* and *performance* are not equivalent. After all, we can each individually improve how well we *perform* our jobs but never achieve desired results—and at the same time, desired results are rarely accomplished without improvements in how people perform. *Performance* is, therefore, considered the combination of the process (that is, performing) and the desired results.[2] We can consider then three levels of performance: *individual* or *team, organizational,* and *societal.*

For some readers, the focus of your needs assessment will be the results achieved by individuals or groups in your organization, also known as *individual* or *team performance.*[3] This first category of performance may deal with the preparation of reports, the production of equipment, or documenting the distribution of funds to local nonprofit groups. Individual performance may relate to the development of a project plan or the results of mentoring colleagues. In all cases, individual or team performance focuses on the accomplishment of desirable results by the individuals, teams, or working groups. Thus, it incorporates improvements in performance and the achievement of desired results.

For other readers, the focus of their needs assessments may relate directly to the results that their organizations accomplish and deliver to clients. *Organizational performance,* the second category of performance, is about the achievement of organizational objectives that lead to beneficial results for the organization, its clients, and its partners.[4] From the delivery of goods or services to the achievement of long-term development objectives, organizational performance is achieved when there is alignment between what an organization uses, does, produces, and delivers. As such, organizational performance is forever bound to individual or team performance, thus making their alignment essential to success.

The third, and final, category of performance has an important role in every needs assessment—*societal performance.*[5] Because individuals, teams, and organizations do not exist in a vacuum, the results they produce are interwoven with the results achieved by the society (from local communities to our shared global society) that they exist within or that they serve. Although the societal connections are not always direct and observable from the level of individual or team peformance (for example, as with team results, when an internal report on customer satisfaction is your product), improvements in performance are most valued when there is alignment between individual, team, organizational, and societal results.

Hence, *improving performance* covers a vast array of topics, disciplines, fields, sectors, technologies, and business models. As such, it is an expedient and pragmatic phrase to use in relation to a needs assessment, because it too can be applied in a host of arenas. From internal decisions about when to develop training, to external choices about how to assist impoverished communities rebuild after a natural disaster, need assessments play a vital role in making informed decisions.

Fundamental to improving performance is the *equifinality principle* of systems theory, which states that in an open system there are always alternatives for achieving desired results. In practical terms, this principle tells you that even when one solution or activity initially seems to be the only way to accomplish results, in reality there are always other options that should be considered (even if you decide in the end to go with your initial selection). This requires a needs assessment approach that focuses on results and that collects data to inform decisions rather than data to justify decisions that have already been made.

At the same time, it is important to remember that all performance is not worth improving. As Doug Leigh (2003) of Pepperdine University points out, "Some results should be improved, some maintained, and some reduced or eliminated." In their book *Performance-Based Instruction*, Brethower and Smalley (1998) point out that "performance improvement interventions always add cost, and only sometimes add value." A needs assessment is a valuable tool for systematically justifying when and where to invest resources after first defining which results are worth accomplishing and then selecting appropriate activities for achieving those results.

The findings of your needs assessment might, for example, determine that although a country's ministry officials are not fully prepared to sustain a development project over time, the cost of training the officials (especially given the high turnover in the ministry) is not a wise investment. In response, you may consider (a) building more partnerships into the project to reduce the long-term dependence on a single ministry or

(b) developing a series of job aids that ministry officials can use as an alternative training program. There are always choices for how to accomplish desired results, including the option of doing nothing at the time. Needs assessments can help you weigh your options, thereby ensuring that you can justify your choices.

What Are the Benefits of a Needs Assessment?

*Needs assessments can be a **systematic** process to guide decision making.* No matter how big or small your choices, the decisions you make each day influence your performance, the performance of others around you, and the performance of your organization and its contribution to society. Systematic processes not only provide initial step-by-step guides, but also offer a foundational set of procedures that you can reflect on, customize, and continually improve in order to enrich your decisions later on.

*Needs assessments can provide **justification** for decisions before they are made.* After all, once a decision is made, it is typically too late to start justifying your choices. Rather, needs assessments proactively identify (a) the performance data that define your needs, (b) the prioritization of your needs, (c) the performance criteria for assessing potential interventions, and (d) the information necessary to justify your selection of one or more activities to improve performance.

*Needs assessments can be **scalable** for any size project, time frame, or budget.* There is no reason to spend US$1,000 to resolve a US$10 performance problem. Likewise, you would not want to take a year and spend thousands of dollars to implement a rigid needs assessment process that would only moderately improve the performance on a small project or program that is about to end. What you want is a process that can be appropriately scaled for the scope of your improvement efforts.

*Needs assessments can offer a **replicable** model that can be applied by novices or experts.* If you build on the lessons learned from previous decisions, needs assessments can offer a replicable process that can be used over and over again and that can be systematically improved upon over time. The fundamental framework for needs assessments provides a flexible structure that you can apply today, tomorrow, and in the future to guide your decisions.

*Needs assessments can provide a **systemic** perspective for decision makers.* Organizations are built around interdependent systems, systems of subsystems, and even social systems that you will never find in an organizational directory. As a consequence, your decisions constantly have rippling effects that move from one system to the next (see box 1.4).

Box 1.4 Example of a Systemic Perspective

The introduction of performance appraisals in your project team is intended to improve the results of your project. This new performance appraisal process, however, could influence what is required of team members as they work in procurement, quality assurance, and technical support. If the systems within the organization are not prepared to support changes in your project team, an overall net-negative effect could occur.

For instance, if organization employees do not have the capacity to complete an increasing number of procurement requests in a timely manner, then improvements to one system—in this case your project team—can influence the performance of other systems inside and outside of your organization.

*Needs assessments can allow for **interdisciplinary** solutions to complex problems.* Unsatisfactory performance in organizations is rarely the result of single problems, issues, or causes. Therefore, performance is rarely improved by single solutions, interventions, or activities. Through their processes, needs assessments encourage you to identify, compare, and—when appropriate—combine the activities that will best accomplish the desired results.

Aren't We Already Doing This?

Yes, no, sometimes, maybe. Most people do use informal or incomplete needs assessment steps to make some decisions in their lives. When you buy a new home, for instance, you will likely take time to collect information on school performance, resale values, neighborhood crime rates, and other essential performance criteria to be used in making your final choice. But when selecting a primary care physician, you may simply go with the one that is most conveniently located to your work or home.

Likewise, sometimes you may use more formal decision-making steps in your professional choices although—more often than not, if you are like most people—you frequently begin your professional decision making with an answer or a solution already in mind.

In most cases, the quality of your informal decision making has been good—and that has likely contributed to your success in the past. Yet, for most of us, decisions are becoming increasingly complex. Most likely, you are often asked to make complicated decisions on a daily basis to keep pace with organizational and global changes and to stay one step ahead of the competition. Although developing a new workshop or creating a new mission statement may have been the answer to many challenges in the past, improving performance now requires the development of sustainable performance systems that address multiple factors that influence individual, team, organizational, client, and societal results.

Dimensions of performance now include individual and organizational capacity; motivation and self-concept; expectations and feedback; rewards, incentives, and recognition; environment, resources, and processes; skills and knowledge; organizational culture; and strategic, tactical, and operational directions.[6]

Solutions presented may include things such as new roads, new computers, more money, more staff members, policy reforms, or any of a thousand ideas that may be useful in improving performance. The challenge is not to find out what ideas people have for improving performance; rather, the challenge is to identify and measure the true gap that exists between the results that should be accomplished and the current achievements and then to match useful solutions to those needs.

Formal and informal needs assessments can—and should—be part of your professional decision making although those systematic processes are not intrinsic to most organizational practice. By regularly conducting formal needs assessments, you can build expertise in the related procedures, customize standardized models for application in your decisions, and then include those steps as inherent characteristics of your informal daily decision making. In this manner, not only can you improve your decisions about what activities to undertake, but you can also internalize informal processes that will improve the results of all decisions you make.

When Should We Conduct a Needs Assessment?

Needs assessments, either formally as part of a major business decision or informally when weighing alternatives, can be of value most days. From determining if (and how) economic policy reforms can be of value to a client country, to deciding when to provide performance feedback to your project staff members, many decisions can benefit from the collection of additional information and the systematic application of that information to your decision making; needs assessments do just that.

Because needs assessments help inform decisions, they can be used *proactively* to identify opportunities to improve performance, *reactively* in response to the consequences of less-than-desirable results, or *continuously* as an integrated component of an ongoing improvement program. Hence, needs assessments are a valuable tool for decision makers at all levels of an organization and in almost any role. From decision makers working to create a new development initiative with other donors, to those charged with improving current efforts (and all combinations in between), needs assessments can be used to guide decisions.

Many conversations can lead to a needs assessment (see table 1.1). Sometimes these conversations are within your organization, and at other times they are with your clients or partners. In the latter case, needs assessment tools may be applied to assist others in identifying their needs and making decisions about what should happen next (potentially leading to new projects). Clients sometimes have well-defined needs, although many times they do not. Other times they may think that they do when, in fact, they do not. Clients usually have a list of desired projects (processes and products, or wants), yet that doesn't mean they have the information to guide useful decisions that achieve results.

Needs assessments, or even the underlying logic of a needs assessment approach, are not however always used to guide decisions. Consequently, decision makers frequently struggle to make justifiable choices. This situation happens for many reasons, including (a) they don't have a clear, mea-

Table 1.1   Sample Paths That Lead to a Needs Assessment

	External examples	Internal examples
Proactive contexts	The minister of education is new to the job and struggling with how to prioritize the national needs, given a very limited budget. His predecessor had initiated many "pet projects" that were based on what he thought would work, but few of the projects achieved any measurable results. The new minister does not want to take that same path.	As a manager, you see the performance requirements of your department changing in the coming years to respond to client realities. In this context, you complete an assessment to determine current and future needs of staff members and their ability to achieve results in the new context.
Reactive contexts	A ministry official is attempting to make a number of informed decisions concerning tax reform as a tool for meeting the debt sustainability goals of her country, but she requires some additional objective inputs from a number of partners.	With a relatively high turnover rate and problems with new staff members not completing assignments, your manager asks you to complete an assessment related to the current orientation program for new staff members.

surable definition of what results are desired or required; (b) they don't have a good measurement of what results are currently being achieved; (c) they are focused only on a single solution that they "want" and are not thinking in terms of alternative solutions; (d) they have very limited information on the options; or (e) they don't have clear criteria for comparing their options. Each of these reasons probably sounds familiar because they are true, to some degree, in almost every organization.

Although assessment opportunities are frequent in conversations, a keen ear is required to note the opportunity (and the value to be added by an assessment). Listen carefully when talking with colleagues, clients, and partners about decisions that could benefit from a clear identification of needs, alternatives, and criteria for making choices.

Needs assessment can also help you avoid missteps. Simple answers to your professional challenges usually won't provide the sustainable results that you are ethically responsible to provide. After all, for every performance problem, there is a solution that is simple, straightforward, acceptable, understandable—and WRONG.[7]

For instance, human resource officers commonly hear managers requesting new or additional training in a variety of organizational areas. Although training may initially seem to be a reasonable solution to the problems being faced by the manager, an informed decision about how to improve performance requires that additional information be considered before rushing ahead with any single solution. Most often, organizational challenges are not linked to any single cause such as the perceived inadequate knowledge or skills of others. Rather, they are brought about by a combination of issues such as misguided incentives, inadequate processes, miscommunication on performance expectations, and other problems.

The following sample statements are good indicators that a needs assessment may be the appropriate next step before making any decisions:

"We *need* to provide more training to people working in the Ministry of Agriculture."

"They really must have this program in place by next year."

"Last week, I decided that introducing *[insert idea]* would be a good place to start building capacity."

"They *need* to go to leadership training."

"If you had *[insert latest technology gadget]*, then you would be more productive."

"You *need* to build X, Y, and Z into your project proposal."

Box 1.5 From A to Z: An Example (Part 1)

New employees in your unit are expected to submit a fundable project proposal within six months of starting. Yet, when data illustrate that 50 percent of new employees are still struggling to achieve this result after one year, then you have identified a performance gap, or *need*. The need, in this case, is defined by the number of months it takes for a new employee to submit a fundable project proposal. Other information, such as management feedback on draft proposals or the number of ongoing projects that new employees supervise, may also be used to further define your need.

Not included in the need are the possible solutions. The need, for instance, is not for more training on proposal writing or partner relationship management, nor is the need for mentoring or new recruiting policies. Each of those solutions may end up being possible activities to improve performance in relation to the need, but

they are not the initial focus of your needs assessment.

Continuing the example, let's say that your needs assessment determines that delays in new employee performance were costing the unit US$500,000 each fiscal quarter (in terms of salary and benefits without achieving desired results). In comparison, a second need that your needs assessment identified was a discrepancy between the current and desired number of projects that engaged partners from multiple sectors. This second need, although not typically measured in quarterly budget reports, must be considered at the same time as the previous need because limited resources will have to be allocated. The second need may be measured in terms of reduced aid effectiveness of development projects and the associated long-term budget implications for the unit in order to draw some general comparisons and to prioritize the two needs.

When you hear these or similar statements about what should be done, it is usually a good time to step back and ensure that you know where you are headed before you take the first step. After all, if you are not headed in the right direction, then you could end up someplace other than where you want to be (see box 1.5).

Are Needs Assessments Just for Reacting to Problems?

In addition to being reactive, needs assessments can, and should, be a proactive tool. You can, for instance, use a needs assessment as a process for working with clients and partners to define future projects. An example of where a proactive approach could be taken would be as part of a government strategy paper designed to look ahead for 20 years to examine possible regional transportation requirements and options. In such situations, the needs assessment provides continual feedback to the planning process about the gaps between current and desired results. The gaps will commonly fluctuate either from year to year or as organizational goals and objectives shift in relation to external pressures or opportunities.

Needs assessments can also be used when working with clients to define new opportunities—that is, opportunities driven by the desired results of the society, community partners, clients, and others (rather than driven by solutions in search of problems).

Continual needs assessments, typically much less formal than initial assessments, can also be used to inform practical and justifiable decisions (see figure 1.2). The monitoring and evaluation results of one project cycle can, for instance, be integrated into a needs assessment that informs the next project cycle. But rather than just building on past project cycles, the needs assessment also infuses new data from internal and external partners into the decision making. If you simply relied on past evaluation reports, then you would probably miss the internal and external changes that are currently shaping the future.

Use needs assessments proactively, continually, and reactively in your organization:

✓ *Proactively* to identify potential opportunities for improving individual or organizational performance

Figure 1.2   Needs Assessment Cycles

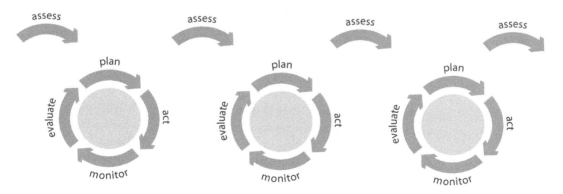

Source: Authors.

✓ *Continually* to monitor your progress toward accomplishing desired results

✓ *Reactively* when new strategic, tactical, or operational objectives are to be achieved

Aren't Needs Assessments Too Rigid?

From practical experience most of us have learned that rigid planning just doesn't work. Life is messy; from natural disasters to changes in government leadership, there are just too many variables to accurately predict or control the future. As the saying goes, "Men plan; God laughs."

Henry Mintzberg (2000), the preeminent management researcher from McGill University, first described this problem in his book *The Rise and Fall of Strategic Planning*, which shed light on how many traditional approaches to planning do not offer the flexibility required for real-world application. More recently, in his book *Tracking Strategies*, Mintzberg (2008) illustrates through a number of case examples how most strategic plans change over time—with some specific objectives being achieved as planned, some dropped as new (or more) information is learned, and some new objectives being created as opportunities arise.

In response, needs assessments (which frequently rely on strategic plans to help define the desired results) cannot afford to be rigid or closed-minded. They must demonstrate, from beginning to end, the flexibility required to inform decisions in complex and ever-changing realities. Your needs assessments should gather information from multiple perspectives, consider a range of alternative activities, and use techniques that give all partners a voice in the decision-making process. Your assessments should do so while maintaining a focus on what desired results are to be achieved (see box 1.6).

In contrast, solution-driven decisions are quite rigid; a solution is selected and then defended against all information that may suggest that alternatives could be of more value. In many organizations, the risks associated with dropping a solution that is already committed to make it very difficult to adjust decisions in response to new realities, thereby leaving many projects to suffer until they are one day forgotten. Use information from ongoing needs assessment activities to continually inform decisions at all stages in the project's life cycle, increasing your agility and your ability to achieve results.

Box 1.6 Gaining Flexibility

1. View needs along a continuum from emerging needs to stable needs.
2. Postpone the selection of a solution until after the needs are well defined.
3. Rely on a diverse set of partners, tools, and techniques to collect information and inform decisions.
4. Compare a number of alternative activities against agreed-upon performance criteria.
5. Focus on systems of improvement activities rather than on single solutions (that is, don't put all your eggs in one basket).

How Does a Needs Assessment Relate to Other Tools You Are Already Using?

Needs assessments are often associated with (that is, drawing on and contributing to) process improvement efforts—including front-end analysis, root cause analysis, and performance analysis. Each of the processes provides a distinct perspective to the analysis of results generated by the needs assessment. For instance, a root-cause analysis will dissect the individual needs derived from the needs assessment to identify and compare the causal factors in an effort to determine which factors are at the foundation of the performance gap and deserve attention. A root-cause analysis is most valuable when you have a well-defined process in place and when you are searching for a human, procedural, equipment, or environment failure in the process that can be improved upon (see box 1.7).

Similarly, front-end and performance analyses build on findings from a needs assessment (and needs analysis) to link the identified and prioritized needs to specific performance improvement activities. From infrastructure investments to training, to recruitment strategies and environmental policy, such analysis procedures can help guide your decisions about what to do in response to priority needs.

Consequently, formal and informal needs assessments are common partners in many (if not most) other essential organizational processes. With needs assessment processes contributing to the foundation, you can then effectively use a variety of analysis procedures and potential improvement activities together to create a multifaceted initiative that improves performance from many angles and perspectives.

Box 1.7 From A to Z: An Example (Part 2)

Most often, you can't prioritize needs without beginning to consider the possible solutions. At this point, the needs assessment transitions from a singular focus on results to a combined focus on results and possible activities. This change in focus is necessary because the estimated cost of activities and their ability to achieve desired results must be weighed when setting priorities—as well as when making decisions about what to do.

Continuing the example (see page 30), your assessment determines that the cost of improving new employee performance is relatively small and that its likely effect on unit performance is significant although the cost of increasing the number of multisector projects is significant and the probable effect on unit performance is moderate at best. This type of information, when associated with well-defined and measured needs, is extremely valuable in making informed decisions about where to place limited resources.

Analyze each need to determine why it is occurring and what potential activities (or solutions) could be of value in closing the gap.

Using this information, along with other useful performance data, begin to set priorities among the multiple needs identified in your assessment. Then begin to compare alternative activities for improving performance.

Your analysis, for instance, of the gap in time required to submit a fundable proposal may have indicated that new employees have the knowledge and skills required to complete the inventory, thus more training for new employees is not going to improve performance. In addition, you may have found that new employees were not being given any feedback on draft proposals for up to six months after the proposals were submitted. Moreover, new employees were more likely to get high scores on their annual performance reviews (and the associated pay increases) if they focused on managing current projects rather than on submitting proposals for new projects. With this information in hand, you could start to identify the factors leading to poor performance and the range of potential activities that may be valuable to improving results.

Isn't an Evaluation the Same Thing?

Not really, though there are similarities. Both assessment and evaluation are important to improving results, but they serve different functions. The distinctive processes differ in the perspectives that they apply when collecting information and guiding decisions. Although many of the same tools are applied in both assessments and evaluations, understanding the difference about how the perspectives are translated into practice requires particular attention.[8]

An assessment perspective, which you apply when conducting a needs assessment, collects information that identifies the gaps between the current results and the required or desired results (or needs), and then it appraises those needs for determining priorities and comparing alternative activities that may help improve performance. Hence, this approach to collecting and analyzing information takes place before any decisions are made about what to do, which vendors to use, or even what products are to be expected. Needs assessments are frequently completed in partnership with planning efforts (such as strategic planning or project planning) to define where a group or organization is headed and how it plans to get there.

In contrast, an evaluation perspective is most commonly applied when initial decisions about what to do (for example, build schools, reform policies, expand HIV/AIDS services) may have already been made and when you are trying to either improve performance (as with developmental or formative evaluations) or determine the value added by current processes (as with summative or impact evaluation). You, therefore, approach an evaluation from a different vantage point than you would for a needs assessment. Your processes and results serve a different, though equally important, function within an organization.

The Organisation for Economic Co-operation and Development's Development Assistance Committee has provided five criteria to consider when evaluating projects: relevance, effectiveness, efficiency, impact, and sustainability (OECD 2011). Evaluations frequently inform, for example, decisions about how (or whether) to improve performance of current efforts; and evaluations are, therefore, sometimes done in partnership with other cost-value analyses (such as cost-benefit, cost-effectiveness, return-on-investment, or cost-efficiency analysis) or ongoing needs assessment efforts.[9]

It is important to note that, in recent years, given an emphasis on achieving results (that is, products, outputs, outcomes, and impacts), more attention has been given by project planners and funders to see evaluation planning as part of the project planning process. Consequently, for those who rightly consider that evaluation efforts start at the beginning of project planning and not at the project's end, we see cases where evaluation and needs assessment are more closely linked even as their functions differ.

If you apply both approaches when they are appropriate, then you are on the way to improving results. Throughout this book, nevertheless, we have made a conscious effort to describe each of the tools and techniques from a decidedly needs assessment perspective.

Don't We Already Know What Works?

Relying on past success is no guarantee of future success. Although decisions should consider the results of past solutions (just as they should look at what others are doing to achieve results), past successes should provide context for decisions rather than constrain them. Too often organizations continue to apply "the same old" solutions well after the solutions have lost their effectiveness—assuming that they were effective to begin with. Successful solutions exist in a point in time and in a certain context, and they have limited transferability to different times and contexts.

Can't You Just Send Out a Survey Asking People What They Want?

No. A survey is not a needs assessment. It is only a tool that may be used in a needs assessment if the circumstances are right to use a survey. Although the individual perspective on what people want to have done is quite valuable in making informed decisions, by itself it is of little value when making decisions. Asking people what they want also sets up the expectation—likely false—that they will get exactly what they want. Thus, we strongly recommend that you don't go down that path.

By going far beyond simply asking people what they want, you can create a needs assessment that collects valuable information from multiple perspectives and that guides justifiable decisions. Use multiple tools and techniques, and stay away from questions that may build unrealistic expectations.

Section Summary

As you can see, needs assessments can be used in many different ways to improve performance. They are distinctive from most other management tools in that they focus on performance (measured gaps in results) and are the precursor to decisions about what to do next. Nevertheless, we use them formally and informally in organizations every day.

In section 2, we will turn our attention from what a needs assessment is (or is not) and will focus on what makes for a useful assessment. From determining the scope of your needs assessment to managing the process, the next section summarizes the steps that can guide a successful assessment.

Notes

1. Roger Kaufman uses *what is* and *what should be*, rather than *current* and *desired*, because the desired results may not always represent what is best for the individual, organization, or society. Although the authors agree with this

perspective, we simply find that the term *desired results* communicates more effectively with development colleagues and partners.

2. Doug Leigh of Pepperdine University refers to *improving performance* as the activities used to accomplish *performance improvement*. Thus, from this perspective, your needs assessment would focus on *performance improvement* (that is, the results) before it would examine alternative methods for improving performance.

3. What Roger Kaufman refers to as Micro Level results or products; planning at this level is operational.

4. What Roger Kaufman refers to as Macro Level results or outputs; planning at this level is tactical.

5. What Roger Kaufman refers to as Mega Level results or outcomes; planning at this level is strategic.

6. Based on John Wedman's performance pyramid model, as found in Watkins and Leigh (2010).

7. An unreferenced phrase frequently used by Roger Kaufman.

8. Based on Watkins and Guerra (2003).

9. A notable exception is *prospective* evaluations. These are, however, less common than the evaluations described here, and they typically serve limited functions in most organizations.

References

Brethower, Dale, and Karolyn Smalley. 1998. *Performance-Based Instruction: Linking Training to Business Results*. San Francisco: Jossey-Bass/Pfeiffer.

Kaufman, Roger, Hugh Oakley-Brown, Ryan Watkins, and Doug Leigh. 2003. *Strategic Planning for Success: Aligning People, Performance, and Payoffs*. San Francisco: Jossey-Bass.

Leigh, Doug. 2003. "Worthy Performance, Redux." http://www.performance xpress.org/0306.

Mintzberg, Henry. 2000. *The Rise and Fall of Strategic Planning*. New York: Free Press.

———. 2008. *Tracking Strategies: Towards a General Theory of Strategy Formation*. New York: Oxford University Press.

OECD (Organisation for Economic Co-operation and Development). 2011. *DAC Criteria for Evaluating Development Assistance*. http://www.oecd.org/ document/22/0,2340,en_2649_34435_2086550_1_1_1_1,00.html.

Rossett, Allison. 1987. *Training Needs Assessment*. Englewood Cliffs, NJ: Educational Technology Publishing Co.

Watkins, Ryan. 2007. *Performance by Design: The Systematic Selection, Design, and Development of Performance Technologies That Produce Useful Results*. Amherst, MA: HRD Press, and Silver Spring, MD: International Society for Performance Improvement.

Watkins, Ryan, and Ingrid Guerra. 2003. "Assessing or Evaluation: Determining Which Approach Is Required." In *2003 Training and Performance Sourcebook*, edited by Mel Silberman. Princeton, NJ: Active Training.

Watkins, Ryan, and Doug Leigh, eds. 2010. *Handbook for Improving Performance in the Workplace*. Vol. 2: *Selecting and Implementing Performance Interventions*. San Francisco: Wiley/Pfeiffer, and Silver Spring, MD: International Society for Performance Improvement.

Williams, Terry, and Knut Samset. 2010. "Issues in Front-End Decision Making on Projects." *Performance Management Journal* 41 (2): 38–49.

Needs Assessment: Steps to Success

Introduction

Because most of us do not conduct needs assessments (such as those typically required to inform decisions in the workplace) each day, the steps to conducting a successful assessment can remain elusive. At the same time there is, of course, no one perfect path to success—nor should there be. Therefore, we have attempted in this section to "boil down" the theories, models, and approaches of needs assessment into clear guidance on how you can manage a successful assessment within your unique context. Along with the management tools provided in appendix A, the guidance offered in this section can start you on the path to success.[1]

How Do You Determine the Scope of Your Needs Assessment?

We can break down decisions into three levels:

- *Strategic* (typically involves goals, objectives, and strategic policies defining the relationship between organizations and the society they serve)

- *Tactical* (includes the policies and procedures put in place to both support strategic decisions and guide operational decisions, thereby defining the goals and objectives of an organization or institution)

- *Operational* (includes all sorts of short- and long-term decisions that typically involve implementing projects or programs and carrying out tasks to produce results)

Needs assessments are routinely used to guide *strategic decisions*, choices that are guided by the needs of society, including the needs of direct clients (such as a government's ministry of education), indirect clients (such as community schools served by the ministry), and others in the society that are the beneficiaries of an organization's efforts (such as the broader population of the country or region). Although your assessment may focus on the needs of a direct client, it is important to recognize and plan for the implications that any decision you make will have on other related societal systems (such as local schools and communities).

Needs assessments also provide valuable guidance for *tactical decisions*, such as when an organization wants to determine what programs and projects should be developed to improve aid effectiveness. Here the focus is on the results of the organization itself, rather than on the contributions of the organization to clients and society. Tactical needs assessments can be used in reactive situations, such as when organizational performance suddenly begins to drift below established expectations. Equally, tactical needs assessments are frequently used proactively to determine if and when opportunities are the right choice. In each case, a needs assessment can help you collect useful information and make justifiable decisions that improve the performance (that is, the achievement of desired results) of your organization.

Operational decisions are also supported by needs assessments. These decisions focus on achieving individual and team results within your organization, and they are best made in alignment with tactical and strategic decisions. Operational decisions include the daily decisions that must be made for projects to be implemented or budgets to be used. They can be short-term decisions (for example, when deciding on the expected results from a staff meeting) or long-term decisions (for example, when setting project management objectives and milestones). In either case, operational decisions are associated with the products of individuals and teams.

Strategic, tactical, and operational decisions—though different in focus—are each essential to success (see table 2.1). Without quality operational decisions, tactical and strategic results would be not achieved. Likewise, without quality tactical decisions, strategic results would not be accom-

Table 2.1 Three Scopes for Needs Assessments

Needs assessment	Results focus	Example 1: Contexts for needs assessment	Example 2: Needs assessment results
Strategic	Results contributed to the society and communities served by the organization and its partners	Ministry officials from five neighboring provinces meet with donor agencies to review the effect of recent global economic changes on their combined populations.	Priority needs include reducing incidence of waterborne diseases and increasing farmland production. The group also indicates that multiprovince projects are preferred, when appropriate.
Tactical	Results delivered by the organization to clients	Changing population needs require more responsive development projects that work across multiple sectors (for example, education, health, agriculture, infrastructure, and so on) and that engage development partners (for example, multilateral and bilateral organizations and nongovernmental organizations).	Priority needs for the organization include increasing the effectiveness of agriculture and health projects, as well as increasing the number of multisector projects that are completed successfully.
Operational	Results produced by individuals and teams within the organization	Your unit within the organization has not been successful in coordinating efforts across multiple sectors in the past, and two such projects have had to be restructured in the past five years (neither being completed within the initial funding period).	The priority needs in the unit include (a) increasing the number of successfully completed multisector projects and (b) increasing the overall number of current projects that are completed on time. Mentoring new staff members, increasing feedback on draft proposals, and monitoring multisector projects biweekly were among the possible activities identified to improve performance.

Source: The framework is based on the multiple works of Roger Kaufman found in the references section, with examples provided by the authors of this book.

plished. If operational decisions are made, for instance, without links to the tactical and strategic implications, then the organization, its clients, the client's clients, and others suffer. At the same time, strategic decisions can provide guidance for subsequent tactical and operational decisions. It is, therefore, the alignment of decisions that is essential.

Many scenarios can commonly lead to needs assessments with differing scopes: strategic, tactical, operational, or all three. The following scenarios may better illustrate examples of when you would select a needs assessment with one or more of these scopes.

Example Uses of a Strategic Needs Assessment

Scenario 1: Environmental and social concerns are changing the requirements that citizens and government agencies have for your organization's products or services.

Scenario 2: Previous strategic planning efforts in your organization have not provided useful guidance for aligning the contributions of your provincial education ministry with the emerging requirements of the impoverished minority populations that you serve.

Scenario 3: Your government agency is responsible for (a) developing 20-year transportation plans for your region, (b) anticipating a range of economic and social changes, and (c) building in consultations with a range of stakeholders (for example, transportation experts, national and community officials, financial experts, and so on).

Scenario 4: New technologies are likely to make the services offered by your organization obsolete in the next five years, and you are looking for new niche markets that your organization may be able to serve in this new development environment.

Example Uses of a Tactical Needs Assessment

Scenario 1: Client satisfaction in your telecommunications organization is historically mixed, but new information is indicating that the retention of clients has decreased and has become a significant financial risk.

Scenario 2: Your transportation organization is struggling to balance workforce capacity, which has too few highly qualified road engineers some years and too many other years, thereby leading to suboptimal project planning and varying satisfaction among clients.

Scenario 3: Results in your water department have been slowly declining in recent years (for example, number of sewer lines completed, quality of water provided, and so on), and it looks as if this year will end with lower results than last year.

Scenario 4: Last year, your organization struggled with approximately 8 percent of the more than 500 employees missing work on the average day. This situation has cost the organization approximately US$180,000 annually and has led to lower client satisfaction ratings.

Example Uses of an Operational Needs Assessment

Scenario 1: Fewer than 40 percent of project leaders in your unit have been adequately identifying emerging risks in their quarterly implementation reports, leading to 10 percent of the projects in your unit being categorized as "at risk of failure."

Scenario 2: Each quarter, electricity department supervisors are expected to meet with their employees to discuss community scorecard ratings. But fewer than half of those meetings take place, thereby resulting in a lack of shared knowledge on community satisfaction with electricity services and where corrective action should be taken.

Scenario 3: It is expected that new employees in your pension agency will be able to accurately input applicant data into the pension management system within six months of being hired. Unfortunately, it currently takes employees 9 to 12 months of practice to enter applicant data with the necessary accuracy.

Scenario 4: According to manager evaluations, more than 60 percent of employees who complete internal training courses do not perform their jobs better after the training.

Both tactical and operational needs assessments begin and end within the organization. Each of the needs assessments relates directly to the ability of the organization and its people to accomplish their goals and objectives. In contrast, the strategic needs assessment begins outside of the organization with the direct and indirect clients that benefit from the products or services of the organization (for example, community members, students, pensioners, and so on). Those direct and indirect clients of the organization are thereby given a voice in setting the long-term direction for the organization through the strategic needs assessments.

Successful needs assessments are not, however, independent from other needs assessments. For an operational needs assessment to be of value, it must be completed within the context of a tactical needs assessment; after all, why improve performance at the individual level if it is not in line with organizational objectives? Likewise, tactical needs assessments are most useful when nested in the results of a strategic needs assessment.

Alignment is essential for success, both in terms of the decisions to be made and the actions that follow those decisions. The goals of an organization are best derived from and aligned with the goals of the broader society in which they function. Likewise, the goals of a project or team are best derived from and aligned with the goals of the organization. The importance of this alignment is, nevertheless, often overlooked, thus allowing decisions to be made—and subsequent actions to be taken—that have little or no chance of accomplishing desired results that span across operational, tactical, and strategic goals.[2]

Managing the scope of your needs assessment requires a sense of balance—balancing strategic, tactical, and operational decisions. At times, you may determine that your assessment requires a 90 percent focus on operational decisions, with just 10 percent of the effort focused on ensuring the links with tactical and strategic decisions. At other times, the context for your assessment may lead you to determine that 50 percent of the effort should be on organizational needs, 20 percent on alignment with societal needs, and 30 percent on alignment with individual or team needs. There is no equation for balancing scope, but rarely would you want to focus exclusively on strategic, tactical, or operational decisions—alignment of the three typically involves some attention and effort.

Where Do You Begin?

To begin any needs assessment, you must determine what decisions the assessment is meant to inform (see box 2.1). For instance, is your organization tasked with reforming education within your country, and is your primarily strategic needs assessment meant to inform those decisions? Or has your division recently undergone budget cuts and, therefore, you want to use a primarily tactical needs assessment to inform decisions on prioritizing limited resources? Or are you concerned that a team you lead is missing too many deadlines and so you want to use a primarily operational needs assessment as a basis for improving performance?

Whatever the case, let the *decisions to be made* be your guide. If you are unclear on what decisions are going to be made on the basis of the results of the needs assessment, then this is a good time to clarify those expectations before you begin to plan, manage, and carry out your assessment. You may have to go back to your boss, the project sponsor, or others in your organization to help clarify how they would like to use the findings of your assessment to guide their choices as well. If conducting the needs assessment was your decision, then clarify the objectives on the basis of the questions to

Box 2.1 Tasks in a Needs Assessment

A useful needs assessment will accomplish the following:
- Focus on results first, solutions second.
- Define needs as gaps in results.
- Align operational, tactical, and strategic performance.
- Systematically analyze needs to inform decisions.
- Consider a broad array of possible activities.
- Compare activities against performance criteria.
- Provide information that justifies the decision before it is made.

which you want answers—answers that will lead to informed and justifiable decisions.

The strategic needs assessment, with its focus on the results required for external partners, generally provides the foundation for successful tactical and operational needs assessments. Without it, you are typically left to rely on assumptions regarding the value of your decisions to clients, communities, and society. In many situations, you may not have the opportunity to formally conduct a strategic assessment as part of your project, but ensuring the alignment of tactical and operational needs with the strategic needs of the external partners and society remains important.

You can, for instance, (a) link your needs assessment to strategic documents (such as the Millennium Development Goals, National Development Strategies, or World Bank Country Assistance Strategies), (b) define strategic needs on the basis of information already collected for other purposes (such as data from the United Nations or Organisation for Economic Co-operation and Development), (c) meet with external partners to verify what you find within your institution, and (d) engage client communities throughout the process by sharing your plans and results. Later, tactical and operational needs can be aligned with these strategic findings to verify that all results contribute to development objectives.

Depending on the history of needs assessments within your organization, it is routine for a combined needs assessment—one that addresses strategic, tactical, and operational questions—to be the right choice. Don't panic if this is the case for you as well. Because all three needs assessments will use similar plans, processes, tools, and techniques, you can typically conduct a more efficient and simultaneous set of assessments than if you conducted them individually. By asking questions regarding all three needs assessments—strategic, tactical, and operational—in one interview, focus group, or survey, you can, for example, save time and money as well as reduce your stress.

Knowing why you are conducting the assessment and what decisions will be made based on its results are the essential foundations for success and are the ideal place to start.

How Do You Conduct a Basic Needs Assessment?

As with any organizational activity, it is best to start your needs assessment with a plan. Your plan will not only help guide the processes within your needs assessment but also help you manage the multiple steps and various partners throughout the assessment.

Depending on the size and scope of your needs assessment (corresponding to the decisions that your needs assessment will guide), you can create a useful plan for identifying needs, analyzing needs, and deciding what to do next (or at least making recommendations). By using this three-step process, you ensure that (a) your assessment focuses on results before solutions, (b) your needs are studied before decisions are made, and (c) your decisions are informed and justified.

For an assessment that is small in scope, you can include in your plan just the primary steps outlined as follows. For an assessment that is larger in scope, add more substeps and details as outlined later in the next section. Your larger-scale assessments will also likely benefit from involving a specialist in needs assessment (or potentially in evaluation) to lead or advise about the assessment. After all, larger assessments will typically involve more questions to be answered, more and different types of stakeholders, more people to gather information from, more information to be analyzed, and more partners in making informed choices. Adjusting the detailed processes within each step of your assessment gives you the flexibility to match your efforts to the desired scope.

That being said, it is important to recognize that although a formal needs assessment will generally follow the same basic steps, having ongoing informal needs assessments can be a necessary tool for responding to changing situations. Even after you complete a formal needs assessment, you should continue to collect information to monitor and evaluate the situation. When you recognize that needs are changing, you should either update the findings of the previous formal needs assessment or begin the process again to update recommendations.

Next are three basic steps that should be included in your plans for a successful needs assessment. In appendix A of this book, you will find additional information, tools, checklists, and resources for managing your assessment.

Identify

The first step in needs assessment is to identify needs (that is, gaps between desired and current results). Although it is often tempting to mix potential solutions (that is, activities or resources) with needs, your assessment will be much more effective if you focus exclusively on results to start. There will be plenty of time for debating potential solutions later in the process. After all, as Henry Kissinger is credited with saying, "If you do not know where you are going, every road will get you nowhere."

1. Identify your internal and external partners for the needs assessment. Colleagues, clients, nongovernmental organizations (NGOs), development partners, and others may all be useful partners in making a quality decision.

2. Determine what data are required to identify needs (that is, gaps) at the strategic, tactical, and operational levels. In other words, what information is required to make an informed and justifiable decision?

3. Determine potential sources of data (for example, community members, documents, and so on) to inform your needs assessment. For instance, is a strategic plan available for the national or provincial government to help guide a tactical-level needs assessment?

4. Make arrangements to collect information that is not already available. Schedule interviews, create surveys, arrange focus groups, collect documents to be reviewed, train focus group facilitators, schedule performance observations, and so forth.

5. Pilot test interview protocols, questionnaires, and other information-gathering tools (see box 2.2).

6. Collect information using a variety of tools and techniques, and include sources that represent varying perspectives on the primary performance issues. Remember to listen—far more than you talk—when collecting information for your needs assessment.

7. Define needs on the basis of performance gaps between current and desired results. Link strategic, tactical, and operational needs to ensure alignment.

Analyze

The analysis process links needs with the information required to make decisions about what actions should be taken. After all, every need does not require immediate action: causal factors must be reviewed, return-on-investment considerations must be weighed, and priorities must be set. At this point, many ideas for solutions or activities to improve results will be offered. These ideas should also be captured during the analysis, though the focus remains on better understanding the differences between current and desired results.

1. Establish an initial prioritization of needs on the basis of size, scope, distinguishing characteristics, and relative importance.

2. Conduct a needs analysis—for the highest-priority needs—to better understand what is working, what is not working, and what the systemic relationships are among needs.

3. Collect information (a) regarding the causal factors (or root causes) associated with what is not working and (b) leading to priority needs. Use multiple data-collection tools and techniques, and ensure that you capture a variety of perspectives.

4. Analyze and synthesize the useful information you have collected about the needs.

Box 2.3 Decision-Making Tools in Part 3.B

Nominal Group Technique
   (A Group Consensus-Building and Ranking Technique)   page 166
Multicriteria Analysis   page 171
Tabletop Analysis   page 180
Pair-Wise Comparison   page 187
2 × 2 Matrix Decision Aids   page 191
Fishbone Diagrams   page 197
Scenarios   page 202
Root Cause Analysis   page 207
Fault Tree Analysis   page 214
Concept Mapping   page 220
Future Wheel   page 228
Performance Pyramid   page 236

Decide

Making complex decisions based on the analysis is the next step (see box 2.3). This step is also often the hardest, given (a) competing interests for certain types of activities to occur, (b) difficulties in agreeing to the criteria to use in making the decisions, and (c) typical realities for negotiation and compromise. Nevertheless, information from steps 1 and 2 will increase the potential for making a justifiable decision that will lead to desired results.

1. Working with needs assessment partners, establish the criteria on which decisions will be made about what to do (for example, cost, time, impact).[3]

2. Identify multiple activities (that is, solutions) that in combination could achieve desired results. There are always multiple options to be considered, so it is important not to become fixated on any one solution until it can be compared with others against the agreed-upon criteria.

3. Evaluate each potential performance improvement activity to assess its value to your improvement effort.

4. Prioritize the identified needs on the basis of the cost to meet the need (that is, closing the gap) versus the cost of not meeting the need (that is, not closing the gap).[4]

5. Summarize your recommendations in a needs assessment report or presentation, and disseminate the information.

6. Evaluate your needs assessment process to determine if changes should be made before you complete your next assessment.

Use the three primary steps (identify, analyze, decide) as a general guide for your needs assessment. For informal needs assessments, these three steps and the recommended substeps may be enough to inform your decision.

How Do You Conduct a Larger-Scale Needs Assessment?

Larger-scale needs assessments typically require a more detailed and formal needs assessment process. If, for instance, you are planning a six-month needs assessment that requires the engagement of several government ministries and donor partners, then the three general steps of identify, analyze, and decide will not be sufficient.

In these cases, Jim Altschuld (2010) suggests that the needs assessment be conducted in three phases: preassessment activities, assessment activities, and postassessment activities.[5] The three previously discussed steps (identify, analyze, decide) can then be integrated into the assessment activities, providing a proactical approach to your assessment (see figure 2.1).

Phase 1. Preassessment

The purpose of this phase is to determine the overall scope and plan for the assessment so you ensure that implementation goes smoothly and generates justifiable information to make decisions. The preassessment phase relies

Figure 2.1 Needs Assessment Phases and Basic Steps

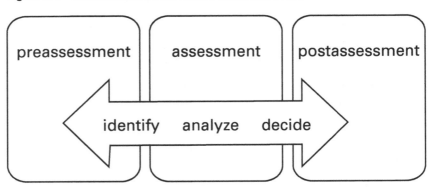

Source: Based in part on Altschuld 2010.

A Guide to Assessing Needs

on using existing information as much as possible, rather than on collecting new information, to inform decisions.

1. With the sponsors of the assessment, determine the overall scope of the needs assessment.

2. Depending on the scope of the assessment, identify the primary performance issues that are leading to the needs assessment. To the extent possible, review existing information (such as earlier reports or surveys) to guide the assessment.

3. Define what data and information are required from the needs assessment to adequately inform decisions. This step may require that you collect some preliminary information from key stakeholders and partners to define objectives and select methods.

4. With others, create a management plan for the needs assessment (see appendix A).

5. Validate your management plan for the needs assessment with colleagues, peers, clients, partners, the assessment's sponsors, and others who will have a stake in the success of the assessment.

Phase 2. Assessment

The purpose of this phase is to implement the assessment in a methodologically sound manner that generates justifiable information to make decisions.

1. Make arrangements to collect the necessary information from the various sources. Schedule interviews, create surveys, arrange focus groups, collect documents to be reviewed, train group facilitators when necessary, schedule performance observations, and so forth.

2. Review protocols, questionnaires, and other information-gathering tools to verify that you capture the necessary information regarding both the current achievements and the desired accomplishments.

3. Collect information by (a) using a variety of tools and techniques and (b) including sources that represent varying perspectives on the primary performance issues.

4. Define needs on the basis of performance gaps between current and desired results.

5. Establish an initial prioritization of needs on the basis of size, scope, distinguishing characteristics, and relative importance.

6. For the highest-priority needs, create a plan for collecting information on the factors that are likely leading to the performance gaps.

7. Collect information regarding the causal factors (or root causes) associated with priority needs.

8. Analyze and synthesize the useful information you have collected.

9. For each priority need and its associated causal factors, identify multiple performance-improvement activities that in combination could address the complete need.

10. Evaluate each potential performance-improvement activity to assess its value to your improvement effort.

11. Use the information to prioritize needs and make recommendations regarding the improvement efforts that will best achieve desired results within the given context.

Phase 3. Postassessment

The purpose of this phase is to underscore that the assessment does not end once priorities have been set. Information from the assessment must be shared and used to guide decisions. Additionally, situations change, and you should routinely collect and assess information as part of ongoing monitoring and evaluation. This phase supports the implementation of recommendations and offers opportunities to take corrective actions where necessary.

1. Summarize your recommendations in a needs assessment report or presentation.

2. Communicate your draft findings to your stakeholders. For larger-scale assessments, this step may involve developing a dissemination strategy, communication strategies, and assessment reports and presentations. It is also good practice to share findings with people who provided information and other inputs for your assessment.

3. Integrate postassessment monitoring and evaluation activities into recommended activities that will be undertaken.

4. Evaluate your needs assessment process to determine if changes should be made before you complete your next assessment.

Build flexibility into your plan, but don't be tempted to take the first plausible solution that shows up and forget about the rest of the assessment that you have designed. Research by Paul Nutt (2008) at Ohio State University illustrates that this tendency, which he refers to as taking an *emergent opportunity*, leads to less-successful results from your decisions than if you follow through with the complete needs assessment, which he refers to as *discovery decision making*.[6]

Nevertheless, you can, for example, complete multiple tasks at the same time to save time and resources. Skipping steps or reversing the order of activities can, however, cause problems or lead to missed opportunities to improve performance. Therefore, especially for needs assessments with a larger scope, include dependencies that illustrate which tasks must be completed before subsequent steps can begin.

Lastly, continually review your needs assessment plan throughout the process to ensure that necessary results have been accomplished before moving on to subsequent, and dependent, tasks. If your assessment drifts away from a focus on performance and results, then it is better to know this change early so that corrective actions can be taken.

Who Should Be Involved in a Needs Assessment?

Needs assessments are rarely successful when performed as an individual activity. Instead, involve others inside and outside your organization to gain multiple perspectives on both the results that should be accomplished and the current levels of performance for comparison. From ministry officials and donor partners to internal managers and volunteers, having various partners represented in your needs assessment will improve the quality of your assessment and will create buy-in to the recommendations that follow.

Building a team (or a committee) to conduct the assessment is also essential to the success of your performance improvement efforts. Not only is a needs assessment typically more work than one individual can do, but also conducting a needs assessment with a single perspective can be dangerous.

Table 2.2   Sample Partners in a Needs Assessment for Regional Planning

	Strategic needs assessment	Tactical needs assessment	Operational needs assessment	Combined strategic, tactical, and operational
Information sources				
Clients	* * *	* *	*	* * *
Customers	* * *	* *	*	* * *
Community members	* * *	* *	*	* * *
Senior managers	* * *	* * *	*	* * *
Functional heads or managers	* *	* * *	* * *	* * *
Performers	*	* *	* * *	* * *
Supervisors	*	* *	* * *	* * *
Suppliers	* *	* *	* * *	* *
Volunteers	* *	* *	* * *	* *
Ministry officials	* * *	* *	*	* * *
Elected officials	* * *	* *	*	* * *
NGOs	* * *	* *	*	* * *
Local community groups	* * *	* *	*	* * *
Needs assessment team				
Executive sponsor	* * *	* * *	* *	* * *
Project manager	* * *	* * *	* * *	* * *
Administrative staff	* *	*	*	* *
Data collection staff	*	* *	* *	* *
Communications staff	* * *	* *	*	* * *

Notes: See pages 39–40 for definitions of strategic, tactical, and operational needs assessments.

　　* = Valued partners who, if available, can improve the quality of your assessment.
　* * = Important partners who, although not essential, contribute to a successful assessment.
* * * = Critical partners whose participation is essential for success.

The varied perspectives offered by others on your assessment team will add significant value to the information that you collect and the decision that you make.[7] Table 2.2 illustrates the relationship of multiple, potential partners for needs assessments of differing scopes.

How Long Will a Needs Assessment Take?

The time required to complete a practical needs assessment depends on many variables, from your previous experiences with needs assessments, to the availability of information within your organization, to the scope of your assessment. As a result, you can complete a quality needs assessment in as little time as a week, whereas more complex decisions may require an assessment that spans several months.

Answering the following questions can help you determine the time required for your needs assessment:

1. What is the scope of your needs assessment: strategic, tactical, operational, or all three? How many and how complex are the performance-related questions that your needs assessment is going to inform?

2. Has another needs assessment been completed within your organization in the past year?

3. Does your organization have a strategic plan that clearly links strategic, tactical, and operational performance objectives? Are data on current performance routinely collected to inform decisions in your organization?

4. Have you previously managed a needs assessment or an evaluation?

5. Do you, or do people working with you on the needs assessment, have experience in collecting, analyzing, and synthesizing information?

6. Are there project deadlines or external events that establish a "must complete by" date for the assessment?

Depending on your responses to these questions, the length of a needs assessment can vary from a few days to a couple of months. After answering the questions, use the needs assessment tools found in appendix A to estimate the number of days required for each assessment activity. Be sure to factor in that many of the steps can be completed simultaneously, but that there are also several that cannot be started until a previous step has been completed.

After all this planning, determine how much time you, and others, have to dedicate to the assessment. Review your commitments to other projects, your upcoming vacation schedule, and other events on your calendar that may extend the amount of time required to complete the assessment. Also factor in that others, especially those whom you are counting on to provide useful information, will be out of town, busy, or on holiday (or vacation) during this time.

We realize that this is no easy formula, and from our experience "easy formulas" typically underestimate the amount of time required to complete a useful assessment. Some experienced professionals estimate how long it will take to complete the assessment, and then double or triple that time to be realistic about how long the assessment will take to complete.

How Do You Manage a Needs Assessment?

Managing a needs assessment is very much akin to managing any other project within an organization. Therefore, in appendix A of this book, we have included a number of needs assessment project management guides, checklists, and resources.

To effectively manage your needs assessment, also consider the following:[8]

- *Involve both internal and external partners from day 1.* A needs assessment is rarely an activity that can be completed successfully without engaging both internal and external partners. From internal partners that represent varied perspectives within your organization to external partners that characterize perspectives of communities, clients, government officials, consultants, suppliers, and others outside of your organization, each group plays an essential role in defining and prioritizing needs as well as in identifying and prioritizing potential activities to improve performance.

- *Get a needs assessment sponsor or champion in top management.* When it comes to a needs assessment, successful project management requires that you have a combination of responsibility (for the results of the needs assessment), authority (to make decisions), and accountability (for the accomplishments associated with assessment). Avoid situations where you are responsible and accountable but have no authority to achieve the necessary results. It is important in most situations that the sponsor delegates to you the authority necessary to make management decisions regarding the needs assessment.

- *Establish measurable goals, objectives, and deliverables.* Needs assessments are best managed through detailed goals, objectives, deliverables, and timelines. Use project management tools, such as Gantt or PERT charts, to guide your project from start to finish.[9] Establish clear and measurable objectives for each phase of the needs assessment, and then track your successful achievements. At the same time, remain flexible. Needs are constantly changing—some are leaving (for instance, when a

A Guide to Assessing Needs

related project achieves positive results, or when your organization shifts its objectives under new leadership), and others are emerging (for instance, when changing global economic conditions strain the limited resources of a developing country). Your assessment—and subsequent decisions—must be able to adjust to these realities.

- *Lead the planning process and the assessment.* Successful needs assessments do not happen by chance or luck. Rather, they are led by an individual (or a team), and they require a blend of leadership and management skills. From motivating team members and guiding decisions to sharing authority and taking accountability, leadership plays an essential role in the success of any needs assessment. It is easy to get so wrapped up in managing the day-to-day activities of your project that your leadership gets lost.

- *Balance time, budget, and quality of needs assessment results.* There is no "perfect" needs assessment; consequently your success depends on finding an appropriate balance of time, budget, and quality of results that can be achieved. As you develop your needs assessment plan and guide that plan through implementation, reflect on these three variables to ensure that you are not losing balance or focus. Roger Kaufman (2006) goes as far as to suggest that "anything worth doing is worth doing poorly, at least at first." In other words, a less-than-perfect needs assessment usually has more value than a needs assessment that never gets done; at least, the former gives a starting place for making improvements.

- *Establish your management style.* There is no ideal management style for all needs assessments. At some times, you may have to be more authoritarian to get things done; at other times, you may want to manage by objectives (and then get out of the way so that people can be successful in their tasks). Establish your *primary* management style early on in the project. If you find that it isn't working for the needs assessment, then reflect on your experiences and select another management style that may achieve better results.

- *Assess your strengths and weaknesses.* To manage a successful needs assessment, know your own strengths and weaknesses (for instance, you may be great at keeping the project organized but less effective in leading focus groups as part of data collection). In addition, it is useful to know the strengths and weaknesses of your assessment team members (for example, one member may be great at conducting interviews but unable to view the perspectives of others when synthesizing information from various sources). Understanding and applying these factors as you assign roles, guide decisions, and manage the daily activities is important to your success—and to the success of the assessment.

- *Communicate early and often.* Keep your partners engaged and active throughout the needs assessment rather than letting them become passive observers (see Greer 1999). These internal and external partners include the assessment team, sponsors, and others who may be providing information to the assessment or using the results to inform their decisions. Consequently, from the time you kick off your assessment until the findings have been communicated, keep your partners involved in the information gathering and decision making to some extent. Whether it is calling them once a week to ask for guidance, e-mailing them sample questionnaires, or holding community information meetings, keeping your partners engaged requires that you do not forget about them for weeks or months at a time. After all, if you lose their interest during the needs assessment process, then it is very difficult to get that interest back during the implementation of recommended activities.

- *Keep your focus on the results (or don't get distracted by processes or potential solutions).* Stay focused on the results to be accomplished by your needs assessment. Frequently, you are so distracted by all of the activities (such as interviews, focus groups, team management, and performance analysis) required to complete a needs assessment that you lose focus of your intended results. Routinely review your assessment's goals and objectives to ensure that all of your decisions are guided by the performance targets. Similarly, when potential solutions (including bridges, roads, new computers, wells, dams, microloans, training, mentoring, and other improvement activities) are mentioned, don't be distracted; stay focused on defining your needs as being gaps in results. In the end, the results of your decisions will be significantly better if you follow through with the whole needs assessment.[10]

Where Does a Project's Logic Model Fit In?

Logic models (also known as results chains, results frameworks, program theory, or log frames) are common planning, monitoring, evaluating, and communicating tools used to guide development projects (see figure 2.2). They display the sequential relationships that describe what the project (or program) uses, does, produces, and delivers—as well as the short-term and long-term desired effects (societal results) of those efforts. The models illustrate the "logic" of how investments (money, time, effort, and so on) are intended to achieve a series of results.

Figure 2.2   Logic Models for Planning, Monitoring, and Evaluating

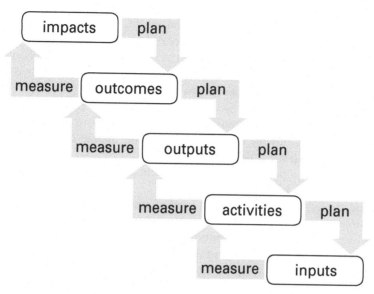

Source: Based on Watkins (2007) and on multiple works by Roger Kaufman, though labels for the three levels of results (impacts, outcomes, outputs) have been modified from his model (outcomes, outputs, products) to reflect the prevalent terminology of the logic model and international development literature.

The logic model works this way: inputs or resources are provided to implement activities. The activities should result in the production and delivery of services or products, which are outputs. These services or products should cause something to change in the desired direction. In the near and medium term, the program's effects are outcomes. The longer-term effects of the program are referred to as impacts. In short, a logic model describes a plausible, causal relationship between inputs and how those inputs will lead to the intended outcomes.

Impacts are the long-term societal results of a project or program. Impacts typically refer to goal attainment and are sometimes referred to as higher-level outcomes. Examples include reduced child mortality and improved rates of economic growth. Achievement of higher-level outcomes is generally beyond the control of those implementing a project, and project implementers should usually not be held solely accountable for achieving them.

Outcomes are the effect or result of activities and outputs at the institutional or organizational level. Outcomes reflect uptake, adoption, or use of outputs by those who are supposed to benefit from the project. Outcomes are what things are changed because of the project or program. Examples include children who have learned more because the quality of their education has improved and who have fewer illnesses because of access to clean water. "Good" outcomes can be measured.

Outputs are the supply-side services or products produced as a result of a project's activities. Examples include the construction of 500 schools, the training of 1,500 nurses, an increase of 20 percent in the production of corn, and a plan for strengthening social protection programs.

Activities are what the project does with the inputs. Examples of activities or interventions include building schools, hospitals, or irrigation canals; training teachers; buying textbooks; developing plans; creating partnerships; and immunizing children.

Inputs are the project's resources, including money, staff, facilities, equipment, and technical expertise.

Logic models typically identify a level of inputs, a level of processes, and then three levels of results. Hence, an important element of a logic model is the differentiation of means (inputs and activities) and results (outputs, outcomes, and impacts) but don't let this cause unnecessary confusion. Some organizations, for instance, prefer to call the three levels of results *outputs, outcomes,* and *impacts*; other institutions refer to them as *products, outputs,* and *outcomes*. Still other organizations use different terminology. The terms are, however, less important than the alignment of results, thereby ensuring that everything a project uses, does, produces, and delivers makes desired contributions to communities and society.

When planning, use logic models (starting with impacts) to determine what results must be accomplished, and then later determine what processes and inputs will best achieve those results. When monitoring or evaluating projects, use the logic model to measure (a) if adequate resources were obtained, (b) if they were used efficiently within the project processes, and (c) then what results (outputs, outcomes, and impacts) were achieved. From here, the project cycle of *assess, plan, act, monitor,* and *evaluate* can begin again.

When available, logic models are an important resource to inform your needs assessment and subsequent decisions. When a model is not available, the results of your needs assessment can easily be used to create one.[11] Within your needs assessment, for example, the logic model can provide a framework for relating current and desired results (see figure 2.3).

Notice that *needs* are only gaps in results, not gaps in activities or inputs. Although your needs assessment should examine gaps for all elements of the logic model, it is important to differentiate gaps in results at the impacts, outcomes, and outputs levels from the activities and resources used to achieve results.

Logic models provide a systemic perspective of projects and offer a useful framework for a needs assessment though your assessment should also look beyond the logic model to ensure that gaps in results are viewed from a systemic perspective. Logic models are predominantly project or program focused, which means they can frequently miss the interdependencies and relationships that span multiple projects, elements critical to making informed decisions. For example, the logic model for a reproductive health project was likely created independent of projects in other

Figure 2.3 Logic Models as a Needs Assessment Framework

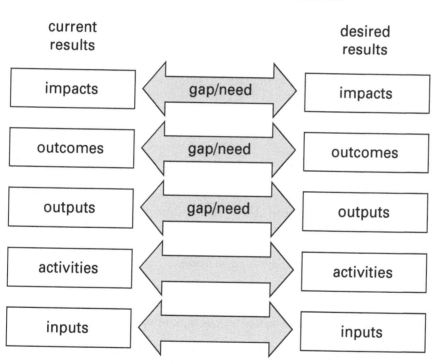

Source: Based on the organizational elements model described in Kaufman (2003) and his other publications. However, it should be noted that Kaufman refers to the three levels of results as *products, outputs,* and *outcomes,* with the latter being those results that primarily benefit society. Kaufman's focus on the beneficiaries' results at each level has distinct advantages over the time-based reference points (such as long- or short-term impacts) that are more common in the logic models literature. Within the Kaufman framework, the primary beneficiaries of *products* are individuals and teams, of *outputs* are organizations, and of *outcomes* is society, thereby making it easier to distinguish and align results during the needs assessment. Nevertheless, given the broad use of logic models literature in international development projects, we will use outputs, outcomes, and impacts throughout this book.

sectors (such as agriculture or transportation) or projects of other development agencies (such as projects funded by NGOs or even those of the client government).

Use logic models as a tool for understanding the relationships of what is used, done, produced, delivered, and contributed to the broader society. Doing so will guide your assessment and will ensure that strategic, tactical, and operational decisions are aligned.

What Types of Data Should You Collect?

Data do not make decisions, but they should play a significant role in supporting your decision making. In his book titled *The ROI of Human Capital*, Jac Fitz-Enz (2009) advises that it is a management imperative to convert data into meaningful information, to turn information into intelligence related to business issues, and then to share that intelligence with others. Needs assessments offer systematic processes for doing just that, thereby providing structure and tools that guide the translation of data into useful information that can be used to make informed decisions about what to do next, which over time creates business intelligence that can be shared with others.

Perspectives on needs assessment also play a vital role in determining (a) which data collection techniques you use; (b), how you ask questions within the technique; (c) what questions you ask; and (d) how you analyze the resulting information to identify, define, and prioritize needs. A combination of discrepancy and appreciative inquiry perspectives is typically valuable to ensure that your assessment determines both what is working well and where improvements can be made.

- A *discrepancy* perspective views needs assessment as a process for identifying and measuring differences and inconsistency between what is and what should be at the strategic, tactical, or operational level.

- An *appreciative inquiry* perspective views needs assessment as a process for engaging people across the performance system so they can build organizations, programs, and projects around what works, rather than exclusively focusing on trying to fix what doesn't.

Given that needs are defined as performance gaps, a discrepancy perspective of data and information is most typically associated with a needs assessment. Discrepancy data are actually quite valuable for informing decisions and improving performance although alone they are not likely enough to consistently make justifiable decisions that will lead to desired results. Likewise, the appreciative inquiry perspective can focus too much on improving activities that are already taking place, without recognizing that improving results may require new activities that address specific weaknesses or future performance expectations. Thus, a combination of the two perspectives is generally recommended for a comprehensive needs assessment.

Discrepancy Data Collection and Information Gathering

Needs assessments and subsequent decisions generally benefit from data and information regarding performance discrepancies. Incomplete projects, missed deadlines, low client satisfaction are discrepancies between desired accomplishments and current achievements that will help shape your assessment and decisions. It is, therefore, useful to collect data and information that can readily describe performance discrepancies. Survey data, interview responses, focus group results, performance observations, document reviews, and other needs assessment tools and techniques described in this book can all be used to illustrate performance discrepancies. For example, the interview question "Given the context of our organization, what would be the desired or expected length of time for a project to go from concept to funding approval, and how long does it currently take?" readily offers discrepancy data that can define a need.

The value of information to illustrate performance discrepancies is not defined by the type of data. Qualitative, quantitative, hard, and soft data can all be used effectively to point out performance discrepancies. Descriptive differences in perceptions can be just as valuable to your needs assessment as numeric data drawn from a database. Information viewed from a discrepancy perspective does not depend on the type of data you have but rather on the point of view you use to compare those data against other information.

Appreciative Inquiry Data Collection and Information Gathering

Focusing exclusively on performance discrepancies can, nevertheless, cast a dark shadow on the many positive achievements within any organization. Taking an appreciative inquiry perspective acts to balance the potentially negative view of performance. By identifying and highlighting the positive achievements, you are adding to your assessment valuable information about what is working well and how you can build on those results.

As you do when looking at performance from a discrepancy perspective, use various assessment tools and techniques when applying an appreciative inquiry perspective. From this perspective, you can also successfully conduct surveys, interviews, focus groups, observations, and reviews and can use other assessment tools. The difference is that rather than looking for gaps in performance, you are identifying the beneficial results of current activities and determining how they can be improved on to achieve future results.[12]

Information gathered from an appreciative inquiry perspective can identify activities that should be maintained or expanded to accomplish desired results. By coordinating these successful activities with the performance improvement activities coming out of your needs assessment, you can increase the likelihood of sustainable improvements.

Collection of Diverse Data

Use a similar integration of qualitative (or quality), quantitative (or quantity), hard (or externally verifiable), and soft (or not externally verifiable) data collection procedures to ensure that your needs assessment is robust

Table 2.3 Examples of Data-Collection Tools and Techniques for Each Data Type

	Hard (externally verifiable data)	Soft (not externally verifiable data)
Quantitative (numeric expressions of a variable)	• Performance data • Budget analysis	• Performance ratings • Scaled surveys (for example, 1 = disagree, 5 = agree)[a]
Qualitative (nonnumeric expressions of a variable)	• Analysis of a list serve • Document review • Focus groups[b] • Multisource performance observations	• Opinion surveys • Individual interviews • Single-source performance observations

Source: Watkins (2007).

a. The results of Likert-type scale surveys are often mistakenly thought of as hard data because they result in quantifiable data. This is a good example of why you should consider data on both dimensions (hard-soft and quantitative-qualitative) because a single dimension may lead to confusion or the use of inappropriate statistical techniques and related conclusions.
b. Focus groups can offer participants the ability to verify the input of other participants, thereby offering external verification of data of individual participants.

and diverse. Each of the different categories of data can be important to your assessment. Each has strengths and weaknesses; therefore, including information from a variety of categories (for instance, soft quantitative and hard qualitative) gives you a more balanced view of the need (see table 2.3).

Likewise, both inductive and deductive approaches to analysis should be considered after you have collected data. Inductive approaches start with a blank slate to identify emerging trends or patterns. Conversely, deductive approaches begin with a framework or model, and then they sort data into the prescribed structure. Both approaches can be effective techniques, and they can complement each other in the same needs assessment. There is, however, no easy formula for determining which approach is appropriate for your assessment. Consider both options for each category of data, and use the approach that best fits your context.

Which Tools and Techniques from This Book Should You Use?

Needs assessments rely on a broad set of common tools and techniques for collecting information and making decisions; many of these tools and techniques are also applied during or after an activity for monitoring, quality improvement, and evaluation purposes. From focus groups and interviews to scenarios and fishbone diagrams, most of the tools are not unique to the needs assessment process; rather, it is the "before a decision is made" perspective applied to each tool that defines the value of a needs assessment.

Your assessment, for instance, may be used to determine what combination of social aid programs will best improve the quality of life for impoverished people living in rural communities. The findings of the assessment could lead to a series of activities that are intended to achieve desired results. However, the context of communities is always changing (for instance, natural disasters occur, changes in government leadership can reduce funding, and emigration patterns change), and the implementation of projects is often quite different from what was intended (for instance, project leaders may not work with community leaders as imagined, project staff members may leave the country, or new technologies may offer unforeseen improvements to the project). Development projects are, therefore, complex and often unpredictable.

Despite this unpredictability, your needs assessment must define and prioritize needs and then must support decisions about what to do. Moreover, your success is frequently measured according to the results of the activities that were recommended in this ever-changing environment. Your assessment, therefore, cannot rely on just one tool (for example, a survey) for collecting information and another (for example, straw polls) for making decisions. Typically, you want to have (and use) a number of optional tools to meet the high expectations.

The needs assessment tools and techniques included in this book offer just a sample of the many ways that you can gather information, make decisions, and improve performance. All the same, it is often challenging to decide which tools or techniques are best for your needs assessment. For some assessments, focus group techniques may be most valuable to ensure partner buy-in. For other assessments, a blend of analytical tools and group decision-making techniques may make the most sense. The choices are, however, rarely easy. For that reason, we have divided the tools and techniques into two categories for needs assessment applications: *information gathering* and *decision making*.

Some of the tools (such as the delphi technique on page 137 or dual-response surveys on page 116) are most effective when you are working with a large number of partners in your needs assessment, whereas others (such as interviews on page 106, fishbone diagrams on page 197, or concept mapping on page 220) can be used equally as well with small or large groups. Similarly, tools and techniques such as surveys and multicriteria analysis can provide useful facts and figures in quantified ways, whereas interviews, case studies, and scenarios provide qualitative information that is also useful in making decisions.

Choosing the right mixture of tools and techniques for collecting information and making decisions is, therefore, much more of an art than a science. Your experiences, background, and confidence in using any of this book's tools and techniques should also inform your decision. If you have the resources to use experts, such as focus group facilitators, interviewers, or return-on-investment analysts, then this involvement will also influence the options you have available for completing your needs assessment.

In addition, we have developed two guides to help you select the appropriate tools for your context. In appendix A, you will find (a) *Tools and Techniques to Consider* and (b) the *Guide to Selecting Tools and Techniques*. These guides can be valuable resources for identifying, comparing, and choosing the tools and techniques for your next assessment.

When Do You Have Enough Information?

Determining when you have "enough" information to make informed and justifiable decisions depends greatly on the decisions you are trying to make

A Guide to Assessing Needs

and the consequences of those choices. Fortunately, when applying many of the collaborative tools and techniques described in this book, it is more easily evident when you have enough information to move ahead or when more information is required to make justifiable decisions.

For example, if you are using a nominal group technique (see page 166) to make a decision, the participants will let you know when more information is required to move on. Likewise, without the necessary data, you will not be able to adequately complete a multicriteria analysis (see page 171) without going back to gather more information. Often, with other techniques, an indicator that you have collected enough data is when you begin to hear the same comments again and again.

When you believe that your assessment has collected enough information to inform a justifiable decision, move on to the next step in your plan. If you get to the decision step and cannot make a decision that is justified by the results of your assessment, then you can always go back to collect any missing information.

Most needs assessments that are done within the context of organizational decision making do not apply statistical standards for sample sizes or confidence intervals. For researchers, guidelines are clear about these issues. Within an organization, however, data from one knowledgeable and experienced staff member may be worth more than survey results from 100 randomly selected staff members. The goal of your needs assessment is to inform a decision, and thus you have a good deal of latitude in determining when enough data have been collected.

As decisions increase in importance, you may, nevertheless, want to examine the statistical standards for sample size and related confidence intervals (as applied in the analysis of quantitative data). For instance, if your needs assessment seeks to identify the needs of HIV/AIDS populations in five countries, and if you determine that a survey is among the data-collection tools to be used to gather necessary information, then it would be important to work with a statistician to determine the appropriate sampling procedures, sample size, and related confidence intervals before conducting the survey.

Although not collecting enough information to inform decisions is one risk in conducting a needs assessment, another risk is the temptation to continue collecting data rather than making a decision. In all assessments, you must take the information you have available at some point and must decide (or recommend) which activities should be used to achieve results. Do your best to strike an appropriate balance between the two risks—having too little or never believing that you have enough—within the context of your assessment.

How Do You Use the Information You Collected to Make Decisions?

To begin, verify that you have the "right" information to make the necessary decisions. From having information that clearly defines the desired results and measures the current levels of performance, to having information on which potential solutions could achieve desired results and knowing how much they could cost, it is important that your needs assessment collects information that could lead to a justifiable decision about what to do.

For each variable that is important to your decisions (for instance, workforce productivity, employee motivation, government policies, client satisfaction, quarterly expenditures, poverty levels, quality of life, and so forth), you should collect data and information regarding both the results that should be accomplished and the results that are currently being achieved. It is also useful to have information supporting how improvements can best be made. Although you can't predict the future, you can use information to support forecasts, scenarios, or anticipated returns on investments.

Alone, determining the size of the gap (desired results minus current results) rarely provides a complete picture. Knowing, for instance, that the desired results of your clients are significantly higher than those outlined in your organization's current strategic plan is valuable information. Organizations are frequently out of touch with their direct and indirect clients.

Likewise, too often we assume that everyone within our organization strives to achieve the same goals and objectives. The reality is that if you were to ask 10 people doing the same job inside of your organization what results they are expected to accomplish, typically you would get at least eight different answers. Document perceptions (or misperceptions) of the desired performance among staff members, and then compare that to the expectations of the organization, clients, and other partners.

Similarly, analyze the information you collect regarding desired performance to gain insights into the priorities of different stakeholders—inside and outside your organization. Routinely in a needs assessment, you will find that groups perceive performance goals differently (for example, headquarters staff members in contrast to field staff members, managers in contrast to clients, or administrators in contrast to trainers). For one group, the desired results are X; for the other group, the goals are Y. Both sets of goals may be right, both may be wrong, or the answer may be somewhere in between. In any case, this analysis yields essential information for guiding your decisions.

A successful needs assessment collects data both to define and understand needs and to identify and compare alternative solutions. The equifi-

Box 2.4 Finding Options: An Example

Through interviews you learn that there are multiple options for reducing the number of waterborne illnesses in rural communities, and then through document reviews you further learn the advantages and disadvantages of each option—as well as the other changes that must take place in the community for each option to be successful.

Likewise, engineering specifications for each option provide useful information on maintenance costs. Using these data, you can make informed decisions about which options will work best in the given country context.

nality principle of systems theory tells us that for any need there are always multiple options for achieving desired results.[13] The data that you collect can help determine which solutions (typically in combinations) should be considered (see box 2.4).

Using information to guide your decisions frequently requires that you first transform raw data (such as productivity reports, performance appraisals, or interview notes) into usable information. Data analysis techniques are typically used to facilitate this transformation. For instance, you may choose a qualitative analysis technique to transform notes from multiple focus groups into thematic responses that illustrate the major findings. Or you may use quantitative correlations to identify relationships between productivity reports and quarterly financial reports.

Many technologies for summarizing quantitative (or numeric) data are now available.[14] Frequencies, averages, and even standard deviations can easily be obtained from spreadsheet data using such programs. These descriptive summaries of the data are usually of more value to decision makers than are pages and pages of raw data. Spreadsheet software also makes it easy for you to illustrate information using graphs, charts, or tables to easily communicate needs assessment findings.

Likewise, numerous pages transcribing the discussions in focus groups or interviews are rarely of great value when making decisions. Instead, use inductive, deductive, or combined approaches to reducing qualitative data so they become pertinent themes and constructive quotes.

Information alone is not, however, enough to consistently make quality decisions. Information has to be moved into useful knowledge through reflection, through links to organizational issues, and by sharing with others to gain valuable perspectives. Many of this book's tools and techniques are designed to facilitate those processes. From tabletop analysis (see page 180) and nominal group technique (see page 166) to scenarios (see page 202) and multicriteria analysis (see page 171), there are many ways to facilitate decision making by helping turn information into knowledge.

Remaining flexible is essential to your needs assessment. Initial conversations will provide guidance on what knowledge is necessary to make informed decisions, but later conversations will frequently transform or expand on these requirements, thereby sending you back to collect more data to inform the pending decisions. Rigid frameworks for determining what data can be collected and what information is necessary to inform justifiable decisions just don't work.

Look at multiple options when looking for solutions, then use agreed-upon performance criteria to assess each of your alternatives (as well as combinations of alternatives). Choose the set of improvement activities that will most likely accomplish desired results in a sustainable manner.

There are, of course, no guarantees. Because your needs assessment focuses on collecting information to inform decisions before they are made, all you have to go on are forecasts, estimates, or "best guesses" of what results can be achieved through various activities. This is just the nature of needs assessments.

Fortunately, from past experiences and through methodical research, you can frequently anticipate future performance with a fair amount of accuracy. Although needs assessments cannot predict all aspects of the future, the characteristics of a systematic assessment increase the likelihood of making quality decisions, thereby giving you the opportunity to make well-informed choices that balance the potential risks and rewards.

What Activities Should You Consider as Solutions?

Do not begin any needs assessment with a solution in mind—not training, not a new high-speed train, not a new HIV/AIDS awareness program, not a new software application, not a reform of economic policy, not even a great motivational seminar by a leading expert in your discipline.

Needs assessments are not worth your time if you are looking only to rationalize a decision that was already made. Rather, enter every needs assessment with a mostly blank slate; then gather information on performance needs, link performance gaps to contributing factors, look for creative ideas, assess solutions, and evaluate alternative activities.

Although you may enter a needs assessment with some ideas and experiences about what solutions may be appropriate to achieve results or what ministry officials want to do, you must hold those possible solutions until they can be evaluated along with the alternatives. Trainers, for example, frequently enter a needs assessment only to rationalize training as the answer to every need. Likewise, experts in developing irrigation systems may find that their needs assessments recurrently justify their creating irrigation systems. After all, nearly everyone feels most comfortable in recommending solutions with which they are already quite familiar from previous experiences. Whether it is digging wells, training teachers, building dams, writing policies, securing loans, or any other activity, prematurely selecting a solution before completing a formal or informal needs assessment rarely leads to sustainable improvements in results. (See also Watkins and Leigh 2010.)

You must put preferred solutions aside, even when others (including your boss or even those who are sponsoring the needs assessment) recommend a plausible solution early in the assessment process. Hold onto such preferred solutions until they can be fairly evaluated. Don't discount them by any means, but don't introduce them as possible solutions unless the results of your needs assessment justify their potential.

Include in your list of optional solutions those that make the most sense within your context. There are always options, so do not settle for the first one or two possible solutions that get mentioned. Press on and listen to what people are telling you during the needs assessment. At the same time, be discerning and include only those that can achieve the desired results within the constraints of your context.[15]

Finally, single solutions rarely achieve sustainable improvements in performance. They typically address only one aspect of an entire performance system. The creation of a performance appraisal program, for example, may be a valuable project for improving performance in a government ministry. But alone, performance appraisals do not address the complete performance system, thereby leaving motivation, knowledge and skills, capacity, incentives, and other elements of performance unattended. Use tools such as the performance pyramid (page 236) to ensure that the activities you select as a result of your needs assessment address the whole performance system.[16]

How Do You Decide Which Activities to Implement?

Deciding (or selecting) which improvement activities will best achieve your desired results given the unique characteristics and constraints of your assessment can be challenging. Begin by using the findings of your needs assessment to link potential improvement activities to the causal factors that are leading to less-than-desired performance. Then evaluate each of your options against performance standards (or criteria) generated in your assessment. You should also evaluate differing combinations of the solutions to determine the appropriate "mix." In many situations, you can then apply participatory techniques such as pair-wise comparison (see page 187) and multicriteria analysis (see page 171) to determine which combinations can best achieve desired results in a sustainable manner.

Several variables should go into determining which activities—or combinations of activities—are "right" for your situation. The variables include the following:

✓ The type of gap—strategic, tactical, operational, or all three—and its level of priority

✓ The causal factors for the need (for instance, conflicting priorities, new skill requirements, lack of clarity, inappropriate incentives)

✓ What the organization or country is already doing (for instance, existing development programs, mentoring, or strategic initiatives)

✓ The ability of the activities to accomplish desired results

✓ The appropriateness of the activities for the organization and its culture

✓ The feasibility of the activities being implemented successfully

✓ The economic costs of the activities in relation to beneficial results[17]

There is, however, no one best way to weigh the variables. In some contexts, the economic feasibility will guide most of the decisions (such as when resources are very limited), whereas at other times the accomplishment of necessary results may drive most of your decisions (such as when responding to a natural disaster). Likewise, many assessments rely on group decision-making tools (such as the nominal group technique on page 166), whereas others rely on analytical techniques (such as the multicriteria analysis on page 171). Therefore, appendix A includes two guides to help you determine which of this book's tools and techniques are most useful to your current assessment: *Tools and Techniques to Consider* (see page 269) and the *Guide to Selecting Tools and Techniques* (see page 273).

When deciding among your options, especially when leading a group toward a decision, it can be helpful to limit the number of potential solutions that are presented. Offering too many options may lead to decision paralysis or create unrealistic expectations of what can realistically be achieved.[18] You may, for instance, want to complete an initial review of the options to remove any that are not going to meet the minimal standards for a workable solution (for example, it is beyond the project's budget). You should inform the group of the options that were removed and why, but then focus the group on analyzing the remaining options to see which can best achieve the desired results within the constraints of your context.

How Do You Know When You Are Done with Your Needs Assessment?

Your assessment should not end until you have enough useful information and knowledge to make the decisions that were the drivers of the assessment in the first place. Therefore, return frequently to the questions you are trying to answer as guides, thus ensuring that time and money are not lost chasing down information that will not help make the pending decisions. Your ability to provide well-informed recommendations regarding the answers to the questions will guide your needs assessment and will help you determine when your assessment is complete.

Needs are not, however, constant artifacts within organizations. New needs emerge on a regular basis, while old needs are either met or made irrelevant. Changes within the organization may shape the permanence of needs, such as when new leadership alters the strategic direction or when other improvement projects achieve desired results. Equally, external changes will influence and shape needs in your organization, such as when government policies shift or a natural disaster affects a community. As such, needs change over time just as individuals, organizations, communities, and whole societies change (see table 2.4). Although your assessment may be very accurate and useful today, it is important to monitor needs and update your assessment whenever significant changes are found.[19]

This instability of needs often requires that needs assessments become a "way of business" rather than a discreet activity; that is to say, although formal needs assessments may be done as time-limited projects, the assessment approach to informing decisions should become an inherent part of the organization's culture.

Most often the results of a needs assessment are summarized in an assessment report or presentation although often the assessment will continue on until the findings have been communicated to most of the assessment's partners. Technically, most definitions of needs assessment end the process when justifiable decisions have been made regarding the activities that will best improve performance. Nevertheless, the findings of the needs assessment are frequently the first resources to be used in the design, development, implementation, and evaluation of any improvement effort. Thus,

Table 2.4 Typology of Needs

Needs	Description	Examples
Continuing needs	Gaps in results that are known from previous assessment and are monitored in an ongoing manner	For a region of the country, the number of HIV/AIDS cases and the percentage of children completing a full course of primary education have remained relatively stable in relation to project goals for the last 10 years and continue to represent significant needs.
Changing needs	Gaps in results that adjust in size, scope, importance, or other characteristics in response to changes internal or external to your organization or community	A rural flood significantly reduces crop production, thereby sharply increasing performance gaps for a number of food- and health-related needs that had previously been stable for several years.
Emerging needs	Gaps in results that emerge when new desired results are identified, or when there are unforeseen changes in current performance	As a result of conflicts in a neighboring country, new immigration patterns are significantly altering the demands placed on local governments, thereby leading to new needs at a time when a large development partner announced a reduction in services in the area.

Note: Case studies that illustrate the various needs of developing countries are included in the United Nations (2004) needs assessment report on the Millennium Development Goals.

your involvement with the needs assessment will frequently lead to continuing contributions throughout the remainder of the improvement initiative (see box 2.5).

As you can see, defining the end to a needs assessment can be difficult for many reasons. Although the formal project steps may come to a close when the final report is written or when a summary presentation is given to stakeholders, the ongoing effects of the needs assessment will frequently keep you engaged in tracking needs over time, in assisting with improvement projects, and in managing subsequent assessment efforts.

Box 2.5 Continuing Role: An Example

If the results of your needs assessment suggest specific reforms to taxation policies to support early childhood development and the development of a rapid social response program within the Ministry of Community Development, then your experiences from completing the needs assessment will likely be of value in assisting in the development, implementation, improvement, and subsequent evaluation of those two activities.

After all, the needs assessment provides the foundation for the selected activities (identifying and defining the results they are intended to achieve), and it simultaneously provides the evaluation criteria on which decisions are made about how to improve results in the future.

What Should Go in a Needs Assessment Report and Presentation?

Although informal needs assessments typically end with just a decision or a choice, most formal needs assessments end with some form of report and presentation. The contents, length, format, and audience for the report and presentation are frequently defined by the norms within your organization. The intent of the report and presentation may be to communicate findings and recommendations to internal partners, external partners, or both. Or a written report may be primarily for external communications, whereas internally a short presentation to the project sponsors may be the custom. It just depends on your organization and the context of your assessment.

The contents of your needs assessment report may also vary widely as determined by several factors, including (a) the audience, (b) the format (for instance, website versus printed report), (c) the scope of the assessment (strategic, tactical, operational, or all three), (d) the type of needs identified (stable, changing, emerging, or all three), (e) the amount and types of data collected, (f) the number of alternative improvement activities considered, and (g) the importance of decisions to be made on the basis of the report (or presentation) (see table 2.5).

Executive summaries are often the most-read part of a report; thus, that section will typically require a significant amount of attention. A good executive summary is typically less than 10 percent of the length of the whole report, including the purpose and scope of assessment, methods used, results found, conclusions and recommendations, limitations, and other

Table 2.5   Typical Contents of a Needs Assessment Report and Presentation

Assessment report	Assessment presentation
Executive summary	Agenda
Introduction	Introduction
Purpose, goals, objectives	Purpose, goals, objectives
Needs	Executive summary
Methods for identifying needs	Needs
Data identifying needs	Methods for identifying needs
Actions considered	Data identifying needs
Methods for identifying alternatives	Actions considered
Data on alternatives	Methods for identifying alternatives
Criteria for comparing	Data on alternatives
Conclusions	Criteria for comparing
Decisions or recommendations	Conclusions
Acknowledgments	Decisions or recommendations
Annex: supporting data	Acknowledgments
Annex: tools and instruments	Additional resources

Note: In her book titled *First Things Fast*, Allison Rossett (1999) provides a useful discussion and set of examples for what can be included in a training-focused needs assessment report.

supportive information that could be important to readers and decision makers. Ideally, the executive summary previews the main report, thereby helping readers build a mental framework for organizing and comprehending the details of the report.

In your organization, however, the reality may be that most of your audience will read only the executive summary—with those most affected by the findings reading the full report. Therefore, many times a helpful heuristic when writing an executive summary is to assume that the audience will not read the full report; thus, you are pushed to be very clear and concise while you include all essential information for making decisions.

Throughout your report, use tables and graphics when appropriate to illustrate data. Readers (or viewers, in the case of a presentation) can benefit from images that summarize data in easy-to-read, easy-to-understand formats. Typically graphics are most valuable when you can illustrate the meaningful relationships among two or more variables in one image (for instance, trend data in the number of children completing a full course of primary education along with data on donor-funded projects completed within the country).

Depending on the context of your report or presentation (such as length, audience, or format), it is important to find an appropriate balance of details and summaries. It can be tempting, for instance, to include pages and pages of detailed data that substantiate your conclusions in an assessment report. But if the audience for your report does not have time to review the data in detail, then it is not a necessary component. In such situations, you can post the detailed data on a web page for interested readers and can simply provide a summary in the written report.

At the same time, your report or presentation must provide enough detail to support your decisions (or recommendations). Readers (or viewers) frequently have high standards for needs assessments, often expecting the assessment to provide clear answers that guarantee future success—which, of course, is unrealistic. Nevertheless, you should strive to meet their standards by including enough data and information in the report or presentation to support your conclusions, recommendations, and decisions.

Finally, you must, as they say, have "thick skin." Almost every needs assessment report or presentation leads to recommendations or decisions that some people support and others do not. The supporters often read the executive summary and are satisfied with the conclusions, even as the challengers closely examine every statement, method, data source, analysis technique, and conclusion to find flaws in your decisions or recommendations. And because needs assessments deal with people, organizations, and forecasting future results, there are bound to be imperfections in every needs assessment. At this point, all you can do is present the facts as honestly as possible. By following this book's systematic processes—as well as by applying its tools, techniques, guides, and checklists—you can, however, minimize the flaws that challengers may use to discount your findings.

Notes

1. For additional information on managing a needs assessment project, you should review Jim Altschuld's 2010 series of five books titled *The Needs Assessment Kit*.
2. The tobacco industry in the United States offers numerous high-profile examples of what happens when decisions are made outside the context of societal outcomes (especially when short-term profits are the dominant guide for decisions).
3. What Peter Drucker refers to as the "boundary conditions" when making decisions (that is, the specifications that answers must satisfy).
4. Based on Roger Kaufman's definition of *needs*.
5. Based on the series of five books by Altschuld (2010).
6. Based on Nutt (2008).
7. See the five-book series by Altschuld (2010) for more on building an effective needs assessment committee.

8. Based in part on Klinder (2005).

9. Useful descriptions and guides for developing Gantt and PERT charts are available at http://www.ehow.com/facts_4844081_between-gantt-charts-pert-charts.html.

10. Research by Nutt (2008) illustrates that ending the needs assessment when the first viable solution is presenting will reduce the beneficial results of the decision.

11. The Kellogg Foundation offers a free guide for developing logic models at http://www.wkkf.org/knowledge-center/resources/2006/02/WK-Kellogg-Foundation-Logic-Model-Development-Guide.aspx.

12. You may also determine that current results do not have to be improved, just maintained. In those situations, you then want to ensure that any improvement activities resulting from your needs assessment do not negatively impact on current results.

13. More specifically, any need within an open system, which encompasses most organizations and organizational activities.

14. Such spreadsheet software programs include Microsoft Excel, OpenOffice Calc (free spreadsheet software), or Google Documents (free online spreadsheets).

15. Too many options can paralyze your ability to make a decision, increase expectations beyond what can realistically be met, or lead to extended second guessing of what you have decided (see Schwartz 2003).

16. Also see http://www.needsassessment.org for audio interviews on numerous training and nontraining performance improvement activities.

17. Based on Stolovich and Keeps (2009).

18. Schwartz (2003).

19. In the overview volume for his five-book series, Altschuld (2010) further identifies seven types of needs that can be examined in a needs assessment. Each category can also be considered in terms of needs that are constant, changing, or emerging.

    1. Present (short-term) and Future (long-term) Needs

    2. Severe vs. Slight Needs

    3. Maintenance/Upgrade Needs (that is, not needs now but will become if results are not maintained or upgraded)

    4. Collaborative Needs (that is, needs that span across multiple organizations and must be addressed together)

    5. Level 1, 2, and 3 Needs (that is, needs of those who receive services, needs of those who deliver services, and needs of the overall system to support the previous)

    6. Asset or Capacity Needs (that is, needs from the perspective of what is working and how to build on strengths)

    7. Retrospective Needs (that is, needs that are assessed during or at the end of a project in conjunction with a formative or summative evaluation)

References

Altschuld, James W., ed. 2010. *The Needs Assessment Kit*. Thousand Oaks, CA: Sage Publications. [A 5-volume series with individual titles]

- Altschuld, James W., and David D. Kumar. 2010. *Needs Assessment Phase I: An Overview* (Book 1 of *Needs Assessment Kit*). Thousand Oaks, CA: Sage Publications.
- Altschuld, James W., and J. Nicholls Eastmond Jr. 2010. *Needs Assessment Phase II: Getting Started* (Book 2 of *Needs Assessment Kit*). Thousand Oaks, CA: Sage Publications.
- Altschuld, James W. 2010. *Needs Assessment Phase III: Collecting Data* (Book 3 of *Needs Assessment Kit*). Thousand Oaks, CA: Sage Publications.
- Altschuld, James W., and Jeffry L. White. 2010. *Needs Assessment Phase IV: Analysis and Prioritization* (Book 4 of *Needs Assessment Kit*). Thousand Oaks, CA: Sage Publications.
- Stevahn, Laurel A., and Jean A. King. 2010. *Needs Assessment: Phase V: Taking Action for Change* (Book 5 of *Needs Assessment Kit*). Thousand Oaks, CA: Sage Publications.

Fitz-Enz, Jac. 2009. *The ROI of Human Capital: Measuring the Economic Value of Employee Performance*. 2009. New York: AMACOM.

Greer, Michael. 1999. "Planning and Managing Human Performance Technology Projects." In *Handbook of Human Performance Technology: Improving Individual Organizational Performance Worldwide*, edited by Harold D. Stolovitch and Erica J. Keeps, 96–121. San Francisco: Pfeiffer.

Kaufman, Roger. 1992. *Strategic Planning Plus*. Thousand Oaks, CA: Sage Publishing.

———. 1998. *Strategic Thinking: A Guide to Identifying and Solving Problems*. Rev. ed. Washington, DC, and Arlington, VA: The International Society for Performance Improvement and the American Society for Training and Development.

———. 2000. *Mega Planning: Practical Tools for Organizational Success*. Thousand Oaks, CA: Sage Publications.

———. 2006. *Change, Choices, and Consequences: A Guide to Mega Thinking*. Amherst, MA: HRD Press.

Kaufman, R., H. Oakley-Brown, R. Watkins, and D. Leigh. 2003. *Strategic Planning for Success: Aligning People, Performance, and Payoffs*. San Francisco: Jossey-Bass.

Klinder, Bernie. 2005. "Step-by-Step Guide: 12 Steps to Project Management Success." http://searchwinit.techtarget.com/news/1063152/Step-by-Step-Guide-12-steps-to-project-management-success.

Nutt, Paul. 2008. "Investigating the Success of Decision-Making Processes." *Journal of Management Studies* 45: 2.

Rossett, Allison. 1999. *First Things Fast*. San Francisco, CA: Jossey-Bass.

Schwartz, Barry. 2003. *The Paradox of Choice: Why More Is Less.* New York: Harper Perennial.

Stolovich, Harold, and Erica Keeps. 2009. "Selecting Solutions to Improve Workplace Performance." In 2007 *ASTD Handbook for Workplace Learning Professionals,* edited by E. Beich. Alexandria, VA: ASTD Press.

United Nations. 2004. "Needs Assessment Report on the Millennium Development Goals." http://www.unmillenniumproject.org/documents/mp_ccspaper_jan1704.pdf

Watkins, Ryan. 2007. *Performance by Design: The Systematic Selection, Design, and Development of Performance Technologies That Produce Useful Results.* Amherst, MA: HRD Press, and Silver Spring, MD: International Society for Performance Improvement.

Watkins, Ryan, and Doug Leigh, eds. 2010. *Handbook for Improving Performance in the Workplace.* Vol. 2: *Selecting and Implementing Performance Interventions.* San Francisco: Wiley/Pfieffer, and Silver Spring, MD: International Society for Performance Improvement.

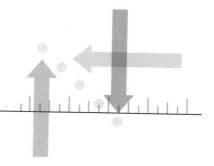

SECTION 3

Needs Assessment: Tools and Techniques

Introduction

Though needs assessments are akin to many other organizational processes from a project management perspective, the characteristics that make needs assessments unique (such as guiding decisions before they are made and focusing on results rather than on solutions) are those that also require a distinctive set of tools and techniques. Although many of the tools you use are not exclusive to a needs assessment—with many being borrowed from scientific research, evaluation, and other disciplines—their application in assessment projects often uses a slightly different perspective from how you may have encountered them before.

In section 3, we have identified 23 tools and techniques that are often applied at varying stages of a needs assessment. The approaches do not represent all of the tools that you might find useful, but rather they are a sample that we believe can expand your options and improve the quality of assessment projects. Rarely would any organization's decision-making culture support the use of each and every technique we describe, though most would benefit from trying tools beyond simple surveys or interviews.

We have broken the tools into two parts for different purposes in the needs assessment process. *Part 3A. Data Collection Tools and Techniques* provides options for you to consider using when you are collecting data to inform your needs assessment. But after you have collected information for the needs assessment, another important step involves making decisions about that collected information. And there are tools to support the decision-making process.

Part 3B. Decision-Making Tools and Techniques offers suggested tools for analyzing and prioritizing issues in the needs assessment process and for ultimately deciding to take action. Prioritizing information and making choices can be a difficult task for both individuals and groups. Instead of making decisions through an informal, ad hoc process, tools are available that can be helpful in ensuring that issues are given due consideration in a participatory decision-making process.

For each tool and technique described in this section, we have applied a needs assessment perspective to its application. That is, we have viewed it from the standpoint of how it is best used to identify and analyze needs so you can make decisions about what to do. In several cases, this perspective required simplifying the tools as they are applied for other reasons, as well as adding new "twists" in other cases to ensure that the goals of your needs assessment can be met. In all cases, our descriptions are intended to introduce tools and techniques rather than provide "the definitive explanation" on how they are to be used. Therefore, at the end of each description, we have included websites, books, and articles that can further guide your use of each tool.

Try a few of them; see how it goes. Learn more about the ones you are most interested in. Build a variety of techniques and tools into your assessment plan. Customize the tools for your organizational context. In the end, you will likely find that a number of tools can improve the quality of assessment projects and the subsequent decision making. Keep those tools, use them again, and improve on them.

Note: For the convenience of our readers, copies of the individual tools are available and can be downloaded as single PDF files at http://www.needsassessment.org.

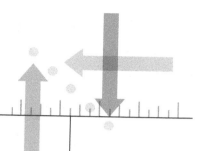

Part 3A

DATA COLLECTION TOOLS AND TECHNIQUES

Part 3A. Data Collection Tools and Techniques provides options for your consideration as you collect data for your needs assessment. After you have collected information for that assessment, you must consider another important step that involves making decisions about your collected data. There are also tools to support the decision-making process. We will explore those tools in *Part 3B. Decision-Making Tools and Techniques.*

DOCUMENT OR DATA REVIEW

Purpose

The purpose of conducting a document or data review is to review a variety of existing sources (for example, documents, reports, data files, and other written artifacts) with the intention of collecting independently verifiable data and information.

Needs Assessment Applications

Many times the information required to complete a needs assessment has already been collected for other purposes. For example, similar data to what you are looking for may have been previously collected for generating other reports, papers, or research. Ministries, government agencies, nongovernmental organizations (NGOs), and other organizations often collect and/or produce the valuable data or reports that can supplement your own data collection as part of your needs assessment. The document and data review process provides you with a systematic procedure for identifying, analyzing, and deriving useful information from the existing documents so you can make informed decisions.

Today, many government agencies, multilateral institutions, and other organizations are making documents and data sets available to the public (see box 3A.1). In 2011, the World Bank, for instance, expanded its access to information policies, thereby making many of its databases and project reports available on its public website. What is available varies widely, ranging from, for example, (a) planning documents related to small development projects in Africa, to (b) evaluation reports on a country's progress toward achieving the Millennium Development Goals, to (c) global information system maps showing crime hot spots in a city, to (d) health sector indicators for a particular nation.

Access to information is, nevertheless, an essential starting place for any document review process. Look broadly for resources that already have the data you require to make decisions. Such resources can save you lots of time and money.

In the context of international development, the documents and data available are heavily biased toward the English language, as well as toward those with ready access to the Internet and basic skills to navigate the databases. Nevertheless, such initiatives are a start toward putting useful information in the hands of the public across the globe. We expect that this trend will grow with governments and organizations that are investing in establishing policies and information systems toward that end.

Advantages and Disadvantages

Advantages

- The information contained in extant data or documents is often independently verifiable.

- The document or data review process can be done independently and without having to solicit extensive input from other sources.

- A document or data review is typically less expensive than collecting the data on your own.

Disadvantages

- Information in the documents or data may represent a perspective that is not aligned with your needs assessment project. For example, the perspective of government reports may not be aligned with those of development organizations.

- Data in the document sources may not be exactly what you want for your needs assessment. For instance, you may want environmental records by village but extant records may document only by province.

- Obtaining and analyzing necessary documents can be a time-consuming process.

- You will not be able to control the quality of data being collected and must rely on the information provided in the documents as you assess quality and usability of the sources.

Process Overview

1. From a list of information required to complete your needs assessment, identify those elements or indicators that may be contained in previously written reports, planning papers, research synopses, or other documents. For instance, if you require statistics on the population growth within a region, then identify several government (or potentially United Nations) reports that provide the necessary information. Both published and unpublished sources can be considered for inclusion, though the validity of unpublished materials can make your quality assurance efforts more difficult.

2. Consider developing a list of characteristics (or attributes) that you are looking for in an existing record; that approach can help you identify a comprehensive list of available resources. For example, (a) do you want to use only data that were collected through internationally funded efforts, or (b) do you want only information that has been published with full disclosure of the participants and of the methods used to collect the

A Guide to Assessing Needs

data, or (c) do you want only records from the past 10 years, or (d) do you need a combination of those elements?

3. For each item of required information that could potentially be found in an existing document, list three to five potential resources for obtaining that information. For instance, imagine that your needs assessment requires information on the number of current employees within a government agency who have the qualifications to perform financial audits. In this case, you want to determine which currently available agency documents or data monitoring systems may include such information, where those documents might be located, and from whom the documents can be obtained.

4. Identify the individual(s) who will be invited to participate in the document review. Most often, you want to invite at least two people to review each document, and you can also be a reviewer when appropriate. Having two or more reviewers improves the reliability of the reviews and gives you the opportunity to compare across reviews.

5. Develop a document or data review protocol, checklist, or examination form that can be used systematically by each reviewer to ensure that valuable information is identified, analyzed, coded, and documented. Be sure to include space at the top of each protocol, checklist, or examination form for the reviewer to describe the document and to state where it is stored if additional information is required later. As appropriate in the protocol, you should ensure that required information regarding both the current results and the desired results will be represented, along with the required information at each level of the program or project results chain.

6. Generate guidelines for using the protocol or checklist or the examination form in the review process. Consider providing a "positive example" of a completed review protocol, checklist, or examination form. Be sure to highlight how information can be recorded on the form to maximize its clarity and usability in the needs assessment process.

7. As each document or data set is reviewed, have the reviewer(s) complete the protocol, checklist, or examination form to verify that all useful information is documented.

8. When all of the relevant files have been reviewed, have all reviewers meet to collectively document the findings of their reviews (or what information has been collected through the document review process). In particular, the reviewers should identify specific instances where informa-

tion from different documents may disagree, where there are instances of multiple documents containing similar information, where additional information may be located, and what information may have to be collected directly through the needs assessment.

9. Collect the reviewers' documented findings from the review process, and codify the findings for inclusion in the needs assessment. Identify any conclusions regarding needs, root causes, and recommendations for addressing identified needs.

Tips for Success

- Be systematic in your review processes. From identifying potential documents and developing a review protocol to collectively reviewing the information attained through the review of multiple documents, systematic processes should ensure that valuable information is not missed during the review.

- Triangulate data to the extent possible. In other words, when the document review yields data or information that may directly feed into the needs assessment, attempt to locate the confirmatory data or information by examining other independent sources. If the data or information can be triangulated, it can increase your confidence in its accuracy.

- When multiple reviewers are tasked with the role of reviewing document sources, provide clear and consistent guidelines to all reviewers on the procedures for completing the protocol, checklist, or examination form. Ensuring that all reviewers receive the same guidelines for the protocol, checklist, or examination form will make certain that the information is identified, analyzed, coded, and documented in a consistent and reliable manner.

Reference

Witkin, Belle Ruth, and James W. Altschuld. 1995. *Planning and Conducting Needs Assessments: A Practical Guide*. Thousand Oaks, CA: Sage Publications.

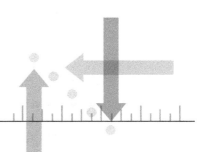

GUIDED EXPERT REVIEWS

Purpose

The purpose of conducting guided expert reviews is to gain informed perspectives from valued experts who are outside the system (for example, education system, transportation system, and so on) on which the needs assessment is focused.

Needs Assessment Applications

Under certain circumstances, you or others associated with the needs assessment can be too familiar (or too unfamiliar) with the processes, procedures, people, tools, resources, performance data, or other variables that influence either current or desired performance to be able to adequately complete a needs assessment. In this situation, reviews by experts (for example, public financial management experts, environmental engineers, organizational development specialists, and so on) provide valuable external perspectives that can inform your decisions.

You should also use expert reviews to provide balanced perspectives when there are even minimal possibilities of internal predisposition or bias that could influence any needs assessment processes or stages. The expert reviews may include collecting data, analyzing information, reporting findings, and conducting other activities that lead to program or project recommendations.

In your needs assessments, guided expert reviews can provide external perspectives on the following:

- Needs (that is, the performance gaps that are the focus of decisions to be made)

- Decisions (that is, the results and recommendations of the assessment itself)

Advantages and Disadvantages

Advantages

- Expert reviews allow you to have a fresh set of eyes that can provide new ideas and insights that might not have come about without the expert's participation.

- The involvement of expert reviewers in the needs assessment process can increase the credibility of the assessment process and findings, thereby potentially increasing stakeholder buy-in.

- The use of expert reviews may allow you to pursue strategies and approaches that make inherent sense for the context in which you may be working but that you might not normally pursue if you did not have the assurance of the expert's careful review.

- Because experts generally bring insights and experiences from other (outside) contexts in which they have worked, the involvement of an expert in the needs assessment may make it possible for you to formally or informally benchmark against other, similar systems or contexts.

- Expert reviews, especially those focused on documents or data files, can often be done at a distance, thereby saving time and resources. For example, you may want expert review performance data to confirm your conclusions, or you may request a review of a pending project proposal; in either case, you could likely e-mail the relevant files or provide access to online databases.

Disadvantages

- It can be a challenge to identify reliable criteria (such as years of development experience, particular technology knowledge, work with specific at-risk populations, and so forth) for selecting experts to involve in the expert review process.

- If the context in which the needs assessment is being conducted is significantly different from the one in which the expert normally works, the extent to which the expert's observations and recommendations are relevant can be diminished.

- As is the case for any other individual, an expert's subjectivity and prior experience may affect the outcome of the expert review process (the effect of this expertise can potentially be mitigated somewhat through the involvement of more than one expert).

- Soliciting insight from experts can be expensive, and it may be difficult to find experts who are able to contribute large amounts of time responding (particularly if the area of expertise is one for which there is high demand).

Process Overview

Getting Started

1. Identify either a need (a gap between current and desired results) or a needs assessment decision (such as prioritizing needs or determining which mix of improvement activities or interventions will work best within your organization) that will be the focus of the guided expert review.

2. Determine what type of expert review you would like the expert to conduct, such as a peer, relevance, or benchmarking review. (a) A *peer review* involves judging the quality of something. For instance, a peer review could involve engaging a public-private sector development expert to assess the quality of a plan developed by a community and its business leaders to help them to address economic development issues for the community. (b) A *relevance review* judges whether an organization's activities are relevant to its mission. An example of a relevance review is when an organizational development specialist works with an organization and engages its stakeholders—management, employees, clients, and others— to understand the strategy of the organization and when the specialist offers an assessment on what could be changed, such as what activities the organization should and should not be doing to meet the goals of the strategy. (c) A *benchmarking review* involves judging the relative standing in an international, regional, sector, or other perspective. For instance, benchmarking reviews assess property rights across countries, thus allowing countries to compare their relative performance.

Finding Experts

Following are some considerations that are relevant when bringing experts on board for an expert review:

1. Generate a protocol (guide) for identifying appropriate experts to invite for the expert review process.

    - This protocol should be based on your understanding of the goals of your needs assessment, as well as the specific context in which the organization functions.

    - Carefully identify the skills and knowledge that someone should possess to be able to meaningfully function as an expert reviewer for the needs assessment, and include those competencies in the protocol.

    - Apply the protocol as you search for potential experts.

2. Identify potential experts from *outside* the system to participate in the review.

    - Experts can be from within the organization (but outside of the unit or division that is the focus of the needs assessment).

    - Or they can be from outside the organization when they have expertise with the performance system or similar such systems.

3. Determine whether you would like experts to be invited as individuals or as teams.

4. Determine whether you would like local or international experts or a combination of both. Consider carefully the benefits and drawbacks of involving experts from other countries. Example benefits and drawbacks include the following:

    - An advantage of involving international experts may be that they bring dynamic new insights to the situation and that they are able to size up the organization's relative standing from an international perspective.

    - A drawback may be that the international expert's ability to leverage his or her expertise may be limited if that expert has no familiarity with the local country context.

    - In some developing country contexts, there may be relatively modest capacity in certain areas of economic productivity, and it may thus be advisable to invite international experts to participate.

    - In many instances, using both local and international experts may provide a mix of the "best of both worlds."

5. As you begin to invite experts, find out about their availability during the time period for the expert review. Because they *are* experts, it is likely

that they are in demand elsewhere too, so you may have to do some creative planning to work around scheduling restrictions while still meeting the goals of an expert review. For instance, if a given expert is not available to come onsite, determine if he or she can review other documentation and reports to give you quality input at a distance (for example, using audio or video conferences).

6. Present the potential experts with unbiased background information on the purpose of their involvement in the needs assessment, and ask each potential expert to evaluate his or her experience and knowledge relative to the specific goals for your needs assessment.

Planning and Conducting the Expert Review

1. Define your objectives for the expert review (or what results you expect to accomplish by the time the review is complete). Be realistic about what objectives can be accomplished. Determine when it is appropriate to use each expert, knowing what they can and cannot do given the constraints of the situation.

2. Generate terms of reference (that is, a scope of work) that can be used by experts prior to arriving on site. Doing so will allow experts to arrive prepared for the task, including giving them time to locate any hard-to-find materials that they may want to consult during the review process.

3. Contact each expert reviewer, and make arrangements for his or her participation. As noted previously, if one or more experts are not available for in-person participation, make arrangements to send relevant documentation that will allow the expert(s) to contribute at a distance.

4. Inform stakeholders and participants of the role of expert reviewer(s).

5. Consider providing metrics or protocols that the experts can use during the expert review. Such metrics or protocols can be valuable in increasing the objectivity and transparency of an expert review process, and they can also increase the chances that the expert review results are aligned with the objectives you defined at the beginning of the process.

6. Collect the necessary background information for each expert reviewer. This information may be valuable later if you have to justify decisions made during the needs assessment.

7. Be sure to include specific deliverables for each reviewer and for each context in which the review is to take place. For instance, do you expect a

written report at the conclusion of each review, or will reviewers be expected to present their findings during a presentation?

Tips for Success

- Develop and maintain a list or inventory of program review experts (especially for larger-scale efforts) to be used for subsequent expert review needs.

- Arrange logistics and provide onsite meeting support. Provide translation and interpretation services, as needed, when engaging international experts.

- Provide experts with specific guidelines or questions that should be used to guide the expert review process.

- Watch out for experts who may have an agenda of their own in completing the review (for example, making recommendations so they can gain future consulting contracts with your organization).

- If you are inviting experts from outside contexts, equip them with some information that will give them insight into the context in which the expert review will take place. This approach is especially important if experts are being invited from foreign countries where cultural and business practices may be significantly different from the context in which your needs assessment is being conducted.

- To the extent possible, schedule the onsite expert's review process during a time when the organization is otherwise functioning in a generally normal way. Scheduling the review process at this time increases the chances that the review will yield relevant results, and it also ensures that others in the organization are not negatively affected by the presence of outside experts.

- Prepare reports on the results of each review. In the reports, identify the relationship of the expert's review to the needs assessment, the goal of the specific expert review, the competencies or expertise of the expert or expert team, the type of expert review conducted, the findings from the expert review, and the potential implications of the findings for the needs assessment.

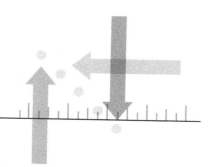

MANAGEMENT OF FOCUS GROUPS

Purpose

The purpose of conducting focus groups is to collect information from a small group (for instance, 5 to 12 participants) in a systematic and structured format (see box 3A.2). An effective focus group is designed around a clear and specific goal. Participants interact with a facilitator who presents the participants with questions designed to yield insight into current or desired results in relation to a specific topic or issue.

Needs Assessment Applications

Attaining the information required to complete a needs assessment will oftentimes require that you interview (or have a focused discussion with) a number of people at the same time. The focus group is an opportunity to gain valuable information related to both current results and desired results at each level of the program or project results chain.

Although focus groups can also be used to identify alternative activities to improve performance, during your needs assessment it is important to

Box 3A.2 Sample Uses of Focus Groups

- Collect information on current performance.
- Validate the results of a survey.
- Define the desired results.
- Identify potential solutions.
- Define strengths and weaknesses of potential solutions.

maintain attention (focus) on the collection of information that will help you identify (a) valid needs (or gaps between current and desired results), (b) evidence to support the validation of those needs, and (c) information that will allow you to prioritize needs before selecting a course of action for addressing the high-priority needs.

Advantages and Disadvantages

Advantages

- Through a focus group format, multiple people can be interviewed at one time.

- Focus group discussions allow members of the focus group to build on each other's comments and reactions. This approach can yield a synergy of discussion around topics or themes.

- Focus groups can help people come to consensus and make challenging decisions (such as prioritizing needs).

Disadvantages

- Group members may not contribute equally to the discussion in a focus group format. More reserved members may not feel comfortable inserting their contributions in the discussion. Other participants may try to dominate discussions.

- Gaining information from the group can be challenging. There is a risk of "groupthink" that can emerge through this process, thus diverting the discussion and making it hard to refocus the group on different issues.

- Discussions may take too long to cover all of the relevant topics and to offer everyone a chance to participate.

- Because of the presence of others, participants may not feel comfortable sharing more sensitive information or views.

- Focus groups are often poorly done, particularly if the focus group facilitator is not experienced in managing focus groups. Focus groups can easily get "off task" if the facilitator does not maintain structure and control throughout the process. (For a helpful sample outline and a sample protocol, see pages 101–105.)

Process Overview

1. From the list of information required for the needs assessment, identify those elements that may best be attained through focus groups. For instance, identification of needs, validation of needs, root causes of needs, and alternative solutions identification, or a combination of these.

2. Prioritize the information requirements for each focus group, and use this ranking to create a facilitator's guide or protocol for each focus group.

3. Select a decision-making technique for each focus group. Although unstructured focus groups may be useful on limited occasions, more structured techniques are often valuable and can ensure that the focus group provides the information you require for making needs assessment decisions. Here are some sample decision-making techniques that you should consider for small groups:

   a. *Critical Incident Technique:* In their responses to focus group questions, participants are asked to provide past events as examples. Each event should include a description of the conditions or context for the event, the people involved in the event, the place of the event, and the associated activities or behaviors of people in the event. The focus of the discussions is then on previous incidents related to the topic rather than on speculations and generalizations.

   b. *Brainstorming:* This technique can be used to quickly generate new ideas or to identify and consider alternative solutions to a given problem. To initiate a productive brainstorming session, you should identify the specific topic that you would like group members to concentrate on. Introduce the topic, and encourage group members to brainstorm freely for a given amount of time. Encourage "on-the-spot" thoughts and ideas. Record all contributions from group members (it is helpful to record their thoughts in a format that is visible to all group members, such as a video-projected concept map or a word processing document). Categorize and combine ideas under overarching headings. Analyze and evaluate the ideas with the group, and prioritize the ideas in terms of their usability in the needs assessment.

   c. *Straw Polls:* An informal voting method that can be used to quickly probe opinions of participants. Straw polls give all participants the chance to give their opinion through a response such as a "yes" or "no" to a question. It is important to recognize that straw polls are not generally considered to be binding, official votes. Instead, they are used to get a sense of the pulse of a group in relation to a specific issue or theme, and they can orient the subsequent discussion. Straw polls can be used effectively in situations where there is a long list of ideas and where you want the group members to eliminate ideas that have little or no support. The straw poll approach lets each group member choose a given number of items from the list for inclusion or elimination.

d. **Round Robin Reporting:** This technique can be implemented in at least two different ways, both of which are based on your having a specific question or suggestion. One approach is to share the question or suggestion with the group members and then to ask all group members to write down their ideas in relation to the question or issue. You next go around the group and have each person take turns to share one idea from his or her list. Continue this process by going around the room until nobody has any ideas left to share. Another approach is to share the question or suggestion with the group and then ask each person to give his or her reactions and ideas in relation to the question or suggestion you presented. In both formats, the round robin approach allows each group member to share equally in the group process, thereby ensuring that no one person dominates the discussion.

4. Create a facilitator's guide or protocol to guide each focus group. Ensure that required information regarding both the current results and the desired results of the needs assessment are represented, along with the required information at each level of the program or project results chain.

5. Locate an experienced facilitator, if possible, as well as a note taker. Using an experienced focus group facilitator will generally lead to better results than if you facilitate the group yourself; however, you may want to be present as a backup note taker during the focus group to capture some of the data firsthand.

6. The facilitator can use the facilitator's guide or protocol to generate a few specific questions that can be used to open the discussion in the focus group (or to come up with the questions, he or she can also consult the information about current and desired results that are based on the needs assessment).

7. Schedule a time for the focus group when the highest-priority participants are all available. Verify that you have both a focus group facilitator and a person to take notes during the meeting, that both are available at the scheduled time, and that both understand what is to be accomplished through the focus group. Arrange for an audio recorder so that the facilitator and note taker can verify information from the discussion when later preparing final notes or a report.

8. Implement the focus group session. The facilitator should remind participants to observe confidentiality of information shared. Allow the facilitator to manage the focus group process. If you serve as note taker for the focus group, avoid being tempted to interrupt the group. You are simply there to record data and to observe the focus group.

9. Immediately after the focus group has ended, the facilitator and note taker should verify that all of the essential information from the group has been captured in a written document.

10. If appropriate, run several focus groups. Doing so ensures that you gather enough information for the needs assessment.

Tips for Success

- Have a clear and specific goal for the focus group (in other words, have and maintain a clear focal point rather than an open conversation).

- Engage a facilitator who is experienced in managing focus groups. Focus groups are not as easy to facilitate as you might expect.

- Create a survey to be given out to participants so you can capture information that may not be discussed in the focus group because of time limitations.

- Carefully present each of your questions to the group, and allow the group members a couple of minutes to think about the question and to record their answers.

- Complete a test run of the focus group so you can identify potential problems, changes to questions, or additional materials that should be available to participants.

- After a question has been answered and before moving to the next question, verbally report back a summary of what you heard. This step confirms for the group members that they communicated what they intended to, and it allows them to make any suggestions for adjustments in the event that their thoughts were not accurately represented.

- Don't be afraid to ask participants to leave if they are not willing to let others in the focus group participate. After all, the goal of the focus group is to gain multiple perspectives on the issues.

- If you are going to record (by video or audio) the focus group, then be sure to get the consent of all participants. Communicate to the group members what will be done with the video or audio recording of the session (for example, who will listen to it, how it will be stored, how long it will be stored, and so on). Such issues have consequences for how open the group members will feel about sharing their true opinions rather than those that they think you (or the organization) will want to hear.

- Write down any observations that you made during the focus group. For example, note if the audio or video equipment failed, if something unexpected took place, and so on. Such notes may help elucidate comments when you analyze the data that you gathered through the focus group.

- Plan for the focus group to take between 40 minutes and 3 hours.

References and Resources

McClelland, Samuel B. 1994b. "Training Needs Assessment Data-Gathering Methods: Part 3—Focus Groups." *Journal of European Industrial Training* 18(3): 29–32.

Witkin, Belle Ruth, and James W. Altschuld. 1995. *Planning and Conducting Needs Assessments: A Practical Guide.* Thousand Oaks, CA: Sage Publications.

Websites

"Brainstorming Process" is available at http://www.businessballs.com/ brainstorming.htm.

"The Focus Group Interview and Other Kinds of Group Activities" is available at http://ppa.aces.uiuc.edu/pdf_files/Focus.pdf.

"Focus Groups—A Needs Assessment Tool" is available at http://www.joe.org/ joe/1992spring/tt2.html.

"Small Group Techniques" is available at http://www.fhwa.dot.gov/reports/pittd/ smlgroup.htm.

A USAID guide for conducting focus groups is available at http://pdf.usaid.gov/ pdf_docs/PNABY233.pdf.

Sample: Focus Group Facilitator Outline and Protocol to Identify Factors Leading to Capacity Gaps in Primary Education

This outline will help lead the facilitator through the four key stages of a focus group, as well as serve as a sample protocol for the focus group. The sample protocol has been developed for a series of focus groups with village, provincial, and national administrators involved with the primary education in a developing country that has a mostly rural population. Such focus groups are part of a larger needs assessment study, and they supplement other data collection approaches that have already been completed.

The focus group facilitator should review this facilitator outline with other organizers of the needs assessment. It will be important to determine if all steps and arrangements for running the focus group have been planned and agreed. Modify this outline as necessary.

Sample of Facilitator Outline for Stages of the Focus Group

1. **Opening Remarks**

   - Explain the purpose of the focus group, how it differs from other types of discussions, and how the information will be used.

   - Encourage disagreement and debate over the issues.

   - Clarify that the group does not necessarily need to reach consensus or make decisions.

   - Describe the facilitator's neutral role, discuss issues about confidentiality of information (where appropriate), and solicit participant questions about the process to reduce anxiety.

   - Provide guidance about how the group will operate (for example, having a time frame, talking one at a time, respecting divergent opinions, no one person speaking for the whole group, having cell phones off, not smoking).

2. **Introductions**

   - Invite members to introduce themselves and to describe their role or relationship to the focus group topic.

   - To stimulate group interaction, have each person speak at least once.

- Establish the group as a safe, comfortable, nonthreatening context for discussion.

- Stimulate members to begin thinking concretely about the issues at hand.

3. **Leading the Focus Group**

- Use the focus group protocol, but diverge where there are emergent data or paths to follow.

- Build on initial questions with follow-up questions. Encourage increasingly deep responses to key questions.

- Connect emergent data from separate questions into a complex, integrated analysis.

- Ensure that all participants who want to comment on a question have the opportunity to contribute and to broaden the information collected.

4. **Closing**

- Signal that the group discussion will end soon.

- Identify and reiterate key themes that emerged from the discussion. Give participants an opportunity to refine the themes.

- Summarize and test with the group the relative weight of certain categories of response.

- Identify differences of perspective, contrasting opinions, and areas of agreement.

- Allow a round of final comments and insights. Thank participants and describe any next steps.

The focus group facilitator should review this facilitator protocol with other organizers of the needs assessment. It will be important to determine if the protocol questions are appropriate for the potential respondents and if they address the main issues of the needs assessment. Beyond working with the needs assessment organizers and focus group, the facilitator may wish to ask for a review by others who know about the topic of the focus group. Modify this protocol as necessary.

Sample of Focus Group Protocol	
Welcome (Where appropriate, modify the script and questions.)	**Script:** Thank you for agreeing to participate in this focus group today. We have interviewed a number of stakeholders of the education system in our country to identify capacity gaps of the primary education system, and now we want to learn more about the *factors* that are leading to those gaps. We are not here to debate or solve the capacity gaps, though if you have suggestions for how to improve capacity, please note them on a sheet of paper. We will collect those ideas at the end of the session. Here are nine common categories of factors that influence capacity and that we will use to guide our discussion. However, you are welcome to suggest others. • **Performance capability.** Do we have the right people in the right jobs to achieve desired results? • **Knowledge and skills.** Do people know what to do, and are they able to do it? • **Motivation and self-confidence.** Do people have the motivation and confidence to achieve desired results? • **Expectations and feedback.** Do we have formal and informal mechanisms to help people know how they are performing? • **Environment, tools, and processes.** Do we have what is necessary to achieve desired results (for example, policies, guidelines, data systems, computers)? • **Incentives, rewards, and recognition.** Do we encourage good performance and recognize the achievement of desired results? • **Resources.** Do we have the resources to achieve the desired results (for example, budget, time, personnel, buildings, books)? • **Goals, strategy, and organizational culture.** Does everyone know what we are trying to achieve and how we will achieve it? Do we have shared norms, habits, and beliefs? • **Coordination within and among ministries and government agencies.** Are the government agencies coordinating appropriately? • **Other.** Indicate other possible factors.
Do you have any questions regarding our goals of the focus group?	Notes:

Questions

Q1: One of the identified capacity gaps is the high variation in teacher commitment to the jobs (from those highly committed and engaged as teachers, to those frequently absent from work). Of the nine common factors leading to capacity gaps on your handout, which do you find are most responsible for the current gap?	Response:
	Follow-up question and response:
	Response:
	Follow-up question and response:
	Response:
	Follow-up question and response:
Q2: A second of the identified capacity gaps is the uneven and late delivery of textbooks for schools and pupils. Of the nine common factors leading to capacity gaps on your handout, which do find are most responsible for the current gap?	Response:
	Follow-up question and response:
	Response:
	Follow-up question and response:
	Response:

Q3: A third identified capacity gap is the increasing absenteeism among third grade girls in our most rural populations. Of the nine common factors leading to capacity gaps on your handout, which do you find are most responsible for the current gap?	Response:
	Follow-up question and response:
	Response:
	Follow-up question and response:
	Response:
	Follow-up question and response:
Q4: The fourth identified capacity gap is the *[insert gap]*. Of the nine common factors leading to capacity gaps on your handout, which do you find are most responsible for the current gap?	Response:
	Follow-up question and response:
	Response:
	Follow-up question and response:
	Response:
	Follow-up question and response:

Note: If you have time remaining, you can cover more remaining capacity gaps. If, however, you are short on time, then start the next focus group with the capacity gaps you were not able to include in this discussion.

Conclusions

Script: Summarize the major factors identified during the conversation, and then ask the focus group members to verify that you accurately interpreted their responses.

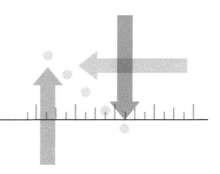

INTERVIEWS

Purpose

The purpose of conducting interviews is to collect information from a single person through a format that may range from structured, to semistructured, to unstructured.

Needs Assessment Applications

Individual interviews can often provide in-depth context, stories, and discussion related to one or more topics that are pertinent to the needs assessment. Such interviews can be done in an environment where the interviewer can ask for elaboration or explanation with follow-up questions. (For a helpful sample checklist and a sample protocol, see pages 110–115.)

Interviews also offer an opportunity for the interviewee to become familiar with the needs assessment and its objectives. Individuals in positions of influence may also appreciate the additional personal attention that the interview can offer as opposed to a survey or focus group.

Advantages and Disadvantages

Advantages

- Interviews typically allow for more focused discussions and follow-up questions.

- Individuals may offer information in interviews that they wouldn't offer in a group context.

- Interviews can be an excellent source for stories and context.

- The interviewer can observe the nonverbal behavior of an interviewee.

Disadvantages

- Time requirements for interviewers and interviewees can be significant.

- Interviews have the potential to reduce the scope and sample for data collection.

- The results of multiple interviews may contradict each other or may be difficult to analyze.

- Interviewees may be biased or may represent only a limited perspective on performance issues and themes.

- Interviews, if not done well, can get off topic and frustrate both interviewer and interviewee (the interviewer can leave without the necessary information to guide his or her assessment; the interviewee can feel that the time was not productive).

Process Overview

1. Create a list of all the information required for completing your needs assessment. Prioritize and align the list of information requirements on the basis of your assessment's objectives and of the participants available for the interviews.

2. Determine what information is required from each interview.

3. Select interviewees who can best provide the information you are looking for in the interviews. Experts are often included as interviewees, but novices should also be considered when questions regarding current (or entry) knowledge and skills are elements in the assessment's considerations.

4. For each interview, create a protocol that will guide the questions that are to be asked.

   a. Determine how structured the protocol should be. A *structured interview protocol* has clearly defined questions and order of questions and can be repeated to elicit the same type of information across different interviewees. A structured interview is preferable when you want to aggregate or generalize information. This approach to interviewing is also preferable when your interviewees are not necessarily experts on a given topic or experienced interviewees (for example, interns seeking to gather information for a needs assessment plan with community leaders). An *unstructured interview* may start with a set of loosely planned questions in the protocol, but the interviewer may alter the questions and the order of questions depending on the information provided by each interviewee. An unstructured interview works best for interviewees who are well-informed about the topic and are able to deviate from a set plan.

b. Determine the types of questions to be included in the protocol. A protocol may include a range of types of questions, including open-ended questions (*What are the possible causes for these identified gaps?*) and closed-ended questions (*Of the six gaps in the handout provided, identify the gap that is most important to address this year*).

c. Leave room in the protocol for the interviewer to take notes during the interview, and include possible follow-up questions to help guide the discussion (see the link in the Websites section of this document for some suggestions on creating an interview protocol).

d. Conduct needs assessment interviews with a formal and systematic process that can be replicated.

e. Ensure that required information regarding both the current results and the desired results of the needs assessment are represented in the protocol, along with the required information at each level of the program or project results chain.

5. Schedule a convenient time and location for the interview. The interview should take place in a friendly location where both the interviewee and interviewer will feel comfortable discussing potentially delicate topics. Describe to the interviewee how the information will be used and the confidentiality of the information provided.

6. Take careful notes during the interview, offering to recap the response of the interviewee whenever there may be confusion. Follow the interview protocol carefully to ensure that you don't have to schedule a second interview to ask questions that may have been skipped. When possible, it is often a good idea to record an interview so you can verify your notes after the interview is complete. Another option is to have a note taker accompany the interviewer.

7. Immediately following the interview review your notes carefully to ensure that you have accurately captured all of the relevant information. If you find any confusion, this is the time to call or e-mail the interviewee to verify information or to ask for clarifications.

8. Relate the findings from each interview to other data sources for verification. For instance, if an interviewee quotes a news article or a research report, then it is typically useful to check that resource to ensure that the facts and figures provided by the interviewee were accurate and presented without bias.

Tips for Success

- Create a friendly and open environment by using active listening techniques (such as recapping, paraphrasing, taking notes, and using friendly body language).

- Refrain from asking leading questions (*"I'm sure you agree that . . ."*) or cutting off an interviewee during his or her response. If you are to avoid cutting off interviewees, it is often helpful to include potential follow-up questions as part of the interview protocol.

- Interviewers should not debate or argue with the interviewees. Interviewers are supposed to gather the views of others, not convince the interviewees of the interviewers' views.

- Using the critical incident technique can be a valuable way to differentiate between perceptions and past experiences. Interviewees are asked to provide past events as examples when they respond to specific questions. Each event should include a description of the conditions or context for the event, the people involved in the event, the place of the event, and the associated activities or behaviors of people in the event.

- Take good notes during the interview (or record it, if the participant is agreeable).

References and Resources

Altschuld, James W. 2010. *Needs Assessment Phase III: Collecting Data* (Book 3 of *Needs Assessment Kit*). Thousand Oaks, CA: Sage Publications.

Altschuld, James W., and J. N. Eastmond Jr. 2010. *Needs Assessment Phase II: Getting Started* (Book 2 of *Needs Assessment Kit*). Thousand Oaks, CA: Sage Publications.

McClelland, Samuel B. 1994a. "Training Needs Assessment Data-Gathering Methods: Part 2—Individual Interviews." *Journal of European Industrial Training* 18 (2): 27–31.

Witkin, Belle Ruth, and James W. Altschuld. 1995. *Planning and Conducting Needs Assessments: A Practical Guide.* Thousand Oaks, CA: Sage Publications.

Websites

"Getting the Lay of the Land on Health: A Guide for Using Interviews to Gather Information" is available at http://www.accessproject.org/adobe/getting_the_lay_of_the_land_on_health.pdf.

"Information Brief: Developing Interview Protocols" is available at http://www.neirtec.org/evaluation/PDFs/PreparingtoCollect5.pdf.

A sample interview protocol is available at http://www.ceismc.gatech.edu/MM_Tools/NIP.html.

A tip sheet on asking open-ended and probing questions is available at http://ppa.aces.uiuc.edu/pdf_files/Asking1.PDF.

A tip sheet on conducting key informant interviews is available at http://ppa.aces.uiuc.edu/pdf_files/Conducting1.PDF.

Tips for using individual interviews as a surveying technique are available at http://ppa.aces.uiuc.edu/pdf_files/Tips.PDF.

The USAID article on conducting needs assessment interviews is available at http://pdf.usaid.gov/pdf_docs/PNABS541.pdf.

Samples of Interview Preparation Checklist and Interview Release Agreement

Interview Preparation Checklist

☐ On what basis was this interviewee selected?

☐ Do I have the time and location of the interview?

☐ What do I know about the interviewee (title, experiences, background, and so on) ?

☐ Has the interviewee been sent information on the topic and focus of the interview?

☐ Should the interview questions be sent to the interviewee before the interview?

☐ Will the interview use closed-ended questions, open-ended questions, or a combination of both?

☐ Do I have some sample follow-up questions identified for each interview question?

☐ What information must I get from the interview?

☐ What information would it be nice to get, but is not necessary, from the interview?

- ☐ Are there documents I should ask for at the end of the interview (reports, files, and so on)?

- ☐ How will I take notes during the interview?

- ☐ Will I record the interview? If so, have I checked the batteries in the recorder? Have I asked the interviewee for permission to record the interview? (See the generic interview release agreement that follows.)

- ☐ How will I transcribe the interview recording (or notes)? Will I have time immediately after the interview to reflect on the answers and to take additional notes?

Interview Release Agreement

Sample Interview Permission or Release Form

(Organization)

(Address)

_____("Interviewer") has informed me that he or she is gathering research for a needs assessment and related Assessments on the subject of _____ (collectively "the Assessment") and has asked me to grant interviews and to otherwise cooperate with the Interviewer in connection with the Assessment.

To assist the Interviewer in preparing the Assessment, I have agreed to be interviewed and to provide information and other materials to be used in connection with the Assessment, including personal experiences, remarks, and recollections, as well as any other documents that I may choose to give to the Interviewer ("the Interview Materials").

I hereby grant and assign to the Interviewer and his or her licensees, successors, and assigns the following rights in connection with the Interview Materials for use as part of the Assessment in any and all reports, versions, and media in perpetuity throughout the world. Indicate your agreement with any of these statements below by checking the boxes and initialing your name next to each agreed item.

☐ The right to **quote or paraphrase using my name** all or any portion of the Interview Materials and to generally use and publish the Interview Materials, including my experiences, recollections, incidents, remarks, and information, as well as any other documents that I may give to the Interviewer.

-- OR --

☐ The right to **anonymously quote or paraphrase** all or any portion of the Interview Materials and to generally use and publish the Interview Materials, including my experiences, recollections, incidents, remarks, and information, as well as any other documents that I may give to the Interviewer in manner where my identity is protected.

☐ The right to use my name, image, voice, likeness, and biographical data.

☐ The right to develop, produce, and distribute the Assessment in any manner that the Interviewer deems appropriate. I understand and acknowledge that the Interviewer's company (which may be the same as mine) will be the sole owner of all copyright and other rights pertaining to the Assessment.

To enable the Interviewer to develop the Assessment in any manner deemed best, I hereby release and discharge the Interviewer and his or her licensees, successors, and assigns from any and all claims, demands, or causes of action that I may have against them by reason of anything contained in the Assessment, or any of the above uses, including any claims based on the right of privacy, the right of publicity, copyright, libel, slander, or any other right.

I acknowledge and agree that I am not entitled to receive any form of payment from the Interviewer or from his or her licensees, successors, and assigns.

Agreed and confirmed:

_____   _____

Printed Name   Date

_____   _____

Signature   Date

Sample of Interview Protocol

Interview Protocol to Identify Teachers' Capacity Gaps in Classroom Teaching Skills and Behaviors

Instructions: Use this protocol to interview principals from provincial schools. The purpose is to obtain information about capacity gaps that teachers have in the area of classroom teaching skills and behaviors.

Introduction	
Welcome (Where appropriate, modify the script and questions.)	**Script:** Thank you for agreeing to participate in this interview. You are one principal in our sample of 58 principals who are from across the country and were selected to provide information on the topic discussed today. In this interview, we will focus on identifying the challenges and capacity gaps that exist among your teachers in the area of classroom teaching skills and behaviors. This interview is part of a broader needs assessment sponsored by the national ministry of education. The overall needs assessment is being conducted so people can understand capacity development issues in the education system—not just related to teachers' skills and behaviors—and then can make decisions on how to address the issues. The information that you provide will not be attributed directly to you.
Do you have any questions regarding our goals?	Notes:
Questions	
Q1. How many years have you served as a principal?	
Q2. How many years have you served as a principal in this school?	

Q3. What is your highest level of education?	☐ High school or secondary education or lower
	☐ Basic university level (for example, associate's degree, Tecnicatura, and so on)
	☐ Intermediate university level (for example, bachelor's degree, Licence, Licenciatura, and so on)
	☐ Master's degree level or equivalent (for example, Master of Business Administration, Maîtrise, Maestria, and so on)
	☐ Postmaster's level or equivalent (for example, All But Dissertation and so on)
	☐ Doctorate level or higher
	☐ Other: Please specify and describe it with regard to the earlier list
Q4. As a school principal, describe your work.	
Q5. How many teachers do you supervise?	
Q6. How many students were enrolled in the school at the beginning of the year (indicate start date of school year)?	
Q7. How many students are currently enrolled in the school now (indicate date)?	

Q8: Drawing on your experiences, can you describe the two or three major capacity gaps related to your teachers' classroom teaching skills and behaviors that limit your school and your province in achieving their educational goals?	Response:
	Follow-up question and response:
Q9: What do you believe are the causes of each of the capacity gaps that you identified in the previous question?	Response:
	Follow-up question and response:
Q10: Are there other challenges that you believe limit the capacity of your province to achieve its educational goals?	Response:
	Follow-up question and response:
Q11: Can you recommend anyone I should meet with to identify related capacity gaps?	Response:
	Follow-up question and response:
Conclusions	
Review	**Script:** Summarize the major capacity gaps identified from the conversation, and then ask the interviewee to verify that you accurately interpreted the responses.

DUAL-RESPONSE SURVEYS

Purpose

The purpose of conducting dual-response surveys is to collect information from a large number of people—typically located in multiple locations—regarding their perspectives on both current and desired performance.

Needs Assessment Applications

Surveys are commonly used for needs assessments, but many types of surveys are available to you. The dual-response survey might be a new tool for you to consider. Surveys can be useful tools for needs assessments because they are relatively easy to develop, their data usually can be clearly transformed into useful information, and surveys (especially web-based ones) can easily be distributed to both large and small groups. Because surveys can require less time to complete than interviews or focus groups, and because they can be sent to people at other locations, they are often used in needs assessments (as well as in needs analyses).

Whereas the traditional single-response survey is a data collection tool used in a variety of organizational activities—such as opinion polling and evaluation—the dual-response survey format provides significant benefits over traditional single-response tools in completing a needs assessment. The dual-response survey, as presented here, collects information regarding both the *current* and *desired* performance, thereby providing clear data regarding the size, direction, and relative priority of performance gaps (or needs). This type of survey gives you more options for analyzing data than does its single-response counterpart, and it provides valuable information that is essential to the unique goals of a needs assessment.

Advantages and Disadvantages

Advantages

- A needs assessment survey allows you to capture the perspectives of multiple groups on a variety of performance-related topics.

- The dual-response format allows the needs assessment survey to simultaneously capture data regarding both the current and the desired levels of performance. Too often needs assessments assume that the desired performance is known and agreed upon by everyone in the organization when in reality this assumption is rarely the case.

- The dual-response format gives you multiple ways to view, analyze, and report on findings, including the size of the needs, the direction of the needs, and the relative priority that participants associate with the needs.

- Surveys offer a variable format where you can ask a few questions or many questions, and likewise you can ask open-ended or closed-ended questions.

Disadvantages

- Survey data are frequently confused with performance data. It is important to remember that survey data rely on the perceptions of those completing the survey. Thus, while a respondent may indicate that his or her perception is that performance is high, the reality may be that performance is low. Nevertheless, knowing the perceptions of those participating in the needs assessment is essential to making informed decisions.

- Many organizations frequently use surveys; as a result, employees can get "burned out" on completing surveys. This reaction can reduce your response rate, increase the number of respondents who complete only part of the survey, or otherwise compromise the integrity of your survey results.

- Surveys do not give you the opportunity to ask follow-up questions to respondents (unlike interviews or focus groups).

- Although surveys may seem easy to prepare, they are often developed poorly. Therefore, it is important to have an experienced survey developer involved in the process of developing a survey, assisting in survey development, determining the survey analysis approach, or reviewing the survey.

Process Overview

1. Drawing from the list of information required for the needs assessment, create a list of the information that you expect to gain from the needs assessment survey. The focus of developing an effective needs assessment survey should always be on the information required to make decisions. This focus will prevent you from asking questions that don't get used in subsequent decision making. (For helpful sample templates to serve as job aids, see pages 125–126.)

2. Create your needs assessment survey for a target audience. Also, consider using multiple versions of a survey to target different audiences or stakeholders. Surveys frequently are best used to collect information from a larger number of people than you would potentially invite for an interview or a focus group.

3. Identify questions to include in your needs assessment. Questions should focus on results and performance, rather than on what resources or changes participants may want. In the Tips for Writing Good Survey Questions section of this tool are many ideas on how to write successful survey questions.

4. Create the survey using the dual-response format. Multiple sections within a single survey can also use different response scales—you simply must clearly communicate those differences to the survey respondents. Table 3A.1. provides examples of three types of rating scales: agreement, satisfaction, and frequency. You can change the associated responses with each level of the Likert-type scales to represent appropriate responses for the questions in your assessment (see example in table 3A.1).

5. Pilot test your survey with participants who are representative of your target audience. When participants have completed the draft survey, calculate the results to ensure that you can use the information attained from each question. Typically, responses to some questions do not provide the useful information you were looking for; thus, changes must be made to the survey.

6. Needs assessment surveys can be done in a variety of formats and media depending on the target audience. Web surveys can easily be created, distributed, and analyzed using Internet-based survey systems. Paper-based surveys can also be effective, especially if members of your target audience may not have access to technology or have the computer skills necessary for completing an online survey. Select the format that you believe

Table 3A.1 Examples of Different Rating Scales

Agreement: 1 = Strongly Disagree; 2 = Disagree; 3 = Neutral; 4 = Agree; 5 = Strongly Agree

Current performance	Survey question	Desired or optimal performance
① ② ③ ④ ⑤	Does the subway usually get me to where I am going on time?	① ② ③ ④ ⑤

Satisfaction: 1 = Very Dissatisfied; 2 = Dissatisfied; 3 = Neutral; 4 = Satisfied; 5 = Very Satisfied

Current performance	Survey question	Desired or optimal performance
① ② ③ ④ ⑤	What is my overall satisfaction with the subway service provided by the city?	① ② ③ ④ ⑤

Frequency: 1 = Daily; 2 = Weekly (3–6 times per week); 3 = Occasionally (3–6 times per month); 4 = Sometimes (less than 3 times per month); 5 = Rarely (once a month to never)

Current performance	Survey question	Desired or optimal performance
① ② ③ ④ ⑤	Does the subway have mechanical failures during my trips?	① ② ③ ④ ⑤

will give you the highest return rate of completed surveys. Ideally, you would want at least 50 percent (often more) of the surveys you send out to be completed. The higher the return rate, the more confidence you can have that your survey results represent the perspectives of the target audience. For national level, highly sensitive, or other important needs assessments, you will want to consult with a statistician about minimum response rates.

7. The data from a dual-response needs assessment can be analyzed using four analysis approaches—discrepancy, direction, position, and demographic differences—to inform decision making. See table 3A.2 for an example of responses from a single survey taker. See table 3A.3 to review how this survey taker's responses would be analyzed using the four analysis approaches.

Analysis 1: Discrepancy

For each question of the needs assessment survey, you should perform a gap analysis by subtracting the value assigned to the *current* column from

Table 3A.2 Example of a Completed Survey

Instructions: Indicate your level of agreement with the survey questions below. Note that desired or optimal performance ratings should be taken in consideration of costs (financial, and other costs) associated with achieving optimal performance. Therefore, take care to avoid giving all responses a rating of 5. (Scale: 1 = Strongly Disagree; 2 = Disagree; 3 = Neutral; 4 = Agree; 5 = Strongly Agree)

Current performance	Survey question	Desired or optimal performance
① **❷** ③ ④ ⑤	a. Does the subway usually get me to where I am going on time?	① ② ③ **❹** ⑤
① ② ③ **❹** ⑤	b. Does the subway station have an adequate number of employees at each station to serve my needs?	① ② **❸** ④ ⑤
❶ ② ③ ④ ⑤	c. Can the subway audio system be heard easily in all train cars?	① ② **❸** ④ ⑤
① **❷** ③ ④ ⑤	d. Is the subway system operated safely?	① ② ③ ④ **❺**

the value assigned to the *desired* column (see table 3A.2). The results of this analysis will identify discrepancies between the *current* and *desired* performance for each variable associated with the performance system. The size of the gap can provide valuable information in determining the perceived acuteness of the need or the extent to which opportunities can be capitalized upon.

The results of this analysis are, however, necessary rather than sufficient for quality decision making. Alone, these results provide only isolated values (data points) that must be put into context through their relationships with the three other analysis approaches.

Analysis 2: Direction

For each question, the positive or negative value of the gap should be identified to differentiate needs (when desired is greater than current) from opportunities (when *what is* (WI) is greater than *what should be* (WSB).

- Positive discrepancies between *desired* and *current* (for example, desired = 5, current = 3, gap = 2 identifies a **need**.

- Negative discrepancies between *desired* and *current* (for example, *desired* = 3, *current* = 4, gap = –1) identifies an **opportunity** (for instance, to reallocate resources).

Table 3A.3 Example of an Analysis of the Completed Survey

Instructions for the survey analyst: For each item, tabulate the gap size by subtracting the current performance from the desired performance. Gap direction will be determined by whether the difference between desired and current performance is positive, negative, or neutral. Once this direction is determined, indicate in the next cells whether the response represents (a) a need, opportunity, or neither and (b) whether the position or priority in addressing the need or opportunity is low, medium, or high. The "analyst comments" column is to be used for summarizing the lengthier comments by the respondent. The example in the table provides analysis for one single respondent, but usually there are many more respondents. Thus, analyzing and aggregating results on a computer spreadsheet is advised.

Survey question	Gap size: *desired – current performance* Gap direction: *positive = need; negative = opportunity*	Need or opportunity	Position or priority	Analyst comments
a. Does the subway usually get me to where I am going on time?	+2	*Need*	Medium	The respondent recommends a reduction in schedule delays. (+2 points: need)
b. Does the subway station have an adequate number of employees at each station to serve my needs?	−1	*Opportunity*	Low	There may be an opportunity to reduce the number of employees at stations during nonpeak hours. (−1 point: opportunity)
c. Can the subway audio system be heard easily in all train cars?	+2	*Need*	Medium	The respondent noted difficulties in hearing the conductor. (+2 points: need).
d. Is the subway system operated safely?	+3	*Need*	High	The respondent indicated a problem with proper door closing during crowded periods. Safety hazard—requires immediate attention. (+3 points: need)

The distinction between needs and opportunities provides a context for discrepancy data, which by itself illustrates only the size of the gap between *current* and *desired* performance. By examining the direction of the discrepancy, decision makers can consider which gaps illustrate needs that have the potential to be addressed through organizational efforts and which gaps identify opportunities that the organization may want to leverage (or maintain) to ensure future success.

Analysis 3: Position (that is, relative priority)

The position analysis illustrates the relative importance or priority of discrepancies from the perspective of the respondents. Although many gaps between *WSB* and *WI* may have equivalent discrepancies and may be in the same direction, the position of the discrepancy on the Likert scale of the instrument can demonstrate the relative priority of the discrepancy in relation to other gaps.

For example, two needs may be identified with a discrepancy of +3, but the first need illustrated a gap between WSB = 5 and WI = 2, whereas the second need illustrated a gap between WSB = 3 and WI = 0. As a result, the interpretation of these discrepancies in relation to each other would indicate a perceived prioritization of the first need over the second. This information can be valuable in selecting which discrepancies are addressed when resources are limited.

Together, three types of analysis (discrepancy, direction, and position) can offer valuable data for identifying and prioritizing needs.

Analysis 4: Demographic Differences (optional)

You may want to view the results of your needs assessment survey on the basis of demographic differences (for example, division, location, position type, or years of experience). Analysis of the results can be reviewed by demographic variables if items related to the desired demographic categories are added to the instrument. If your organization has collected data regarding the demographics of respondents to the survey, then you should complete an analysis for *discrepancy*, *direction*, and *position* for each demographic on a section, subsection, or item basis, depending on the level of information required for decision making.

Tips for Success

- An abundance of literature exists about survey development, implementation, and analysis. Developing surveys is not as easy as it may seem, so consult survey literature and survey developers when preparing your survey.

- You should pilot test any survey questions with representatives from the target audience.

- Before releasing your survey, plan ahead on how you will analyze the results.

- If you have diverse audiences, you should not try to write one survey that fits all audiences.

- You must plan to follow up with participants who have not completed the survey after a few days so you can remind them of the importance of their participation.

- If you must have survey results from an important stakeholder group to be able to make informed decisions, you should oversample that group to ensure that you get enough responses. In other words, if you want 50 returned surveys, then you would send out 200 surveys to the group in hopes of getting at least a 25 percent response rate rather than sending out 100 surveys with hopes of getting a 50 percent response rate.

Tips for Writing Good Survey Questions

- Ensure a common understanding.

- Start with the more interesting questions for the audience.

- Don't try to impress participants with big words.

- Don't write leading questions.

- Avoid double negatives or questions with multiple meanings.

- Stay focused: don't ask more questions than you require for making decisions.

- Put your questions in a logical order (for example, use sections or topic area headlines to organize questions).

- Verify that questions make sense for both response columns (current and desired).

- Don't let your survey get too long (for example, it should take participants no more than 15 minutes to complete).

References and Resources

Altschuld, James W. 2010. *Needs Assessment Phase III: Collecting Data* (Book 3 of *Needs Assessment Kit*). Thousand Oaks, CA: Sage Publications.

Altschuld, James W., and J. N. Eastmond Jr. 2010. *Needs Assessment Phase I: Getting Started* (Book 2 of *Needs Assessment Kit*). Thousand Oaks, CA: Sage Publications.

Kaufman, Roger, Ingrid Guerra-López, Ryan Watkins, and Doug Leigh. 2008. *The Assessment Book: Applied Strategic Thinking and Performance Improvement Through Self-Assessments*. Amherst, MA: HRD Press.

Websites

An inexpensive and easy-to-use survey development and deployment tool can be found at http://www.surveymonkey.com.

Another site that offers complete online survey services, including the development, deployment, and analysis of dual response and traditional surveys, is at http://www.evaluationsolutions.com.

Samples of Job Aids

Survey Template

Satisfaction Scale: *1 = Very Dissatisfied; 2 = Dissatisfied; 3 = Neutral; 4 = Satisfied; 5 = Very Satisfied*

Sample Instructions: Indicate your level of agreement with the survey questions in the table. Note that desired or optimal performance ratings should be taken in consideration of costs (financial and other costs) associated with achieving optimal performance. Therefore, take care to avoid giving all responses a rating of 5. (Scale: *1 = Very Dissatisfied; 2 = Dissatisfied; 3 = Neutral; 4 = Satisfied; 5 = Very Satisfied*)

Current performance	Survey question	Desired or optimal performance
① ② ③ ④ ⑤	a.	① ② ③ ④ ⑤
① ② ③ ④ ⑤	b.	① ② ③ ④ ⑤
① ② ③ ④ ⑤	c.	① ② ③ ④ ⑤

Analysis Template

Instructions for the survey analyst: For each item, tabulate the gap size by subtracting the current performance from the desired performance. Gap direction will be determined by whether the difference between desired and current performance is positive, negative, or neutral. Once this direction is determined, indicate in the next cells whether the response represents (a) a need, opportunity, or neither and (b) whether the position or priority in addressing the need or opportunity is low, medium, or high. The "analyst comments" column is to be used for summarizing the lengthier comments by the respondent. The example in the table provides analysis for one single respondent, but usually there are many more respondents. Thus, analyzing and aggregating results on a computer spreadsheet is advised.

Survey question	Gap size: *desired – current performance* Gap direction: *positive = need;* *negative =* *opportunity*	Need or opportunity	Position or priority	Analyst comments
a.	0 1 2 3 4 5 Positive or Negative	Need or Opportunity	High Medium Low	
b.	0 1 2 3 4 5 Positive or Negative	Need or Opportunity	High Medium Low	
c.	0 1 2 3 4 5 Positive or Negative	Need or Opportunity	High Medium Low	

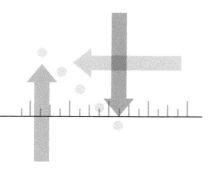

SWOT+

Purpose

The purpose of conducting a SWOT is to identify, organize, and prioritize the strengths, weaknesses, opportunities, and threats (or SWOTs) that influence the planning, design, development, implementation, and evaluation of almost any program or project.

Needs Assessment Applications

Identifying a list of SWOTs is a common brainstorming technique used in organizational planning. Developing a list alone, however, rarely provides the useful information required to guide a needs assessment. Instead, you should combine the benefits of brainstorming with an approach that defines the relationships among the identified SWOT factors, and then you should use those relationships to guide decisions about what to do next.

The resulting SWOT+ technique asks SWOT informants to assign values to each of the items on the SWOT list. Thus, in certain cases, the items on the list that are of highest value may be acted on first, and the items with lesser importance might need to be recognized but never acted on.

Advantages and Disadvantages

Advantages

- A SWOT builds on the value of a process that is already familiar in most organizations.

- SWOT factors are prioritized in relation to other SWOT factors, rather than simply listed and given equal value.

- A SWOT engages a group in defining the relationship among SWOT factors.

Disadvantages

- Assigning of values to each SWOT factor can be challenging for group members.

- Additional time is required to move from the SWOT factors to their relationships to the recommendations about what should be done next.

Process Overview

1. Decide on a focus for your SWOT+ analysis. For instance, are you looking for SWOT factors that influence just your project or unit, or SWOT factors that affect the entire organization? This context will provide boundaries for the discussion and will help you identify SWOT factors that will best guide your needs assessment.

2. Identify internal and external stakeholders for the SWOT analysis. These partners should represent an array of perspectives around the performance issue at the center of your needs assessment.

3. In a meeting (or by e-mail), have group members identify SWOT factors from their perspectives. In most situations, begin your SWOT analysis by asking participants to simply brainstorm ideas to fit into the following four categories:

   Strength: An internal competence, valuable resource, or attribute that an organization can use to exploit opportunities in the external environment

   Weakness: An internal lack of a competence, resource, or attribute that an organization requires to perform in the external environment

   Opportunity: An external possibility that an organization can pursue or exploit to gain benefit

   Threat: An external factor that has the potential to reduce an organization's performance

4. When you have identified an adequate number of SWOT factors (6 to 10 per category is typically enough), sort them into a SWOT matrix (see table 3A.4).

5. To enhance the SWOT factors, ask the group members to define their relative value or importance within the context. Do this by using a continuum along each of the X and Y axes of your SWOT matrix (see figure 3A.1). Use the continuum of internal-to-external control for the X axis and the asset-to-liability continuum for the Y axis. Individual factors can then be plotted within the matrix according to their relationships to other factors.

6. Place a mark (for example, S1, S2, and so on) for each SWOT factor where it intersects along the two continuums, thus defining its relationship to other SWOT factors. Figure 3A.1 shows how value assignments were given to each item on the SWOT list (from table 3A.4) and were plotted on the matrix.

7. Use the plotted SWOT factors to determine which factors should be fixed immediately, which should be improved on over time, which should be sustained, and which should be monitored (see figure 3A.1).

Table 3A.4   Traditional SWOT Matrix

SWOT Analysis
Community Public Transportation SWOT

Strengths	Weaknesses
S1 = Four new subway stations have been completed in the past year; three more are expected in the next two years.	W1 = Approximately 18% of subway and bus mechanics are expected to retire in the next five years.
S2 = There is a growing demand—a 15% increase in subway riders in the past year.	W2 = Development of new bike lanes in the city center has been delayed.
S3 = The past year saw a 3% increase in "overall satisfaction" among subway riders.	W3 = Increased subway and bus fees have reduced the ability of poorer citizens to afford public transportation.
Opportunities	**Threats**
O1 = Increasing fuel costs may push more people to public transportation.	T1 = Increasing fuel costs increase bus costs.
O2 = Biking and walking to work are becoming more popular.	T2 = The roads in the city center are clogged during rush hours, increasing commuting times and delaying bus schedules.
O3 = National subsidy is possible to help finance reduced fee transit cards for elderly and disabled populations.	T3 = Labor costs are increasing.
	T4 = Delays in delivery of new buses and subway cars from manufacturers are averaging 4–6 months behind schedule.

Figure 3A.1   Expanded Versions of the SWOT Matrix (SWOT+)

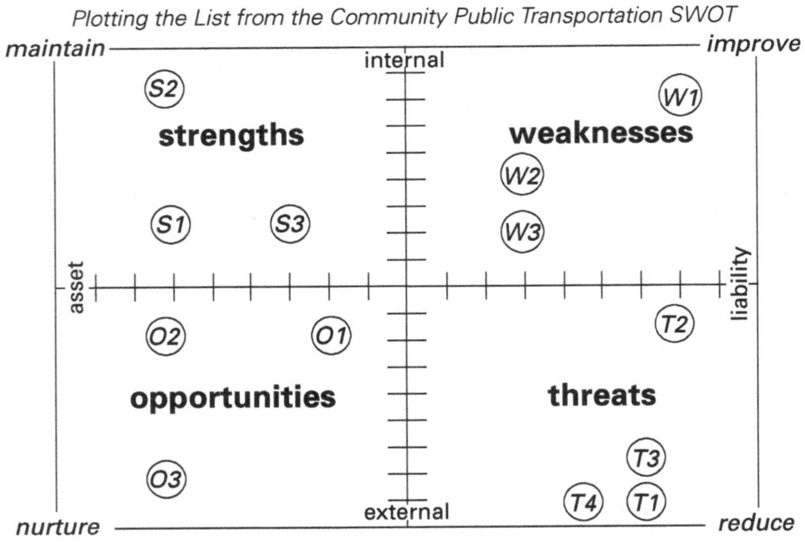

Plotting the List from the Community Public Transportation SWOT

Note: The letters and numbers within the quadrants correspond to information provided in table 3A.4.

8. With each SWOT factor plotted into the matrix from table 3A.4 , prioritize the factors in order of importance for achieving desired performance objectives.

9. Use the prioritized list of SWOT factors to guide your decisions. You can see that with this information visually plotted, the participants can go a step further and can discuss the relationship among the items plotted; (a) which items to act on and in what order and (b) which items can possibly be monitored for now, but perhaps never acted on.

Tips for Success

• When identifying SWOT factors, use an open brainstorming process that allows all participants to share their ideas.

• Avoid ambiguous SWOT factors; link each factor to a specific and measurable indicator to ensure that everyone is using the same operational definition of the factor.

- Work to build consensus around the placement of SWOT factors within the matrix; keep in mind that often there are many opinions about where individual factors should go on the continuums of internal–external and asset–liability.

References and Resources

Leigh, Doug. 2006. "SWOT Analysis." In *The Handbook of Human Performance Technology*, edited by J. Pershing, 1089–1108. San Francisco, CA: Jossey-Bass/Pfeiffer.

Watkins, Ryan. 2007. *Performance by Design: The Systematic Selection, Design, and Development of Performance Technologies That Produce Useful Results.* Amherst, MA: HRD Press, and Silver Spring, MD: International Society for Performance Improvement.

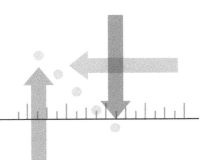

WORLD CAFÉ™ (WITH "SPEED DATING" VARIATION)

Purpose

The World Café is a format for collaborative conversations designed to yield deeper insights into pressing collective issues. The collaborative conversations bring together stakeholders in group settings to formulate directions (or ideas, opinions, and so on) concerning needs, next steps, and solutions.

Needs Assessment Applications

The World Café format has gained in popularity over recent years because it is an easy approach to gathering information through collaboration; also it is a generally quick and usually fun process. (See http://www.theworldcafe.com for more information on the approach.) The following discussion draws on the trademarked World Café approach, but it has been adapted for needs assessment purposes.

When used in a needs assessment context, the World Café approach offers a useful, fluid framework for structuring a productive, problem-solving discussion among a group of participants who typically would have diverse perspectives (but, in many cases, they could have shared or common perspectives). Because of the way in which the conversations are structured, participants circulate about the room, cross-pollinating ideas and building upon one another's suggestions. This approach lends itself well to needs assessment because it can provide unique opportunities for gathering information when other techniques would not be appropriate, viable, affordable, or useful.

Advantages and Disadvantages

Advantages

- This approach can be used with a large and diverse group of participants and stakeholders.

- A collaborative setting allows for transparent decision making.

- The approach can yield more nuanced data and findings than can structured interviews or focus groups.

- The flexible technique can be applied in many settings and for different objectives.

Disadvantages

- The "results" of World Café sessions are subject to interpretation.

- The findings of this approach will depend largely on which stakeholders participate.

- The approach requires substantial advance planning for determining key discussion questions.

Process Overview[1]

1. Have organizers determine in advance the targeted questions that will address the key objectives for holding the World Café.

2. Seat groups of four or five people at small tables or in clusters. Each table is led by a host who has been given some guidance about duties of facilitating the table work.

3. Set up progressive (usually three) rounds of conversation of approximately 20–30 minutes each.

4. Encourage both table hosts and members to write or draw key ideas using the markers and paper provided.

5. When groups have completed the initial round of conversation, ask one person to remain at the table as the host while the other group members become ambassadors. Ambassadors carry key ideas, themes, and questions from their first group into their new conversations.

6. Ask the table host to welcome the new guests and to briefly share the main ideas, themes, and questions of the initial conversation. Encourage the ambassadors to link and connect ideas coming from their previous table conversations as they listen carefully and build on each other's contributions.

7. In the third round of conversation, either have people return to their first table or have them continue traveling to new tables. Sometimes facilitators will add a new question in the third round of discussion to help deepen the exploration.

8. After several rounds of conversation, initiate a period of whole-group discussion.

Tips for Success

- Clarify your purpose, and keep in mind the reason for gathering your group. Design the session with targeted questions and issues in mind.

- As an important component of the World Café approach, create a welcoming environment so participants can share their ideas. Consider how your invitation and the meeting's location will contribute to a hospitable atmosphere.

- Have your World Café explore only one question or a set of related questions. Remember that choosing questions that are of central importance to your meeting objectives and, for that matter, to your participants can produce powerful results.

- Importantly, encourage participants to be active contributors of their ideas and perspectives while allowing those who wish to participate by simply observing to do so.

- Remember that in the World Café design, participants circulate about the large group and take ideas from each small group's discussion to the next table as they become ambassadors. Typically, one participant stays behind as a host, sharing the previous group's ideas with the new arrivals. By using the center of the small-group tables as spaces for drawing with markers, your facilitators and hosts can draw attention to the illustrations and diagrams created as an example of a shared, collaborative vision.

- Encourage participants to sharpen their listening skills as they go into the World Café. Encourage participants (a) to listen rather than plan their response to the current speaker, (b) to be open to being influenced by another's ideas, (c) to listen for deeper questions and insights that may emerge in the group discussion, and (d) to listen for what questions are not being asked or for what is not being spoken.

- To tie in the whole group's progress, first ask each table to spend a few minutes brainstorming about what has emerged in their World Café rounds that has been most meaningful. Depending on the range of ideas that have emerged, the ambassadors and table participants might want to prepare a summary list of the ideas. The list could include those items that were suggested frequently, but it could also include ideas that were suggested less often but that could represent an important and perhaps underrepresented view. Because the World Café is meant to collect expansive ideas around an issue, under many circumstances it will be useful to think beyond the "top five" type of items and to dig deeper about items that were not suggested as frequently. After this period, begin a whole-group discussion. Perhaps tailor this exercise into thematic clusters by asking people from each table to share one thing that they found new or surprising, and then asking others to share ideas and observations that build on that one thing. Ask the whole group the following questions:

    - If there were a single voice in the room, what would the group say are the key takeaways?

    - What deeper questions are emerging as a result of these conversations?

    - Do we notice any patterns emerging? If so, what do these patterns point to?

    - What do we now see and know as a result of these conversations?

"Speed Dating" Variation

As with speed dating events—where single adults meet to have timed interactions with other singles so they can determine if there is a match—adding a similar set of timed and focused conversations among pairs of participants can be a useful variation of World Café. The same general World Café setup would occur, but instead of starting with small groups for 20 minutes, you would start with paired participants talking and brainstorming together for about 5 to 8 minutes.

Following two or three rounds of the paired conversations, you would then begin the process of sharing ideas on white boards or through index cards handed to a facilitator. This information would then be collapsed into the whole-group session of the World Café. This variation on the format allows for more sharing by each participant and potentially for an even deeper conversation on issues (with a reduced threat that a single person would dominate a group conversation).

Notes

1. Based in part on "Café to Go" in World Café (2008) at http://www.theworld cafe.com/pdfs/cafetogo.pdf.

References and Resources

Brown, Juanita, and David Isaacs. 2005. *The World Café: Shaping Our Futures through Conversations That Matter*. San Francisco, CA: Berrett-Koehler Publishers.

Brown, Juanita, David Isaacs, Eric Vogt, and Nancy Margulies. 2002. "Strategic Questioning: Engaging People's Best Thinking." *The Systems Thinker* 13 (9).

Brown, Juanita, David Isaacs, Nancy Margulies, and Gary Warhaftig. 1999. "The World Café: Catalyzing Large-Scale Collective Learning." *Leverage Magazine* (33): 1–2.

Websites

"Café to Go: A Quick Reference Guide for Putting Conversations to Work" is available at http://www.theworldcafe.com/pdfs/cafetogo.pdf.

Additional World Café information is available at http://www.theworldcafe.com/.

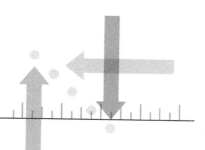

DELPHI TECHNIQUE

Purpose

The Delphi technique is a powerful approach that can be used (a) to gather data and opinions from experts (such as identifying primary performance constraints) or (b) to lead to a group decision (such as making recommendations about what to do). The Delphi technique is also referred to as the Delphi method, Delphi approach, Delphi activity, or Delphi study. It was developed by RAND during the 1950s for warfare forecasting, and it relied on panels of experts to provide information in a systematic and iterative manner.

Needs Assessment Applications

The Delphi technique is a data collection tool that you can use to solicit insight from a group of experts in a structured way. In a needs assessment, the Delphi technique is typically used to gain expert input for defining needs, to identify desired results, to prioritize causes, or to recommend solutions. The intention with the Delphi technique is for the iterative process not only to solicit insight from experts, but also to ultimately reveal the areas where experts have consensus in their views. This consensus expert insight can be an invaluable source of information to support decision making about things such as needs, goals, and anticipated outcomes.

The Delphi technique uses a "layered," or iterative, strategy to gather information and arrive at consensus about a specific subject, situation, need, or goal. The technique is similar to the nominal group technique (see page 166 in part 3B) in terms of its structure. One of the unique features of the Delphi technique, however, is that the information solicitation and consensus-building processes can be done through either postal or electronic mail. The Delphi technique can be used for planning, problem solving, decision making, or data collection. The information that is generated through this technique typically (a) provides insight about a variety of different alternatives, (b) seeks to correlate expert insight on a specific subject, (c) provides the background information necessary for decision making, or (d) reveals consensus in expert opinions about a particular subject or theme.

Advantages and Disadvantages

Advantages

- The Delphi technique is versatile in terms of its potential application and can, therefore, be used to tackle a very wide variety of issues, subjects, and situations.

- Through this technique, you have the option of setting up a broad and dynamic panel of experts from a variety of disciplines and professional sectors (for example, donors, community organizations, government officials, and academia).

- Location is not a constraint in terms of access to expert insight. This technique accommodates data collection through either postal or electronic mail, making it possible to involve experts from almost any part of the world.

- The iterative process of the Delphi technique promotes reflective and evaluative contributions from experts.

- The technique enables the natural group process of sharing and evaluating ideas and expert insight without the need for an in-person meeting format. Because the objective of the Delphi technique is to achieve convergence, as opposed to divergence, in expert perspectives, it promotes a nonconfrontational format for communication and exchange. Expert contributions also remain anonymous to other participants in the expert panel, which may help participants to feel more at ease with fully and honestly providing their insights and opinions.

- The structured and step-by-step nature of the technique makes it very democratic in nature, giving each invited participant an equal opportunity for contribution.

- Quantitative analysis of the data from a Delphi study is relatively simple and can be done using spreadsheet software (such as Microsoft Excel).

Disadvantages

- If the coordinator of a Delphi activity fails to (a) select a representative expert panel, (b) select a good initial question, or (c) follow the recommended implementation steps for the technique, the outcomes of the activity may be compromised.

- If the Delphi technique is conducted through postal mail, the time required for the process can be lengthy, particularly if the panel of expert participants is located in a variety of different countries. If you decide to use the Delphi approach with postal mail, you should expect to allocate between one and three months for data collection.

- The technique requires sustained involvement from the participants. Participant dropout is, therefore, a risk.

- The viewpoints and judgments that are collected through the Delphi technique are subjective in nature. Thus, the extent of accuracy and comprehensiveness of the data may, in some instances, be uncertain.

- The Delphi technique, although generating valuable information, should not be used as the sole source of information for making definitive decisions about needs or future strategies.

Process Overview

The procedure for the Delphi technique essentially consists of four steps: (a) planning, (b) setting up the expert panel, (c) administering questionnaires, and (d) interpreting final data for decision making.

Planning

1. Form a small group of colleagues to work with you on implementing and monitoring the Delphi study. The Delphi depends on the group's ability to identify and engage a number of experts on the topic, which is often challenging for one individual to manage.

2. Use the list of information required for the needs assessment to determine the specific issue, purpose, scope, and focus of the Delphi study.

3. Develop a time line for the Delphi activity. This time line should include intended deadlines for (a) setting up the expert panel, (b) sending out each

of the questionnaires, (c) receiving responses to each of the questionnaires, and (d) analyzing and interpreting the final results from the Delphi.

4. Determine how you will define *consensus* from the responses you receive. For example, does a simple majority (51 percent) represent consensus, or is greater agreement required?

5. Create the first questionnaire for the Delphi study. Ensure that the questionnaire clearly aligns with the scope and purpose of the Delphi.

   a. The questionnaire can consist of one single question that targets the specific focus area of the Delphi. If a single question is used, make sure that it is an open-response question (that is, a question that allows the respondent to submit his or her own answer rather than being forced to choose an answer). An example might be a question asking experts to identify all possible causes of a specific performance gap.

   b. Plan on testing the questionnaire before you distribute it so you can make sure that it is worded correctly to elicit the types of information that you are looking for.

Setting Up the Expert Panel

1. Select a panel of experts to match the scope and purpose of the Delphi study. The initial panel should typically consist of between 30 and 50 participants, though more may be warranted in some cases. The specifics of the kind of panel that you create may differ depending on the specific goals of the assessment. Here are some tips:

   a. Although a larger panel will generate more information on the focus of the activity, it will also increase the data to be analyzed in each phase of the Delphi.

   b. The panel should include individuals who are experts in the focus area of the study.

   c. It is advisable that you select participants who have both conceptual and applied (practical) understanding of the focus areas of your Delphi activity.

   d. If the focus area of your Delphi endeavor extends over several sectors, you may want to invite experts representing each of those sectors.

   e. You should try to screen the panel to make sure that you have selected a group of participants who represent diverse perspectives about your focus area.

2. Prepare and distribute a letter to invite the experts you want to participate on the expert panel. The letter should include the following:

   a. The specific scope and purpose of the Delphi

   b. The general process that will be used in the activity

   c. The anticipated time commitment the expert will be asked to make (This commitment should include the amount of time that you expect the expert will require to complete each questionnaire, as well as the span of time over which the Delphi activity will take place.)

3. Remember that sustained participation of the expert panelists is essential to the success of the Delphi activity. Consider following up the invitation letters with a telephone call to each invitee.

Administering Questionnaires

1. Send out the questionnaire that you prepared during the planning phase. Make sure that you include directions on when and how responses should be returned (for example, "Please submit your responses to this questionnaire by replying to this e-mail. The deadline for submitting responses is April 2.").

2. Code the responses by identifying all the elements or factors that are referred to in the responses you receive. For example, if you asked experts to identify all "possible factors contributing to a performance problem," then your task is to identify each statement referring to a "possible factor" in the responses. Next, you compile all those statements of possible factors into one single list. Make sure that the duplicate references are removed and that each factor represents only one idea or construct.

3. Create a second questionnaire using the list of elements that you compiled in step 2, directly above. In your instructions to this questionnaire, ask the respondents to rate each element on the list in terms of importance or relevance to the focus of the Delphi. For example, provide a scale as follows: *"Low Importance = 1 2 3 4 5 = High Importance."* Ask respondents to rank each element in the list while using that scale. Make sure that you include directions on when and how responses should be returned.

4. Tabulate the results from the second questionnaire by calculating the mean (average), median (middle), and mode (most) scores, as well as standard deviation (dispersion of scores around the average) and inter-

quartile range (percentage of similar responses). Each can be calculated in spreadsheet programs such as Microsoft Excel.

5. Using your analysis, determine where there is consensus among the experts. Typically median (middle) scores, along with interquartile ranges, are of the most value in determining consensus although how you define consensus can vary from project to project. In their article, Hsin-Ling Hung and his colleagues (2008) identify a number of important considerations in defining and calculating consensus.

6. Drawing from the results of the second questionnaire, develop a third questionnaire with the items from the second questionnaire that had the greatest consensus among the experts. Depending on the context, you will want to determine an appropriate "cut score" for consensus to be able to reduce the list.

7. Conduct a third and fourth round of questionnaires, calculating consensus among experts using the results of each.

8. Remember that research indicates most Delphi applications reach stable consensus among experts (in other words, few changes from one round to the next) after four rounds. If you do not see this consensus, then you can use additional rounds of data collection (five or six in total) or can consider including both median scores and interquartile ranges for each element in the fifth round to help the experts move toward consensus. When you find stability in responses from one round to the next, you can then use those findings in your needs assessment.

Interpreting Final Data for Decision Making

1. Report the final results to the panel of experts; they will be interested.

2. Use the results to focus in on the specific issue, purpose, and scope of the Delphi study, and use the insight from the expert panel as guidance in your needs assessment decisions.

Tips for Success

- Consider seeking endorsement from an influential person for the Delphi activity. This endorsement may help you to solicit and sustain involvement from the experts you wish to involve in the activity.

- Remain in contact with participants throughout the Delphi activity. For example, consider calling each of the experts after you have sent them the invitation to participate. In addition, follow up personally with participants who do not respond to the subsequent questionnaires.

- If possible, plan to provide incentives to participants at each round in the Delphi activity. Incentives can be of either a material or a nonmaterial nature. Following up with thank-you cards or other personalized communication may play an important role in keeping participants involved.

References and Resources

Hung, Hsin-Ling, James W. Altschuld, and Y-F. Lee. 2008. "Methodological and Conceptual Issues Confronting a Cross-Country Delphi Study of Educational Program Evaluation." *Evaluation and Program Planning* 31 (2): 191–98.

Websites

One of the earliest reports on the development of the Delphi technique is "The Use of the Delphi Technique in Problems of Educational Innovations" by Olaf Helmer-Hirschberg, which is available at http://www.rand.org/pubs/papers/2006/P3499.pdf.

An article on the art of the Delphi technique is available at http://findarticles .com/p/articles/mi_6820/is_4_12/ai_n28482367/?tag=content;col1.

A descriptive definition, including a history of the technique and valuable resources, is available at http://en.wikipedia.org/wiki/Delphi_method.

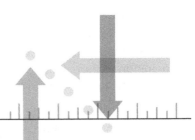

PERFORMANCE OBSERVATIONS

Purpose

The goal of a performance observation is to accurately document the steps, procedures, tools, and decisions used to accomplish current performance (see box 3A.3).

Needs Assessment Applications

To fully understand what is involved in accomplishing current results, you should use performance observations to document the current individual or team processes. Performance observations can, thereby, provide essential information in the analysis of current performance (or information that is helpful in determining what is working and what is not working in the current process).

Information from the performance observation can then be compared and contrasted with information from other sources (such as interviews with expert performers, statistical performance measures, task protocols and procedures, best practices for the task, and performance standards for desired performance).

Box 3A.3 Sample Uses of Performance Observations

- Identify procedural breakdowns in current delivery of HIV/AIDS medications.
- Modify procurement process to reduce redundancies.
- Reduce the time required to conduct inspections to identify potholes in roads.
- Improve team member collaboration.

Advantages and Disadvantages

Advantages

- By observing without interfering, you can create a performance observation that accurately documents the steps, procedures, tools, and decisions made in completing a task.

- Performance observations don't rely on the perspectives or memories of performers to define how tasks are currently completed.

- Performance observations can be done by multiple members of the needs assessment team to validate the findings.

Disadvantages

- Performance observations require the time and related expenses of having an observer to document the current performance.

- Observations alone may miss some of the decisions and other nonvisible aspects that go into performing a task (especially with regard to complex cognitive tasks).

- Observers may introduce biases into the needs assessment. Therefore, it is important that observers are trained in the observation process and are sensitized about biases and the need for objectivity. Having multiple observers can also be a way to address issues of observer bias. Observers should also be aware that those being observed might change their behavior, change what they say or do, or say or do things they think the observer would want to hear. The observer should consider options on how to conduct the observation to avoid influencing the person(s) being observed.

Process Overview

1. After needs (or gaps between current and desired performance) have been identified, use performance observations to document the current processes, procedures, tools, and decisions that helped achieve current results. To begin, identify essential tasks involved in the achievement of current performance (for example, develop a concept note, monitor procurement transactions, or review project reports).

2. For each essential task involved in the achievement of current performance, determine which tasks can be observed during the needs assessment. For instance, if a task will not be completed again for another 12–18 months, then it is unlikely that you can include a performance observation of that task in your needs assessment.

3. Remember that performance observations are rarely done as an exclusive information-collection process because observations should involve minimal interactions with the performers (which could be distracting and could compromise the validity of the observation). Plan to integrate your performance observations with other processes such as post-performance interviews, document reviews, or performer focus groups.

4. Before observing the completion of a task associated with the performance, review any documentation on the processes, procedures, tools, or decisions that may be used in completing the task. Having an idea of what steps are coming next can help you to focus your observations.

5. Create a performance observation protocol or checklist to ensure that you systematically assess the current performance. This step will also be valuable if multiple reviewers will be observing the performance or if multiple tasks are to be observed.

6. Select the performers to be observed. It is frequently helpful, when possible, to observe the performance of both an expert and a novice so you can isolate potential differences. For most needs assessments, as compared with performance evaluations, it is useful to inform the performer that he or she will be observed and to schedule time to debrief him or her after the observation.

7. Observe the performer while he or she completes the task. During the observation, the observer should not interfere with the performance. For example, do not stop the performer to ask questions or make suggestions; hold questions and comments until the post-observation debrief. Use the observation protocol to track activities and to make observations about how the task is completed.

8. After the task is completed, meet with the performer to debrief him or her on the observation. During the debrief, ask questions to (a) identify any unique characteristics of the observed performance that may not be relevant to your assessment (for instance, unrelated activities or interruptions that took place during the observation), (b) determine if the observation is representative of task performance by others, or (c) find out

what recommendations the performer would offer for completing the task more efficiently or effectively.

9. Write a summary report of the findings from each performance observation. Include these in the report: background information on the task, performer, and performance environment; notes from each performance observation; notes from each observation debrief; and your comments or recommendations that are based on observations.

Tips for Success

- Observe the complete performance of the task being reviewed; you don't want to leave early and potentially miss critical steps, tools, or decisions. However, for tasks that are completed over several days or weeks (such as developing a project plan), it can be useful to conduct performance observations that focus on select subtasks.

- Make arrangements early in the needs assessment process if you want to observe performance, especially for tasks that are not completed on a routine basis within the organization.

References and Resources

McClelland, Samuel B. 1994c. "Training Needs Assessment Data-Gathering Methods: Part 4—Onsite Observations." *Journal of European Industrial Training* 18 (5): 4–7.

Website

A how-to description on Find, Use, Manage, and Share Information (FUMSI) is available at http://web.fumsi.com/go/article/use/2491.

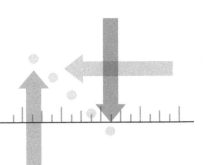

TASK ANALYSIS (HIERARCHICAL OR SEQUENTIAL, IF-THEN, AND MODEL-BASED)

Purpose

The purpose of a task analysis is to systematically describe, document, and analyze the activities, procedures, processes, and resources that are used by individuals or groups to accomplish current results.

Needs Assessment Applications

A task analysis explains the processes and inputs that are being used at this time to accomplish results. Consequently, a task analysis defines what individuals and teams both are doing and should be doing to contribute to current results. As part of a needs assessment, this vital tool can inform both the diagnosis of needs and the detection of potential remedies for improving performance.

In many ways, a task analysis process parallels the performance analysis process although the former begins with the results currently being achieved, whereas the latter begins with the desired results that should be accomplished in the future. Sometimes these starting places are one and the same. Yet, from their unique vantage points, the two processes parallel each other as they identify the tasks, processes, procedures, tools, and resources that are used to achieve results.

Your focus during a task analysis is on systematically documenting what individuals or groups are doing (or should be doing). From observable processes and behaviors to scripted procedures and organic creativity, it is important to detail current events so that they may be compared with desired events when identifying future actions.

Advantages and Disadvantages

Advantages

- A task analysis can attain a clear definition of what resources, processes, and results are related to current tasks that are (or will be) related to your program or project.

- By using a task analysis to systematically review the completion of current tasks and their results, you will ensure that your needs assessment will be better prepared to make recommendations regarding changes to current procedures and new tasks.

- A task analysis will help you to identify both what is working well and what is not working as well within the current organization.

Disadvantages

- Effective task analyses require time and resources that may not have been included in your initial planning.

- Completing a task analysis is usually more complex than completing the task itself. For complex tasks, you will likely want to use a task analysis expert.

- It can be challenging to determine (a) if and how the completion of tasks would change because of needs assessment recommendations and (b) how those changes would influence other parts of the system.

Process Overview[1]

1. Identify key positions and tasks related to the completion of results within your results framework. For example, if your results framework identifies food safety inspections conducted by the state health and agriculture agencies as an essential result for improving performance in the overall food safety system, then you would want to identify which positions and tasks within the agencies are (or would be) responsible for the successful completion of food safety inspections.

2. Select a task analysis method. Several systematic task analysis methods can be applied, each with advantages and disadvantages depending on the context. As a result, use a mix of task analysis methods during any needs assessment. Three possible methods are (a) hierarchical (sequential), (b) if–then, and (c) model-based.

a. ***Hierarchical (Sequential) Task Analysis***

(1) This kind of analysis identifies both the component steps in completing the given task and their hierarchical (or sequential) relationship to one another. When desired results are not being accomplished, use the hierarchical analysis to provide insights into the obstacles preventing success. Equally, when desired results are being accomplished, use the analysis to detail the constructive processes that lead to accomplishment of objectives.

(2) To begin, you should review, observe, and document each step taken by the performer in completing the task. Verify the appropriate sequence of steps for accomplishing results, and identify the resources (for example, supplies, computers, or other employees) used to complete the task. Routinely, processes will involve steps that cannot be observed. Talk with the individuals or teams that perform selected tasks to identify both internal and external behaviors. Most often, a hierarchical task analysis requires a combination of observation and interviews with expert performers.

(3) For example, a task analysis may identify that receptionists complete the following steps in accomplishing a performance objective for the pension office:

- Check voice mail messages.

- Take detailed and accurate notes on each voice mail message.

- Send e-mail to district pension officers along with voice mail messages.

- Copy managers on e-mail messages sent to their respective pension officers.

- Clear phone messages after e-mail messages have been sent.

(4) Depending on the level of detail required for making useful decisions, additional analysis may be done on any single step within the process to determine more detailed actions taken by the expert performer (for example, what steps are required to check voice mail messages). The level of detail required for a task analysis varies greatly from initiative to initiative. Balance (a) the desired level of detail for making improvement decisions with (b) the available time and resources.

(5) Create a graphic depicting the tasks and their relationships (see figure 3A.2).

b. *If-Then Task Analysis*

(1) If–then analysis applies process logic to the determination of the important decision steps for completing a task. This analysis technique can be useful when you have multiple decision steps. For example, for the task of using a word processing software application, you might include "*If* a word in the text is underlined in red, *then* right-click on the word to identify options for revising the spelling of the word." As tasks gain in complexity, multiple decisions must typically be made by the performer. The if–then analysis becomes an effective technique for identifying and documenting decisions and behaviors that cannot be observed.

(2) In a manner similar to the hierarchical analysis technique, you can use both observations and interviews with expert performers to complete an if–then analysis. In addition, combinations of methods are commonly used to identify the constituent steps in completing many complex tasks.

(3) Continuing the example, receptionists in another pension office might identify the following steps for achieving the same performance objective:

- Step 1: Check voice mail messages when you arrive at work. If there are messages, then take detailed notes on each voice mail message.

Figure 3A.2   Example of a Hierarchical Task Analysis Graphic

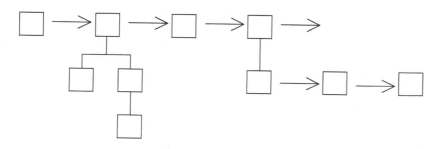

- Step 2: If the voice mail was for a pension officer, then e-mail the pension officer the contact information and message from the voice mail (and proceed to step 4).

- Step 3: If the voice mail message was for a manager, then forward the voice mail to the manager using the *8 feature of the phone.

- Step 4: Copy (or inform) the managers about e-mails going to their respective pension officers.

- Step 5: If you have completed steps 2, 3, and 4 for all voice mail messages, then delete phone messages.

(4) Create a graphic depicting the tasks and their relationships (see figure 3A.3).

c. *Model-Based Task Analysis*

(1) Use a model-based analysis when the task being reviewed is vague or difficult to define. Because many "soft skills" or professional tasks (for example, demonstrating leadership, group problem solving) are characterized by their elusive definitions and reliance on situational context, model-based analysis can provide you with essential information for describing how performance objectives get accomplished in these situations. In completing a model-based analysis, you work closely with performers to develop a model or framework for completing the task. Performance is then the result of applying the model even when there are ambiguous guidelines for performing the task.

Figure 3A.3   Example of an If-Then Task Analysis Graphic

(2) For example, for the soft skills task of mentoring pension office employees, the analysis may identify the following performance model:

> Describe for the employee the optional techniques that may be used to complete his or her work. In mentoring the employee, use one or more of the following techniques: (a) use examples of other current and previous employees, (b) have the employee form a mental picture of performing the work at his or her desk, (c) demonstrate successful performance of the work-related tasks, (d) have the employee practice the work steps and then provide immediate feedback to the employee, and (e) suggest additional training opportunities offered within the organization.

(3) Use interviews (or focus groups) with expert performers to define a model for a task. After a model is developed, expert performers should again review the procedures and options to ensure that the model adequately represents a framework for accomplishing desired results. The ability of a model to represent the successful completion of a task depends on the flexibility of the model. If your model-based analysis does not result in a flexible framework that can be applied in a variety of contexts, then review the task using another task analysis technique.

(4) When possible, create a graphic depicting the tasks and their relationships (see figure 3A.4).

3. To collect information in a task analysis, use a combination of interviews, observations, intensive observations, focus groups, surveys, document reviews, data reviews, and other techniques.

4. After the initial task analysis is completed and as a useful step, have the participants in the analysis review your findings to provide clarifications and corrections when appropriate. Depending on the complexity of your tasks, several rounds of revisions may be required.

5. Write a summary report of the findings from the task analysis.

6. Remember that the task analysis is an essential ingredient to a needs assessment and should be used as a point of comparison with other assessment data (for example, surveys, interviews, focus groups) to inform your decisions.

Figure 3A.4   Example of a Model-Based Task Analysis Graphic

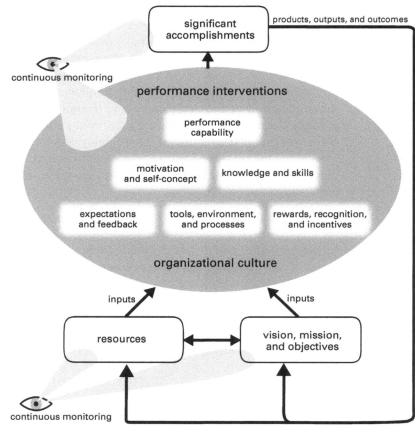

Source: The example is the performance pyramid model found in Wedman (2010). Reused with permission. Also available at http://needsassessment.missouri.edu.

Tips for Success

- Strive to be very systematic in your analysis.

- Communicate openly with those participating in your analysis to assure them that the results of the analysis will be used only for improving results and not for placing blame.

- Remember that actions speak louder than words; it is better to observe individuals performing a task than to simply ask them what they do.

Note

1. Based in part on http://www.nwlink.com/~donclark/hrd/tasks.html and Watkins (2007).

References and Resources

Jonassen, David H., Wallace H. Hannum, and Martin Tessmer. 1989. *Handbook of Task Analysis Procedures.* Westport, CT: Praeger Publishers.

Watkins, Ryan. 2007. *Performance by Design: The Systematic Selection, Design, and Development of Performance Technologies That Produce Useful Results.* Amherst, MA: HRD Press, and Silver Spring, MD: International Society for Performance Improvement.

Wedman, John F. 2010. "Performance Pyramid Model." In *Handbook of Improving Performance in the Workplace.* Vol. 2: *Selecting and Implementing Performance Interventions,* edited by Ryan Watkins and Doug Leigh. San Francisco: Wiley/Pfeiffer, and Silver Spring, MD: International Society for Performance Improvement, 51–80.

Website

Tasks and Task Analysis is available at http://www.nwlink.com/~donclark/hrd/tasks.html.

COGNITIVE TASK ANALYSIS

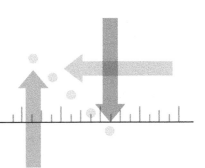

Purpose

The purpose of a cognitive task analysis (CTA) is to systematically define the decision requirements and psychological processes used by expert individuals (or performers) in accomplishing results.

Needs Assessment Applications

A standard task analysis explains the processes and inputs that are being used at this time to accomplish results. As a consequence, a task analysis defines what individuals and teams either are doing or should be doing to contribute to current results. In the completion of a needs assessment, the task analysis is a vital tool for informing both the diagnosis of needs and the detection of potential remedies for improving performance.

In a CTA, however, cognitive analysis methods focus on the psychological processes underlying the completion of a task. For example, CTA may be used when one is trying to understand how master teachers are able to manage student behaviors in classrooms. CTA should be used whenever complex decisions are required (such as when multiple contributing variables and options must be weighed by the performer) and when few observable behaviors can be identified. Subtle cues from the performance context and the experience of expert performers are often discovered through the CTA technique. Of the many tools and techniques offered in this book, CTA is one of the more difficult approaches to undertake.

Advantages and Disadvantages

Advantages

- A CTA generates detailed, precise information on the nature of expert performance in a specific task of interest.

- When implemented correctly, CTA techniques provide highly valid sources of information on expert cognitive processes.

- A CTA provides systematic procedures (rather than hit-or-miss steps) for ascertaining expert cognitive processes.

Disadvantages

- Analysis of the data gathered during a CTA can be time-intensive.

- CTA does not always capture other noncognitive attributes necessary for accomplishing results (such as physical capabilities, access to resources, and interpersonal relationships).

- The results of a CTA can be misleading when expert performers have performance capacities beyond that of others (for example, a CTA can be done with high-performing professional athletes, but implementation of cognitive processes alone will not duplicate performance).

- Completing a task analysis, especially a CTA, is usually more complex than completing the task itself. For complex tasks, you will likely want to use a task analysis expert to get useful results.

Process Overview[1]

Collect Preliminary Knowledge

To kick off the CTA process, identify some key cognitive tasks to study (for example, how master teachers manage classroom behavior) that are important elements in the achievement of particular results (for example, improvements in student performance on tests). In particular, identify those cognitive tasks that merit *detailed* study through CTA. As you proceed through the following steps, pay special attention to (a) tasks that are important, frequent, and highly critical cognitive tasks within the job performance that you are studying and (b) tasks or problems that are within the job performance and that allow for discrimination between expert and novice performance (such tasks are referred to as *representative tasks*).

1. Develop some general understanding of the domain area (for example, training of teachers) in which the CTA will be conducted and of the common terminology used in that domain area. This understanding will make it a lot easier to conduct an effective CTA.

2. Identify experts who are good candidates (for example, master teachers) for serving as subjects of the CTA (ideally two or more experts should be identified for participation). Experts with recent experience in both performing and teaching the cognitive skill are generally considered to be good candidates for participation.

3. Identify the knowledge structures associated with the task area through one or more of the following substeps:

   a. ***Document review and analysis:*** Review any written materials that you can locate and that provide relevant information on the tasks you have identified as being of interest. Documents could include job descriptions, reports, training materials, and so on. By reviewing available documents and research, you are better prepared to conduct interviews with experts, and you are able to (later on) identify discrepancies between extant training (performance support materials) and expert performance.

   b. ***Observation:*** Observe an expert conducting the tasks and procedures of interest to the CTA (for example, teaching a classroom subject to high school students). Record the actions and conditions that are naturally a part of the process of executing the tasks that are of interest. Make special notes of points in the task-completion process where it seems that the expert is engaged in decision making, analysis, or other critical cognitive tasks.

   c. ***Unstructured interviews:*** When you are conducting an unstructured interview, it generally is helpful if you have been able to do a document analysis or observation beforehand. For the interview, your goal is to ask the expert direct questions that will give you more information about the tasks and to sort through preliminary questions that may help you in preparing for structured interviews that you complete later in the process. Because the interview is unstructured, you may opt to take a "go with the flow" approach for the interview, or you may ask the expert to focus on a specific aspect or task related to the domain area.

Identify Knowledge Representations

Using the results from the preliminary knowledge data collection, identify the subtasks and knowledge that are associated with each of the primary tasks that you are interested in studying further. Generally, an effective approach for visually organizing this information is by creating a visual representation of the relationship between the tasks, subtasks, and knowledge associated with the domain of interest. Concept maps can be an effective approach to visually representing the knowledge and task structures.

Use Focused Methods to Gather Information

1. If the CTA will be conducted by someone other than you, identify someone to serve as the cognitive task analyst. Note that it is highly desirable to choose this individual carefully. Ideally, it is someone who can interact comfortably with the subject matter expert and who can learn domain- and task-specific terminology efficiently.

2. Choose one or more of the following methods to work with the expert(s) to identify, cluster, link, and prioritize the critical cognitive decisions that are routine in expert performance. All of these knowledge-gathering methods can be used with expert performers. If you intend to also gather information from novices, however, it is recommended that you select either *structured and unstructured interviews* or *concurrent verbal protocol analysis* as knowledge-gathering methods, because the other techniques assume a high level of domain knowledge.

   - *Structured and unstructured interviews:* One approach is to ask the expert (for example, a master teacher) to list (a) all of the steps involved in completing the subtasks (for example, how to call on students, how to deal with misbehaviors, and so on) that are part of the larger task (for example, classroom management) that you are studying; (b) key decision points, and when those decision points appear; (c) procedures that can be used to make decisions between alternate options; (d) conceptual knowledge required to tackle the subtasks; and (e) ways that the expert determines when the conditions call for beginning the process for completing the subtask(s).

- **Concurrent verbal protocol analysis:** To begin a protocol analysis, you should work with experts to identify a good "representative task" in the task area. An example could be how a master teacher would deal with a disruptive student. Develop a problem or scenario around that representative task, and ask several experts (such as master teachers) to review and modify the problem or scenario before using it for knowledge gathering.

  To begin understanding the task (for example, the process of dealing with disruptive students), you should schedule time with the expert in a quiet location where you have audio or video recording capabilities. Prepare and train the expert for solving problems aloud by giving him or her instructions on how to think aloud, as well as by giving the expert the chance to think aloud while solving at least two or three sample problems so that he or she can get comfortable with the verbalization process. Next, present the main problem or challenge to the expert. Record all of the verbal utterances of the expert as he or she solves the problem. It is very important that you avoid interrupting the expert at any time during the problem-solving process. If possible, gather verbal protocols from several experts for the same problem, and pay special attention to problem-solving steps and strategies used by all or most of the experts.

- **Applied cognitive tasks analysis:** In this approach, you conduct three structured interviews. Each interview generates a separate product. Through the first interview, you develop a *task diagram* that gives a broad representation of the task and specifically allows you to hone in on complex cognitive processes that merit further consideration. The second interview yields a *knowledge audit*, which probes the expert on the skills and knowledge applied to tackle specific component tasks or decision points in the overarching task process. The third and final interview involves presenting the expert with a specific and relevant scenario designed to elicit insight into the cognitive processes used by the expert in the scenario context. The compiled and analyzed results from the applied cognitive tasks analysis are represented in a *cognitive demands table*.

- **Critical incident (or decision) method:** This procedure begins with the expert identifying a situation in which he or she had to apply expertise to a critical and uncommon situation relating to the task area of interest (for example, a classroom where students were starting physical fights). The expert describes the incident, and the analyst works with the expert to create a time line for the incident. The analyst then works with the expert to try to identify key points on the incident time line when decisions had to be made (for example, when to intervene to prevent fights in classrooms). From there, the analyst closely questions the expert to identify perceptual cues and prior knowledge that were used in the decision making, as well as alternative decisions that could have been made. An understanding of those key decision points, as well as of the representative tasks that experts can perform and that novices have difficulty performing, is an important result of using the critical incident method.

3. Develop a protocol for each of the knowledge-gathering methods selected. Next are recommendations for the design of the protocols for each of the knowledge-gathering techniques:

- ***Protocol for structured and unstructured interviews:*** Develop instructions and questions for interviews, focusing on key decision points, procedures for choosing between different options at decision points, and domain knowledge.

- ***Protocol for concurrent verbal protocol analysis:*** Develop a protocol that provides participants with information on procedures for verbalizing thought sequences, as well as a few simple problem-solving tasks that can be used to practice the verbalization process. The protocol should conclude with the presentation of the main problem (based on the representative task).

- ***Protocol for applied cognitive task analysis:*** Develop instructions and questions for each of the three interviews. For the task diagram, come prepared with paper, sticky notes, markers, or a computer to diagram the tasks. For the knowledge audit, come prepared with some idea of what the possible knowledge and skills would be so you are able to probe for more information. For the third interview, prepare scenarios for the expert to discuss.

- ***Protocol for critical decision method:*** Develop instructions and questions, focusing on key decision points, procedures for choosing between different options at decision points, and domain knowledge in use in the critical incident identified by the expert.

4. Apply the knowledge-gathering technique. It is highly advisable that you record the knowledge-gathering session in either audio or video format (video format is justified in cases where the task includes psychomotor actions). Make sure that you have the expert's permission in

advance to record the session. Because people generally do not feel immediately at ease with being recorded, and because the knowledge-gathering exercise may be unfamiliar to the expert, it is highly recommended that you run through with the expert an example session of the exercise before conducting the actual knowledge-gathering session. This suggestion is particularly relevant if you choose to implement a concurrent verbal protocol analysis, an applied CTA, or the critical decision method.

Analyze and Verify Data Required

1. If you have recorded the knowledge-gathering session(s), transcribe the recorded information into a text-based format.

2. Prepare the transcripts for further categorization and synthesis by coding them. Pay special attention to diagnosing and characterizing key decision points on the basis of the techniques used, the cues signaling the decision points, and the inferences made.

3. After coding has been completed, organize the data from the transcripts into a format that summarizes and categorizes the data.

4. Provide a copy of the formatted results from the knowledge-gathering session to each of the experts from whom you gathered data. Allow the experts to make any suggestions for changes or clarifications.

5. Integrate edits and adjustments recommended by the experts.

6. Compare the formatted results for each of the expert knowledge-gathering sessions, and verify that the formatted results reflect the knowledge representation for the task area.

Format Results for Intended Application

1. Using the formatted results from the expert knowledge-gathering sessions, create a single model task analysis, representing all the skills, knowledge, and strategies used by the experts when functioning in the task area.

2. Write a summary report of the findings from the CTA.

3. The task analysis is an essential ingredient of a needs assessment and should be used as a point of comparison with other assessment data (for example, surveys, interviews, focus groups) to inform your decisions.

Tips for Success

- Strive to be very systematic in your analysis.

- Remember that actions speak louder than words; it is better to observe individuals performing the task than to simply ask them what they do.

- Also remember that expert performers have often internalized or made habitual many of the key decisions that go into performing the related steps within the task. This internalization makes completing a cognitive analysis challenging. Aid expert performers in communicating their cognitive processes by using techniques such as card sorting, process tracing, or concept mapping.

Note

1. Based in part on Clark et al. (2008). Also available at http://www.cogtech.usc.edu/publications/clark_etal_cognitive_task_analysis_chapter.pdf.

References and Resources

Clark, R. E., D. Feldon, J. J. G. van Merriënboer, K. Yates, and S. Early. 2008. "Cognitive Task Analysis." In *Handbook of Research on Educational Communications and Technology*, 3rd ed., edited by J. M. Spector, M. D. Merrill, J. J. G. van Merriënboer, and M. P. Driscoll, 577–94. Mahwah, NJ: Lawrence Erlbaum Associates.

Watkins, Ryan. 2007. *Performance by Design: The Systematic Selection, Design, and Development of Performance Technologies That Produce Useful Results.* Amherst, MA: HRD Press, and Silver Spring, MD: International Society for Performance Improvement.

Witkin, Belle Ruth, and James W. Altschuld. 1995. *Planning and Conducting Needs Assessments: A Practical Guide.* Thousand Oaks, CA: Sage Publications.

Websites

"Applied Cognitive Task Analysis (ACTA)" (by Militello and Hutton) is available at http://www.class.uidaho.edu/psy562/Readings/Militello&Hutton(1998).pdf.

"Cognitive Task Analysis" (by Clark, Feldon, van Merriënboer, Yates, and Early) is available at http://www.cogtech.usc.edu/publications/clark_etal_cognitive_task_analysis_chapter.pdf.

"Cognitive Task Analysis" (from NATO) is available at http://ftp.rta.nato.int/public//PubFulltext/RTO/TR/RTO-TR-024/TR-024-$$ALL.pdf.

"Cognitive Task Analysis for HPTers" (presentation slides generated by Stone and Villachica) is available at http://www.dls.com/1090_CTA_Panel.pdf.

"Protocols for Cognitive Task Analysis" (from the Institute for Human and Machine Cognition) is available at http://www.ihmc.us/research/projects/CTAProtocols/ProtocolsForCognitiveTaskAnalysis.pdf.

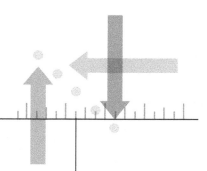

Part 3B

DECISION-MAKING TOOLS AND TECHNIQUES

As seen in *Part 3A. Data Collection Tools and Techniques*, this book provides options to consider using as you collect data to inform your needs assessment. However, once you have collected that information, another important step is required as you make decisions about using the data. And there are tools to support your decision-making process.

Part 3B. Decision-Making Tools and Techniques suggests tools for analyzing and prioritizing issues in your needs assessment process and, ultimately, for deciding to take action. Prioritizing information and making choices can be a difficult task for both individuals and groups. Instead of your making decisions through an informal, ad hoc process, this part describes tools that can be helpful in ensuring that issues are given due consideration in a participatory decision-making process.

NOMINAL GROUP TECHNIQUE (A GROUP CONSENSUS-BUILDING AND RANKING TECHNIQUE)

Purpose

The nominal group technique is used to engage in consensus planning so you can prioritize issues and make decisions.

Needs Assessment Applications

The nominal group technique can be a valuable tool for facilitating group decision making, and it can also be useful for data collection (such as for generating a list of the possible causes of a particular problem). The theorists who originated this technique used the term *nominal* (meaning *in name only*) to express the bringing together of a group that is assembled for the purpose of pooling ideas around a particular issue and ranking those ideas. We can also think of this technique simply as a *group ranking technique*. The technique provides a structured process for working with group members to prioritize their ideas, concerns, or other decision inputs in a format that is both inclusive and consensus-building.

During data collection, for instance, a nominal group technique can help a group of community members as they prioritize their list of public services that are provided by the city and that are inadequately addressing community expectations. This dynamic group decision-making process is flexible enough that you may use it multiple times at different steps within your needs assessment—whenever a group with multiple perspectives has to make a difficult decision.

Advantages and Disadvantages

Advantages

- The nominal group technique is more structured than the ordinary group discussion approach.

- Through a nominal group technique, everyone in the group is given an opportunity to contribute to the discussion and decision, thereby avoiding a situation where one person dominates the group process.

- The nominal group technique can be used with small (3–9 people) groups as well as with larger groups (for example, 10–30 people).

- By using the nominal group technique, you can get a sense of priority concerns that are represented among the group's members.

Disadvantages

- The synergism that is experienced in more open-ended group discussions may not develop as easily in the nominal group approach.

- The nominal group technique may feel somewhat mechanical to some participants. This situation can be circumvented to some extent by ensuring that the facilitator shows flexibility in process and implementation.

- Although the nominal group technique can be used with a range of group sizes, it is hard to implement the technique effectively with large audiences unless you plan very carefully beforehand.

Process Overview

1. From the list of decisions to be made during your needs assessment, identify those elements that may best be attained through the nominal group technique.

2. Create a facilitator's guide or protocol to guide the group. In the protocol, ensure that all participants are given multiple opportunities to contribute to group decisions. At the same time, the process must intentionally and continually move the group toward a decision, rather than letting discussions continue without advancing. The guide should offer

the facilitator a fair amount of flexibility to modify the process when the group requires additional information or when subdecisions must be made prior to other decisions.

3. Schedule a time for the group when the highest number of priority participants are available. Verify that you have a group facilitator available at the scheduled time.

4. To begin the exercise, give each group member some paper and a writing implement.

5. Present the session's single topic to the group members. For example, the group members could be presented with a context for why the group is meeting and could be asked to "identify what results you should be accomplishing but are not able to accomplish at this time," "list all of the things that could be improved about . . . ," or "list which of the factors causing the performance gap should be our priorities for the next year." Only one key question should, however, be used in a session so that you can maintain a clear focus and objective.

6. Give the group members an opportunity to ask any questions that come to mind or to discuss anything that helps to elucidate the scope and specifics of the topic. In other words, accommodate interaction that will help increase clarity for the discussion.

7. Ask the group members to take time (generally a few minutes) to think about the topic and to write notes for their responses. Encourage group members to write down their thoughts in a bulleted, abbreviated format.

8. On a turn-by-turn basis, ask each group member to share a response with the group. As each group member shares his or her response, write it on a flip chart. Invite the group member to elaborate if necessary, but do not allow other group members to ask questions, challenge, or otherwise discuss the responses (to avoid subtle peer pressure, disagreements, arguments, unwanted embarrassment, and other undesired behaviors or emotions).

9. After all group members have given one response, go around the room again and ask each group member to give a second response, and then a third. Continue this process until all answers have been written on the flip chart sheets. Ask participants to scratch items from their individual lists as those points are added to the flip charts (to avoid duplication). Again, group members should not discuss the responses, but the

facilitator may ask for clarifications to ensure an accurate response is recorded.

10. Hang the flip chart sheets next to one another so all sheets can be seen at the same time by all group members. Assign a letter to each discrete contribution on each flip chart sheet. To facilitate discussion, give each item on the flip charts a unique letter.

11. Give each group member a stack of index cards. Ask each member to identify, for example, the five responses that he or she feels is most important, identifying each response on a separate index card by the letter it has been assigned on the flip chart.

12. Next, ask the group members to rank the five responses they selected in order of priority, from one to five (five being the highest priority and one being the least high priority). They should do this on their index card by writing the rank order value of each response next to the letter for the response. When the group members are done, ask them to reorganize their index cards in alphabetical order.

13. Reading from the flip chart, go through the list of responses in alphabetical order. As you read aloud the letter corresponding with a response, ask each group member to state the rank (if any) that they gave it.

14. Aggregate all the ranks for each response on the flip chart. The responses with the highest aggregated value constitute the top priorities for the group.

15. If necessary, a second or third round of rankings can be done to further reduce the responses and to advance the group toward a decision.

Tips for Success

- Each nominal group session that you conduct should last between 30 minutes and four hours. Each session should present only one key question to the participants.

- Arrange to have the following supplies available at the group meeting site: flip chart, masking tape, markers, paper, index cards, and pens or pencils.

- If you are working with a large group, consider assigning individual participants to smaller groups, with an assigned leader for each group.

References and Resources

Witkin, Belle Ruth, and James W. Altschuld. 1995. *Planning and Conducting Needs Assessments: A Practical Guide.* Thousand Oaks, CA: Sage Publications.

Websites

"Expressed Satisfaction with the Nominal Group Technique among Change Agents" is available at http://cogprints.org/4767/01/Gresham.pdf. (This is a dissertation document; however, the literature review provides interesting and in-depth information on the use of the nominal group technique.)

"Nominal Group Technique" is available at http://syque.com/quality_tools/ toolbook/NGT/ngt.htm. (This website includes a worked example of the technique being implemented.)

"Using Nominal Groups" is available at http://ppa.aces.uiuc.edu/pdf_files/ NomGroup1.PDF.

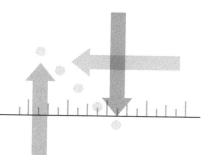

MULTICRITERIA ANALYSIS

Purpose

The purpose of multicriteria analysis is to systematically provide a quantitative comparison across multiple options.

Needs Assessment Applications

Multicriteria analysis is a valuable tool for making decisions on the basis of information collected during a needs assessment. This analysis technique, which is based on the multi-attribute utility analysis frequently used by engineers and architects to select materials,[1] provides a systematic process of assigning and weighing quantitative (or numeric) values to a variety of potential performance-improvement programs and projects. Thus, it provides you with a justifiable process for determining what actions should be taken. As such, multicriteria analysis is a worthwhile tool for comparing across potential improvement activities, which can be particularly beneficial in organizational sectors (such as financial, manufacturing, aviation, construction, disaster management, and so on) that especially value quantitative and systematic comparisons of alternatives.

Advantages and Disadvantages

Advantages

- Multicriteria analysis offers a systematic and quantitative analysis procedure for comparing potential options. This method can be especially valuable if one alternative improvement activity is particularly popular (for instance six sigma, training, coaching, wells, roads, irrigation systems), even though it might not be the most useful activity for accomplishing desired results.

- Additional variables can be added to the comparison as the field of potential interventions or activities is narrowed. In the end, you can make justified recommendations based on the interventions or activities that score best across a variety of variables.

- Variables in the analysis (for instance, cost, time, expected outcomes) can each be given a weighting that reflects the priorities of the project. For example, if budgets are very tight, then scores related to costs of alternative activities may be weighted at four times the value of expected time to implement the activities.

Disadvantages

- Multicriteria analysis requires a higher level of effort than does some other analysis procedures because information regarding each potential solution (intervention, activity, and so on) is necessary for accurate comparisons. As a result, additional time and resources may be required; therefore, you may prefer to use this method only for high-cost or high-priority needs.

- The multicriteria analysis process can be manipulated by only selecting comparison variables that favor a preferred activity. Or other participants can manipulate their weightings on variables so they produce the results they desire. Such challenges can be controlled, but you have to be aware of the risk in order to ensure that this manipulation doesn't happen to you.

Process Overview

1. Understand that the multicriteria analysis process typically begins when two or more alternative interventions or activities have been identified as potential solutions to a need. Although you can complete the analysis for as many potential solutions as you have, the time and effort required to collect valid information for comparison typically will necessitate that you limit the analysis to the most likely contenders. (For helpful sample templates to serve as job aids, see page 179.)

2. Identify (a) the most important criteria to making the decision and (b) the performance criteria (attributes or characteristics) required of

alternative solutions. Typically, consider no more than five to eight attributes for any decision. Example criteria could include the following:

- Results you can expect after six months
- Total time required
- Number of outputs
- Client satisfaction
- Feasibility of implementation
- Environmental impact
- Ability to accomplish desired outcomes
- Cost of the activity over the first year
- Safety expectations
- Number of people who will be working on the project in the first month

3. Note any "must have" (or "must not have") attributes. For instance, if an activity or intervention must not cost more than the budget set by the organization, then this attribute provides a cap at which alternatives that go beyond the budget are no longer considered. Likewise, if minimal improvements in results must be demonstrated after three months, then potential solutions that cannot meet those specifications should also be dropped.

4. Depending on the context of your decision and as a useful technique, apply weighting to the diverse criteria. The weights differentiate criteria according to their relative importance to the decision. For example, as you select among alternative irrigation technologies, the cost criteria may be twice as important to the decision as the time it will take to implement the technology.

5. To establish weights, discuss the criteria with those who will be part of the decision-making process. During the discussion (which could apply a survey, interview, or focus group technique as an alternative), you should ask questions to establish the relative importance of each performance criteria that you identified in the previous step.

6. In both establishing criteria to apply and weighing those criteria relative to one another, use a number of techniques[2] either separately or in combination, including the following

   a. To assist decision makers, consider using a 100-point system (or ratio method). For instance, of the 100 total possible points, a decision maker may assign 60 points to the maximum achievement of desired results, 40 points to cost, and 20 points to the number of staff members assigned to the project. Each value can then be divided by the total so that a percentage can be calculated. For example, if participants indicate a weight, on average, of 70 out of 100 for the cost criteria, then .70 would be the weight assigned to cost.

b. Use hypothetical tradeoffs to prioritize criteria or set weights. For instance, ask partners whether they would prefer for the project to be completed several months late and achieve all of its objectives or for it to be completed on time but not achieve all of its objectives. Those establishing the criteria, thereby, have to make tradeoffs regarding which criteria are most important or should have the greatest weight in the decision.

c. Also include costs in the establishing of weights by using the pricing-out method combined with tradeoffs. This method would, for example, ask those establishing the criteria if they would prefer for the project to be completed two months late but on budget or for the project to be completed on time but 2 percent over the set budget.

d. Consider the *swing method*. Imagine, for example, that all of the criteria being considered were at their worst possible level (for instance, the project achieves none of its goals), then ask those establishing the criteria to identify which criterion they would want to "swing" to the highest potential level (for instance, the project achieves all of its goals), and assign this criterion 100 points. Next, ask which of the remaining criteria would be second-most important and swing its potential value. In points, how does the second criterion relate to the previous criterion (for instance, completing the project on budget might be assigned 80 points in relation to 100 points for completing all project goals)? Apply this method until you have identified the criteria to be applied or assigned weights to each criterion.

7. See how the examples in tables 3B.1 and 3B.2 illustrate how applying weighted criteria can influence the results of a multicriteria analysis. Now that you have your criteria (and weights for each when appropriate), it is time to rate each alternative activity on each of the criteria. It is important to use the same scale for each attribute. For example, if you select a scale from 1 to 10 for rating the attribute of client satisfaction (with 10 being given to alternatives that will achieve the highest levels of client satisfaction), then you would also rate the cost attribute from

Table 3B.1   Multicriteria Analysis Table Example

**Comparison of Regional Government-Sponsored Alternatives for
Providing Temporary Shelters after a Natural Disaster**
Ratings: 1–2 = very low, 3–4 = low, 5–6 = medium, 7–8 = high, 9–10 = very high

	Criterion 1 rating Speed in meeting needs	Criterion 2 rating Affordability (per unit)	Criterion 3 rating Quality of the shelter	Criterion 4 rating Durability (up to 12 months)	Criterion 5 rating Ease in coordination	*Average rating*
Alternative 1 Canvas tents (small, per family)	9	7	3	2	9	6.0
Alternative 2 Canvas tents (large, 4–6 families)	7	9	3	2	9	6.0
Alternative 3 Construction of temporary wooden structures	4	5	6	7	5	5.4
Alternative 4 Trailers, prefabricated	4	1	9	10	2	5.2

1 to 10 for each alternative (with 10 being given to the alternatives whose cost are most closely aligned with the desired budget).

8. Create a table or spreadsheet with the performance attributes listed in the columns along the top and the potential solutions listed in the rows. For each alternative intervention or activity, include an estimate for each performance criterion.

9. Review the results of the analysis. Just because a single alternative scores the highest doesn't always mean that it is by itself the right choice. In tables 3B.1 and 3B.2, for instance, alternatives 1 and 2 scored the highest overall in the unweighted comparison, suggesting that a combination of alternatives might be desirable. However, in the weighted example, where the option to assign relative value to each criterion was applied, alternative 1 was somewhat superior to alternative 2.

Table 3B.2   Multicriteria Analysis Table Example (with Weighted Criteria)

Comparison of Regional Government-Sponsored Alternatives for Providing Temporary Shelters after a Natural Disaster
Ratings: 1–2 = very low, 3–4 = low, 5–6 = medium, 7–8 = high, 9–10 = very high

	Criterion 1 rating Speed in meeting needs	**Criterion 2 rating** Affordability (per unit)	**Criterion 3 rating** Quality of the shelter	**Criterion 4 rating** Durability (up to 12 months)	**Criterion 5 rating** Ease in coordination	*Sum of weighted ratings*
Weights	.30	.20	.15	.15	.20	
Alternative 1 Canvas tents (small, per family)	9 × .30 = **2.70**	7 × .20 = **1.40**	3 × .15 = **0.45**	2 × .15 = **0.30**	9 × .20 = **1.80**	6.65
Alternative 2 Canvas tents (large, 4–6 families)	7 × .30 = **2.10**	9 × .20 = **1.80**	3 × .15 = **0.45**	2 × .15 = **0.30**	9 × .20 = **1.80**	6.45
Alternative 3 Construction of temporary wooden structures	4 × .30 = **1.20**	5 × .20 = **1.00**	6 × .15 = **0.90**	7 × .15 = **1.05**	5 × .20 = **1.00**	5.15
Alternative 4 Trailers, prefabricated	4 × .30 = **1.20**	1 × .20 = **0.20**	9 × .15 = **1.35**	10 × .15 = **1.50**	2 × .20 = **0.40**	4.65

10. In most needs assessments and as a useful approach, consider a combination of alternative activities rather than viewing each option as mutually exclusive. You might find that combining alternatives accomplishes desired results and mitigates the potential risks of any activity on its own. In the earlier example, even though alternative 1 (small tents) ranked highest, there might be some basis for choosing a combination of the top three alternatives (small and large tents, plus wooden structures), and eliminating the remaining alternative (prefabricated trailers).

11. Use the results of the analysis and your interpretation of those results as you present decision makers with recommendations about which alternative solutions they should consider.

A Guide to Assessing Needs

Note: Also consider using the multicriteria analysis technique to prioritize or rank needs (that is, gaps in results). In this application of the technique, you would work with decision makers to identify the criteria on which they would compare needs in order to set priorities (for example, the numbers of people affected by the continuation of the need, the availability of partners to help address the need, the costs to meet the need, the increasing severity of the need over time, and so forth). Then ask decision makers to compare each option using those criteria.

Tips for Success

- Don't get carried away with adding too many variables to the comparison. It is best to stick to the top five or six highest-priority variables and then to collect valid information for each alternative intervention or activity.

- Remember that no rule says you can select only one activity or solution. As you complete the analysis, keep in mind that a combination of one, two, three, or more potential activities or solutions may be the right choice for your organization and the identified need.

- As another alternative, ask participants to choose from options that include different levels of performance characteristics (for example, would you choose a solution that achieves 80 percent of the desired results over the next three years if it costs twice as much as the solution that achieves 50 percent of the desired results?). Each question in this format should include at least two of the performance characteristics at opposing levels so that you can move participants toward making a decision about which are the higher-priority characteristics in relation to the others. This procedure is an adaptation of analytic hierarchy process, another form of multicriteria analysis.

- Use multicriteria analysis in conjunction with other tools and techniques described in this section to ensure that valuable decisions are made about which performance-improvement programs and projects should be implemented.

Notes

1. The technique also uses elements of the simple multi-attribute ranking technique (SMART), which is an alternative used by engineers for applying the principles of multi-attribute utility analysis.

2. Borcherding, Eppel, and von Winterfeldt (1991) compared four methods for establishing weights; the results of the research indicated that a mix of methods was typically best, with no one technique being superior to the others.

References and Resources

Altschuld, James W. 2010. *Needs Assessment Phase III: Collecting Data* (Book 3 of *Needs Assessment Kit*). Thousand Oaks, CA: Sage Publications.

Altschuld, James W., and J. N. Eastmond Jr. 2010. *Needs Assessment Phase II: Getting Started* (Book 2 of *Needs Assessment Kit*). Thousand Oaks, CA: Sage Publications.

Borcherding, K., T. Eppel, and D. von Winterfeldt. 1991. "Comparison of Weighting Judgments in Multiattribute Utility Measurement." *Management Science* 37 (12): 1603–19.

Roth, R., F. Field, and J. Clark. 2011. "Multi-Attribute Utility Analysis." http://msl1.mit.edu/maua_paper.pdf.

Witkin, Belle Ruth, and James W. Altschuld. 1995. *Planning and Conducting Needs Assessments: A Practical Guide.* Thousand Oaks, CA: Sage Publications.

Websites

"Analytic Hierarchy Process" can be found at http://en.wikipedia.org/wiki/Analytic_Hierarchy_Process.

"Answers to Frequently Asked Questions about Decision Analysis" can be found at http://www.infoharvest.com/ihroot/infoharv/infoharvestfaq.asp.

Multiattribute utility models can be found at http://www.ctg.albany.edu/publications/guides/and_justice_for_all?chapter=9&PrintVersion=2.

Samples of Job Aids

Multicriteria Analysis Template (no weights)

	Criterion 1	Criterion 2	Criterion 3	Criterion 4	Criterion 5	Average rating
Alternative 1						
Alternative 2						
Alternative 3						
Alternative 4						

Multicriteria Analysis Template (with weights)

	Criterion 1	Criterion 2	Criterion 3	Criterion 4	Criterion 5	Sum of weighted ratings
Weights	Insert weight	Insert weight	Insert weight	Insert weight	Insert weight	
Alternative 1						
Alternative 2						
Alternative 3						
Alternative 4						

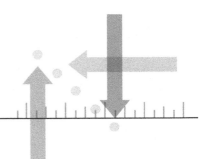

TABLETOP ANALYSIS

Purpose

Tabletop analyses are facilitator-led discussions that are used in a wide variety of settings to identify gaps, performance deficiencies, and communication problems in a given system.

Needs Assessment Applications

Tabletop analyses can be used as a decision-making technique for numerous needs assessment applications. They can identify gaps in performance at several levels (individual performance, unit or group performance, or organizational performance). In addition, they can *identify gaps within systems*, such as communication breakdowns or poor resource allocation). Finally, a tabletop analysis can *identify, analyze, and evaluate potential solutions* to a performance problem.

A tabletop analysis is a discussion-based activity in which a group of participants works with a facilitator. A problem or need, which is based on a specific performance area (such as municipal sanitation services), is presented to the participants. The participants then (a) systematically work through, discuss, and refine the problem focus; (b) develop a strategy for analyzing the problem; (c) collect data on the basis of the analysis plan; (d) analyze the data to determine the specific performance gaps; and (e) identify potential solutions for the performance gap. The participants and facilitator use a collaborative problem-solving approach to identify and find solutions to performance-related problems. The outcomes from this exercise allow you to identify and analyze the actual performance and to identify potential sources (and solutions) for a given performance area.

Advantages and Disadvantages

Advantages

- You do not require access to a lot of resources to conduct a tabletop analysis. This technique is not expensive to use in terms of material requirements.

- Tabletop analyses are usually conducted over a time frame of only a few hours, so the time requirements for participants are minimal. Note, however, that the time required to effectively prepare and analyze the tabletop analysis is longer.

- Employee participants learn about the needs assessment process and key issues (such as goals, gaps, actual, and ideals) through their active participation and are, therefore, able to create awareness of such issues in their on-the-job environment.[1]

- The tabletop analysis is an effective technique for

  - Reviewing and analyzing existing plans, procedures, and policies

  - Identifying any factors inhibiting effective performance

  - Handling breakdowns in communication between groups or systems

- Tabletop analyses promote buy-in for both the process and the results of the exercise, because stakeholders and representatives from the organization are an active part of the process.

- Tabletop exercises generally require participants to review performance-related documents and to participate actively in discussions about the performance environment. The tabletop analysis can, therefore, yield much information in a short time span, potentially reducing the necessity for extensive use of other techniques and tools to complete the needs assessment.[2]

Disadvantages

- The tabletop analysis process is a discussion-based approach to analyzing performance within a system. Because no simulation and no on-the-job performance observations are conducted, the tabletop analysis may not be a true test of the effectiveness of a system's performance.

- An essential ingredient for the tabletop analysis is the active participation of key representatives from the system where the performance gap is sus-

pected to be. If you are not able to secure the involvement of key participants, the effectiveness and accuracy of the tabletop analysis will be ham-
pered significantly.

- Active participation and dialogue are an essential part of this technique.
  If the facilitator cannot enable a high level of active engagement during
  the technique, then the amount of insight gained from the activity is very
  limited.

- The activity requires two sessions (or meetings), with some work being
  done by group members in between sessions.

Process Overview

Planning and Preparing

1. From the list of information required for the needs assessment, determine the specific scope of the tabletop analysis by focusing on what functions or elements should be analyzed through the tabletop analysis and
   on who should participate in the tabletop analysis.

   a. When identifying the functions or elements, ask, "What is the specific
      performance area, and what are the key procedures or operations that
      should be analyzed by the tabletop analysis participants?"

   b. When selecting participants, ask, "Who are the specific individuals
      who should take part in the exercise?" Examples of individuals inter-
      ested in municipal sanitation could include sanitation department
      managers and supervisors, sanitation workers, staff members from the
      mayor's office, commercial business owners, and community mem-
      bers—among others.

2. Schedule the tabletop analysis activity, and invite the appropriate participants. Introduce the participants to the tabletop analysis by (a) introducing them to the concept of a tabletop exercise and (b) explaining how
   the tabletop analysis is being used in the context of the needs assessment.
   Set the tone for the collaboration process and the ground rules for the
   activity, if appropriate.

3. If possible, arrange to have an experienced facilitator coordinate the implementation of the tabletop analysis.

4. Make arrangements for a comfortable meeting facility that provides conditions for the use of projection technology, if appropriate.

Conducting the Tabletop Analysis: First Session

1. Use the broad information identified during the planning and preparation stage. To kick off the tabletop analysis with the participants, focus on building consensus about the problem to be tackled and the desired outcomes from the tabletop analysis. Introduce the problem to the participants (for example, community frustration with sanitation services), and engage them in a brainstorming discussion as they explore questions and issues such as the following:

   a. Effect of the problem on the community

   - Garbage is piling up in some communities. Residents complain of rodents, smells, and other related problems to the mayor's office.

   b. Factors potentially contributing to the problem

   - The community has increased urbanization, inadequate housing, garbage truck breakdowns, inadequate inspections, and shortages of sanitation workers.

   c. Questions that should be answered to analyze the problem

   - How does the community plan to address housing shortages?

   - What can be done in the short and long term to address increases in garbage quantity?

   - What are options for recycling and reducing community consumption?

   d. Expected outcomes of the tabletop analysis

   - Recommendations will be made to the sanitation department to address the different causes of the sanitation complaints.

   e. Strategy for using the results from the tabletop analysis

   - The organizers of the tabletop analysis will follow up with community leaders on recommendations and will bring back this group in six months to discuss changes that have and have not occurred.

2. Work with the participants to generate a specific problem statement. Write the problem statement and the expected outcomes of the tabletop analysis in a prominent place, so that both the participants and the facilitator can refer to the list during the remainder of the activity.

3. Facilitate a discussion to develop a strategy for analyzing the problem. Begin the discussion by asking participants to identify the following:

a. Describe the specific types of information required to answer the key unknowns about the problem. These types of information should be structured in general categories such as (a) ideal performance, (b) current (actual) performance, (c) performance gaps, (d) causes of performance gaps, and (e) solutions to performance gaps.

b. Name the sources that can be consulted to gather each type of information that participants identify as part of the analysis. Sources of information may include documents, individuals, performance observations, work products, and so on. Ask participants to identify, to the extent possible, the specific source of information (for example, the specific documents that provide information on ideal performance).

c. As the participants identify the information necessary, verify that the information requirements are aligned with the purpose statement. Ask, "Will this information help you find answers to your original problem and to the outcomes you wish to achieve?"

4. After the list of sources has been identified, make the arrangements necessary for locating any document sources that participants identified and that have not been located yet. In addition, schedule the interviews and meetings that are required to gather information described in the analysis plan. Assign interview responsibilities to participants as required.

Conducting the Tabletop Analysis: Second Session

1. Ask the participants to reconvene and to work through the data that were identified during the first session so they clearly formulate the current and ideal performance for the problem area explicated in the purpose statement.

2. Guide the participants in creating a systematic listing of the conditions, procedures, and tasks that would, under ideal circumstances, take place. Encourage participants to refer to the document sources and collected data as this list is created. Create the list on a flip chart or whiteboard so that it can be seen by all participants.

3. Ask the participants to review the list of ideal tasks, procedures, and conditions and to verify its completeness and accuracy.

4. Next, ask participants to refer to the documents and data that were collected so they identify specific gaps in the performance area. Emphasize that gaps, rather than causes, should be identified. Also verify regularly that the gaps that are being identified are directly related to the purpose

statement for the tabletop analysis. If appropriate, work with the participants to group together gaps that have common attributes. Write the list of gaps on the flip chart or whiteboard.

5. After the gaps have been identified, ask participants for insight about potential causes of each of the gaps, as well as for potential solution strategies. Work through the list of gaps in a systematic manner, and write possible solutions for each gap (or group of gaps) on the flip chart or whiteboard. Solutions should be aligned with the original purpose statement and should be evaluated for feasibility.

6. To conclude the tabletop analysis, evaluate the results from the analysis against the expected outcomes that were listed during the first tabletop analysis session. If there is consensus that the expected outcomes have been achieved, then conclude the discussion by working with the participants to determine what to do with the results from the analysis. For example, a debriefing session could be conducted with key stakeholders to report on the results of the analysis and to discuss the solution strategies that were identified. Alternatively, the decision could be made to use additional data collection techniques to validate the results from the tabletop analysis.

Tips for Success

- Carefully select the participants for the tabletop analysis. Consider including experts, decision makers, supervisors, and current employees in the activity. The specific participants in the tabletop analysis should be aligned with the specific goal of the activity.

- Because facilitation is an essential ingredient for the success of the tabletop analysis, select an experienced facilitator for implementing this technique.[3] The facilitator should be well informed about the topics of discussion, including potential areas of sensitivity among tabletop participants.

- Develop and distribute materials about the goal, focus, and purpose ahead for the scheduled activity of the tabletop analysis. These materials will ensure that the tabletop analysis can get under way most efficiently.

- Limit the length of each tabletop analysis session. Each session should generally not last more than 3–4 hours.

- Consider recording the actual tabletop analysis, thereby giving you the option at a later date to revisit the information shared during the activity.

If you decide to record the session, make sure that you inform all of the participants and that you identify a secure way of storing the recorded data so that participants do not have to be concerned about their participation in the tabletop analysis negatively affecting them professionally.

- Control the size of the group for the tabletop analysis. To be effective and manageable, the size of the group of participants should generally range from between 5 and 15 participants.

Notes

1. See http://www.hss.doe.gov/nuclearsafety/ns/techstds/docs/handbook/hdbk1103.pdf.
2. Ibid.
3. Ibid.

Websites

An example of the technique applied in instructional design context can be found at http://www.nwlink.com/~donclark/hrd/needsalt.html#various2.

The U.S. Department of Energy handbook on tabletop needs analysis is located at http://www.osti.gov/bridge/servlets/purl/459762-JeQi3h/webviewable/459762.pdf.

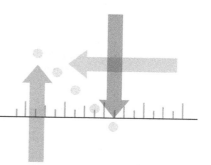

PAIR-WISE COMPARISON

Purpose

The pair-wise comparison technique is used when you have multiple options to prioritize. It helps you to narrow the options according to a set of agreed-upon criteria. It may be used to prioritize or rank needs (that is, gaps in results) or possible solutions (that is, interventions or activities) to address those needs.

Needs Assessment Applications

A pair-wise comparison is a simple, yet effective, tool for facilitating group decisions that are based on the information collected during a needs assessment. This analysis technique is a worthwhile tool for prioritizing needs, determining the relationships among multiple causal factors, or recommending potential improvement activities. Whenever you have multiple options or alternatives to consider, you can quickly use a pair-wise comparison to advance group discussions toward a decision. (For a helpful sample template to serve as job aids, see page 190.)

Advantages and Disadvantages

Advantages

- A pair-wise comparison is easily done and can be completed quickly during a group discussion to progress toward a decision or recommendation.

- Criteria for comparing options can remain informal, thereby letting participants make judgments that are based on their experience and expertise.

Disadvantages

- Pair-wise comparisons do not provide the level of detail or sophistication of a multicriteria analysis (see page 171).

- Although criteria for making comparisons are discussed within the group, each participant may apply varying criteria (without public disclosure to other group members) when making comparisons.

Process Overview

1. Make sure that the analysis process begins (as is typical) with (a) two or more needs, (b) two or more alternative interventions, or (c) activities that were previously identified as potential solutions to a need. Although you can complete the analysis for the number of potential needs solutions that you have, the time and effort required to collect valid information for comparison typically necessitates that you limit the analysis to no more than five or six of the most likely contenders.

2. List the possible options in both the first column and the first row of the pair-wise comparison table (see table 3B.3). Working with those who will be making the decision or recommendation, discuss the performance criteria required of alternatives.

Examples of Criteria for Comparing Needs and Solutions

Example criteria for comparing **needs** could include the following:
- Number of people influenced by the continuation of the need
- Availability of partners to help address the need
- Anticipated costs to meet the need
- Increasing severity of the need over time
- Alignment of the needs with the institution's mission

Example criteria for comparing **solutions** could include the following:
- Total time required
- Cost of the activity over the first year
- Environmental impact

Table 3B.3 Sample of a Completed Pair-Wise Comparison Table

	Option A Playground equipment	**Option B** Benches	**Option C** Picnic tables	**Option D** Tree and flower planting	**Option E** Walking paths
Option A Playground equipment					
Option B Benches	B				
Option C Picnic tables	A	B			
Option D Tree and flower planting	D	D	D		
Option E Walking paths	E	B	E	D	

Note: This example presents some options preferred by community members for a new community park, which is part of a larger municipal project to build and improve green spaces in the city. In the example, the number of pair-wise "wins" is as follows: A (playground equipment) = 1, B (benches) = 3, C (picnic tables) = 0, D (tree and flower planting) = 4, E (walking paths) = 2. By using this example, you might concentrate your group discussions going forward more on building a park that emphasizes trees and flowers, benches, and walking paths. But you might also consider that you may not have had a representative number of young parents with children in your pair-wise session. This example gives one set of rankings at one point in time and is a good reminder that multiple sessions may be needed with different groups to get a representative picture of community preferences.

- Results expected after six months
- Feasibility of implementation

3. Talk with others about the most important criteria (or attributes) to making the decision (time, cost, number of outputs, client satisfaction index, number of injuries, ability to accomplish desired outcomes, and so on). Typically, consider no more than two to three criteria for any decision.

4. If you are in a group setting, write the agreed-upon criteria on a whiteboard or flip chart.

5. Ask participants who will be making the decision or recommendation to keep each of the discussed criteria in mind as they compare each option using the pair-wise comparison table in table 3B.3. For example, is Option A or Option B the preferred option according to the discussed criteria? Then, is Option A or Option C the preferred option, and so forth. Continue until all options have been compared.

6. Have participants count the number of times each option appears in the table. The option that was selected the greatest number of times, in comparison with the alternatives, is the leading option.

7. Review the analysis carefully, noting that this technique does not directly facilitate the comparison of combinations (for example, Option A combined with Option C). Discuss with participants the results of the analysis so that you can make decisions or recommendations, with the analysis results being one of the primary inputs to the decision.

Websites

An example of pair-wise comparisons applied to voting can be found at http://www.pbs.org/teachers/mathline/concepts/voting/activity3.shtm.

Examples worked through to illustrate the technique can be found at http://deseng.ryerson.ca/xiki/Learning/Main:Pairwise_comparison.

Sample of Job Aids

Pair-Wise Comparison Template

	Option A	Option B	Option C	Option D	Option E
Option A					
Option B					
Option C					
Option D					
Option E					

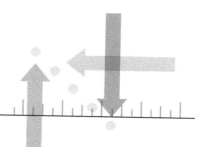

2 × 2 MATRIX DECISION AIDS

Purpose

The purpose of a 2 × 2 matrix decision aid is to examine multiple perspectives on issues identified during a needs assessment. A number of perspectives can be compared in the 2 × 2 matrix format (for instance, risks vs. rewards, your view vs. the view of others, what you know vs. what you don't know, or urgency vs. importance). Therefore, we have combined these techniques on the basis of their shared similarity of using the 2 × 2 matrix to represent alternative perspectives.

Needs Assessment Applications

Needs (or gaps between current and desired results) are viewed from many perspectives within an organization, which can make the findings of an assessment challenging to prioritize and to turn into justifiable decisions. For example, when gaps between current and desired results are identified, the perspectives of individuals directly associated with the performance (for example, public service providers) will often differ from the perspectives of those who depend on the results (for example, general public, customers, and so on). Likewise, perspectives on the amount of potential risk that can be tolerated in relation to the potential benefits will also vary across individuals and groups—including the views of partners internal to your organization (such as managers from other units, technology specialists, and others) and those external to your organization (such as government agency staff members, development partners, community groups, and others).

Use 2 × 2 matrix decision aids to assist in identifying the priorities, selecting solutions or activities, facilitating group discussions, or verifying that you have examined the issues identified in the needs assessment from multiple viewpoints. Although examples of 2 × 2 matrix decisions aids are used in this guide to illustrate the value of the technique, you can substitute these examples with other examples within the context of your assessment. The 2×2 matrix format allows you to compare and contrast a variety of perspectives in an easy-to-complete format.

Advantages and Disadvantages

Advantages

- A 2×2 matrix decision aid can ensure that multiple perspectives are considered when needs assessment findings are prioritized.

- The results of a 2×2 matrix decision aid can help you communicate with others when prioritizing needs, identifying appropriate solutions, or justifying decisions.

- You can use a 2×2 matrix decision aid to expand on needs assessment findings, including information on the preferences of differing groups regarding what should be done in response to identified needs.

- A 2×2 matrix decision aid allows for potential positive and negative consequences to be considered prior to decision making.

- Using this technique, you can compare and contrast the value of taking an action (or selecting a need as a high priority, or implementing a solution) to *not* taking an action (or not selecting a need as a high priority, or not implementing a solution). Too often the latter—decisions not to do something—are not considered for their potential consequences or payoffs.

- A 2×2 matrix decision aid ensures that multiple perspectives are included in decisions regarding all needs and potential solutions, thus avoiding a situation where needs assessment data are simply used to confirm preexisting perspectives about what should be done.

Disadvantages

- A 2×2 matrix decision aid can be more limited than other tools or techniques (for example, SWOT or brainstorming) for generating ideas about what to do next.

- A 2×2 matrix decision aid typically requires that all stakeholders value the perspectives and potential differences between groups within the organization.

- The analysis of this technique is only as useful as the quality of information available from the needs assessment.

- Identified comparative characteristics in each "cell" of the 2 × 2 matrix decision aid are only listed, and not prioritized or given differentiating weights.

Process Overview

1. Create either a list of the needs (or gaps in results) that were already identified in the needs assessment process or a list of the potential activities (or solutions) that you are considering as recommendations that are based on the needs identified during the assessment. It is best not to mix the two (needs and solutions). If you want to gain perspectives on both the prioritization of the needs and the prioritization of potential interventions, then conduct two separate applications of the 2 × 2 matrix decision aid.

2. Identify representatives from other groups with varying perspectives on the issue (for instance, agency managers, new employees, field employees, central or headquarters employees, donor institution representatives, government ministry officials, community members, or other development partners).

Example of Differing Perspective[1]

1. Provide the representatives with the issues identified during the needs assessment (for instance, needs or potential activities), and ask them to prioritize these issues according to their perspective.

2. Prioritize the same list of issues from your perspective as well. If you are working with a team on the needs assessment, then this prioritization can be done as a team through a variety of group decision-making techniques.

3. With a priority list from each group, place the highest priority data elements into the 2 × 2 matrix decision aid. Consider including your priorities in comparison with the priorities of another group (see table 3B.4). Or compare the priorities from differing groups, leaving out your perspective (see table 3B.5).

4. Review the complete 2 × 2 matrix decision aid—along with recommendations of how to expand the needs assessment to address gaps between

Table 3B.4   Differing Perspectives Example A: Prioritizing Needs (Youth Employment)

	High priorities of city youth	Low priorities of city youth
High priorities of city employment agency	• Low youth employment rate • Few internship opportunities with local businesses	• Low employment rate for aging populations
Low priorities of city employment agency	• Few youth recreation centers open in evenings • Moderately high education fees for youth training courses	• Decreasing retention rate of city employment agency employees

Table 3B.5   Differing Perspectives Example B: Comparing Potential Solutions (Organizational Performance)

	High priorities for new employees	Low priorities for new employees
High priorities for managers	• Performance specific training • Redesigned new employee orientation	• New hiring standards • Renewed emphasis on standardized interviewing procedures
Low priorities for managers	• Improved mentoring program • Quarterly performance feedback system	• Motivational workshops

what is known and what is unknown from each perspective—with your needs assessment partners.

Example of Risk vs. Rewards

1. Provide the representatives with the issues identified during the needs assessment (for instance, needs or potential activities), and ask them to identify the associated risks and rewards for each issue. For example,

    • What are the associated risks and rewards of addressing or not addressing the identified need?

- What are the associated risks and rewards of implementing or not implementing this activity?

2. Note that the analysis combines perspectives to examine the risks and rewards of taking or not taking action. Work with assessment partners to come to an agreement about the risks and rewards included in each 2 × 2 matrix.

3. Create a 2 × 2 matrix to illustrate the associated risks and rewards for each issue (see tables 3B.6 and 3B.7).

4. Review the complete 2 × 2 matrix with your needs assessment partners, along with recommendations of how to expand the needs assessment to address gaps between what is known and what is unknown.

Table 3B.6 Rewards vs. Risks Example C: Addressing Needs (Project Completion Delays)

	Address need (takes too long to complete projects)	**Do not address need** (takes too long to complete projects)
Rewards	• Reduces the time to complete projects • Makes project completion as important as project initiation	• Maintains focus on project initiation
Risks	• Distracts managers from other strategic priorities • Increases the cost of projects	• More projects are at risk of failure to meet goals • Country needs change before a project can be completed

Table 3B.7 Rewards vs. Risks Example D: Implementing Solutions (Employee Mentoring)

	Implement mentoring program	**Do not implement mentoring program**
Rewards	• Knowledge sharing • Better engagement of new staff members	• Saves time and money • Do not have to place additional burdens on managers
Risks	• Encourages sharing of bad habits • Requires time of managers	• New staff members are not able to perform roles as soon • Knowledge of staff members continues to leave when they leave

Needs Assessment: Tools and Techniques

Tips for Success

- Before getting started, discuss with participants the specific goals you are hoping to accomplish by using the 2 × 2 matrix decision aid.

- Work with group members to include factors in all four quadrants of the matrix. Leaving quadrants of the matrix empty will limit your ability to make quality decisions.

- Focus each 2 × 2 matrix on just one need or potential solution. It can be tempting to save time by combining needs or solutions, but doing so typically leads to general discussions rather than to a focused decision.

- Strive to include at least three items in each of the four cells of the 2 × 2 matrix.

- Remember that a decision not to take action (or not to address a need, or not to implement a solution) is a decision that carries potential risks and rewards, just as does a decision to take action.

- The book by Alex Lowy and Phil Hood (2004) contains more than 50 examples of 2 × 2 decision aids that can be used to improve performance.

Note

1. The differing perspectives example is loosely based on the Johari Window activity used by psychologists.

References and Resources

Beach, E. K. 1982. "Johari's Window as a Framework for Needs Assessment." *Journal of Continuing Education in Nursing* 13 (1): 28–32.

Lowy, Alex, and Phil Hood. 2004. *The Power of the 2 × 2 Matrix: Using 2 × 2 Thinking to Solve Business Problems and Make Better Decisions.* San Francisco: Jossey-Bass.

Witkin, Belle Ruth, and James W. Altschuld. 1995. *Planning and Conducting Needs Assessments: A Practical Guide.* Thousand Oaks, CA: Sage Publications.

Website

"Risks versus Rewards Worksheet" is available at http://www.lifehack.org/articles/lifehack/risks-versus-rewards-worksheet.html.

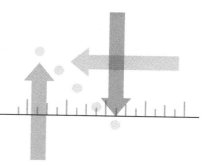

FISHBONE DIAGRAMS

Purpose

The fishbone diagram—so called because of its resemblance to a fish skeleton—is a cause-and-effect diagram that can be used to identify the potential (or actual) cause(s) for a performance problem. Fishbone diagrams provide a structure for a group's discussion about the potential causes of a problem.

Needs Assessment Applications

Fishbone diagrams are often used in needs assessment to assist in illustrating and communicating the relationships among several potential (or actual) causes of a performance problem. Likewise, these graphical representations of relationships between needs (or discrepancies between desired and actual results) offer you a pragmatic tool for building a system of performance-improvement interventions—for instance, a combination of mentoring, using job aids, training, enhancing motivation, and arriving at new expectations—around the often complex relationships found across potential (or actual) causes.

Advantages and Disadvantages

Advantages

- Fishbone diagrams permit a thoughtful analysis that avoids overlooking any possible root causes for a need.

- The fishbone technique is easy to implement and creates an easy-to-understand visual representation of the causes, the categories of causes, and the need.

- By using a fishbone diagram, you are able to focus the group on the big picture as to possible causes or factors influencing the problem or need.

- Even after the need has been addressed, the fishbone diagram shows areas of weakness that—once exposed—can be rectified before causing more sustained difficulties.

Disadvantages

- The simplicity of a fishbone diagram can be both its strength and its weakness. As a weakness, the simplicity of the fishbone diagram may make it difficult to represent the truly interrelated nature of problems and causes in some very complex situations.

Process Overview

1. Identify gaps between the results (or performance) that are required for the successful accomplishment of your program's or project's results chain (also commonly referred to as a results framework, logic frame, or logic model) and the current achievements to date.

2. Generate a clear, concise statement of the need(s). Make sure that everyone in the group agrees with the need as it is stated. For example, the application of modern agricultural techniques among the population is at 25 percent, and the aim of your program or project is for 75 percent of the population to use modern techniques (leaving you with a gap or need of 50 percent).

3. Using a long sheet of paper or a white board, draw a horizontal line. This line will be the spine of the fish. Write the need along the spine, on the left-hand side.

4. Identify the overarching categories of causes of the need. Brainstorming is often an effective technique for identifying the categories of causes. For each category of causes, draw a bone—a line at a 45-degree angle from the spine of the fish. Label each bone (see figure 3B.1) with the cause categories; for instance, categories could include materials, knowledge or skills, time, motivation, incentives, performance feedback, and others.[1]

5. Have the group brainstorm to identify the factors that may be affecting the cause or the need or both. For each category of causes, the group

should be asking, "Why is this happening?" Add each "why" to the diagram, clustered around the major cause category it influences.

6. Repeat the procedure by asking, "Why is this happening?" for each effect until the question yields no more meaningful answers (see figure 3B.2).

Figure 3B.1 A Basic Fishbone Diagram

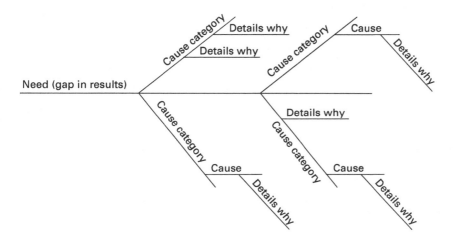

Figure 3B.2 An Annotated Fishbone Diagram

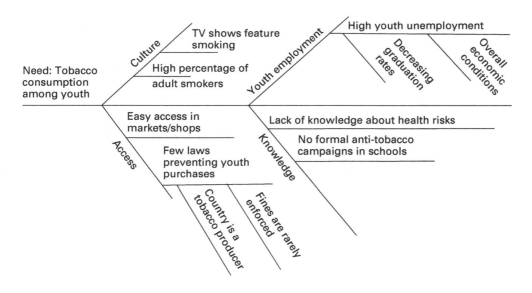

7. When the group has reached a consensus that the diagram contains an adequate amount of information, analyze the diagram. In particular, look for causes that are appearing in more than one section of the diagram.

8. Circle anything that seems to be a root cause for the need. Prioritize the root causes, and decide to take action, a move that may involve further investigation of the root causes.

Tips for Success

- Make sure that the group has consensus about both the need and the characteristics of the cause statement before beginning the process of building the fishbone diagram.

- If appropriate, graft (add) branches that do not contain a lot of information onto other branches. Likewise, you can split branches that have too much information into two or more branches.

- Make parsimonious use of words while populating the fishbone diagram. Only use as many words as necessary to describe the cause or effect.

Note

1. Also see the performance pyramid tool (page 236) for additional categories that may be applied.

References and Resources

Altschuld, James W. 2010. *Needs Assessment Phase III: Collecting Data* (Book 3 of *Needs Assessment Kit*). Thousand Oaks, CA: Sage Publications.

Altschuld, James W., and J. N. Eastmond Jr. 2010. *Needs Assessment Phase II: Getting Started* (Book 2 of *Needs Assessment Kit*). Thousand Oaks, CA: Sage Publications.

Gupta, Kavita, Catherine M. Sleezer, and Darlene F. Russ-Eft. 2007. *A Practical Guide to Needs Assessment*. San Francisco: Pfeiffer.

Witkin, Belle Ruth, and James W. Altschuld. 1995. *Planning and Conducting Needs Assessments: A Practical Guide*. Thousand Oaks, CA: Sage Publications.

Websites

Cause analysis tools (American Society for Quality has an example of a fishbone diagram) are available at http://www.asq.org/learn-about-quality/cause-analysis-tools/overview/fishbone.html.

The fishbone diagram (Six Sigma has templates for making fishbone diagrams in Microsoft Word and Microsoft Excel) is available at http://www.isixsigma.com/index.php?option=com_k2&view=item&id=1416:the-cause-and-effect-aka-fishbone-diagram&Itemid=200.

"Use a Fishbone Diagram to Help Attack Complex Problems" (from TechRepublic) is available at http://articles.techrepublic.com.com/5100-10878_11-6092236.html?tag=nl.e053.

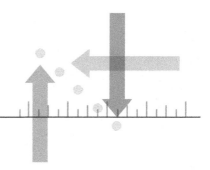

SCENARIOS

Purpose

The purpose of scenarios is to provide contextual explorations of the potential strengths and weaknesses of different combinations of performance-improvement interventions. Scenarios are most useful in situations where the number of possible directions is large or where there is a large degree of uncertainty.

Needs Assessment Applications

The best decisions are typically made when you can compare and contrast the potential benefits and the potential risks of each decision. The same is true in needs assessment, especially when it is time to recommend what to do next according to your needs assessment findings.

Use scenarios during this stage of your needs assessment to provide examples of different combinations of performance-improvement activities. For instance, scenario A could be a mentoring program paired with some training and a job aid, whereas scenario B could be a management performance feedback tool paired with training, new work policies, and a new rewards structure. By comparing both the benefits and the risks of alternative scenarios, you have a foundation for recommendations about the appropriate balance of risk and reward for your program or organization.

Advantages and Disadvantages

Advantages

- Scenarios allow decisions to be made by examining multiple alternatives rather than single solutions.

- Instead of simply reviewing options as discrete alternatives, scenarios can provide contexts for making decisions. Scenarios are especially valuable when you are dealing with a complex situation in the context of the needs assessment.

- Decision makers often value scenarios for their ability to provide a visual illustration of different alternatives within the organization's context.

- Multiple scenarios can also be used to contrast positive and pessimistic views, thus providing a balanced perspective.

Disadvantages

- Developing realistic scenarios can be time-consuming, and there is no guarantee of what results will actually be yielded as the situation in the scenario is implemented.

- Scenarios can (but should not) limit decision makers to examine only the combinations of activities or solutions included in the presented scenarios.

Process Overview

1. Complete the identification of needs (gaps in results) and the associated analysis of causal factors.

2. Identify sets of potential activities or solutions that will assist in accomplishing desired results while also addressing the potential causes of problems with the current performance.

3. For each set of potential activities, create a scenario based on the results your program or organization could realistically expect to accomplish and the risks associated with the implementation of each set (including economic, time, and opportunity costs). Each scenario should use the same concrete time frame (for example, 1 year, 18 months, 3 years) and should apply similar constraints that could affect implementation.

4. In each scenario, describe the factors that are internal and external to the organization and that are likely to increase or decrease the successful achievement of desired results. Here are some ideas to consider when developing the substance of a scenario:

   a. Build uncertainties and unexpected events into each scenario.

   b. Use information on trends and on the character of the organization to write each scenario.

   c. Write each scenario so that it seems plausible. Choose names used in the scenario carefully; they can communicate a great deal to the reader.

   d. It is generally a good idea to make each scenario about one page long.

   e. Give each scenario a short and meaningful title.

5. Develop two or three scenarios for each of the sets of potential activities (or solutions) that meet the requirements dictated by the performance pyramid tool (see page 236) by Wedman (2010). Scenarios can be written from several perspectives (for example, yours, the agency management's, a community member's). Therefore, it is important that you describe each scenario from a similar perspective (thus ensuring that you are comparing "apples to apples").

6. After a solid draft of each scenario has been developed, validate the scenarios with experts and others who are familiar with the situation. Make any changes recommended by the scenario reviewers before sharing the scenarios with decision makers.

7. Schedule time with the groups or individuals who will be making decisions about which activities to implement.

8. Provide at least two or three scenarios to the groups or individuals selected for participation. Often, it is helpful to provide varying perspectives in different scenarios, including both positive and pessimistic views. If your scenarios are longer than a page or two, provide the scenarios to the decision makers before the meeting.

9. Discuss each scenario with the participants, highlighting the strengths and weaknesses exhibited in the context described in each. (Scenarios are best estimates of how the interventions would be implemented and how the results would be accomplished; thus, decision makers must

take into account that later implementation may or may not mirror the scenario's description).

10. Ask group members to rank each scenario and to provide alternative combinations of the activities that could be used for a second round of scenarios (if desired).

11. After you have finished administering the scenarios, you may be asked to write a report discussing the results. If so, it is generally a good idea to include summaries of the scenarios, as well as an overview of how scenarios were shared with participants. Keep your report short, highlighting key data without overburdening the readers with too much detail. Include observations and conclusions, and provide some suggestions for next steps.

Tips for Success

- Create multiple scenarios, with each scenario having a unique balance of risk and benefits that are based on multiple perspectives within the organization.

- Don't paint too rosy a picture within each scenario. The scenarios should be realistic and should show no preference for one set of activities or solutions over another.

- Inform decision makers that they don't have to select a scenario but that other combinations can also be developed, depending on the balance of rewards and risks that the organization is looking for in the program or project.

References and Resources

Watkins, Ryan. 2007. *Performance by Design: The Systematic Selection, Design, and Development of Performance Technologies That Produce Useful Results.* Amherst, MA: HRD Press, and Silver Spring, MD: International Society for Performance Improvement.

Wedman, John F. 2010. "Performance Pyramid Model." In *Handbook of Improving Performance in the Workplace.* Vol. 2: *Selecting and Implementing Performance Interventions,* edited by Ryan Watkins and Doug Leigh, 51–80. San Francisco: Wiley/Pfeiffer, and Silver Spring, MD: International Society for Performance Improvement.

Witkin, Belle Ruth, and James W. Altschuld. 1995. *Planning and Conducting Needs Assessments: A Practical Guide.* Thousand Oaks, CA: Sage Publications.

Websites

Examples of scenarios (from Arizona State University) are available at http://cals.arizona.edu/futures/sce/scemain.html.

Scenarios: An explorer's guide is available at http://www-static.shell.com/static/aboutshell/downloads/our_strategy/shell_global_scenarios/scenario_explorersguide.pdf. (This document from the Shell Corporation is written for people who want to build scenarios and for those who want to help develop scenario-thinking skills.)

Scenarios Toolkit developed for The European Centre for the Development of Vocational Training is available at http://www.cedefop.europa.eu/EN/Files/6009_en.pdf.

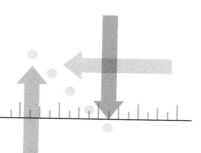

ROOT CAUSE ANALYSIS

Purpose

The goal of a root cause analysis (RCA) is to identify the contributing causal factors that have led to a performance problem.

Needs Assessment Applications

Identifying gaps between current and desired performance is the primary goal of a needs assessment, yet alone this information is not adequate for making decisions about what to do to improve performance. An RCA is, therefore, a useful tool for examining the contributing factors that are preventing current achievements from matching your desired accomplishments (see box 3B.1). An RCA offers a systematic process that can help you determine which processes, procedures, tools, or policies (or combination of the three) are limiting performance and leading to the needs found in your assessment.

Identified root causes can then be targeted by the solution recommendations coming out of the needs assessment. Later, the results of the RCA can

---

Box 3B.1 Sample Uses of Root Cause Analysis

- Separate problems from symptoms when conceptualizing new projects with clients or partners.
- Identify factors causing a project to be at high risk of failure.
- Determine why a policy reform did not accomplish desired results.
- Resolve questions about how corruption entered a project.

---

also be monitored to ensure that organizational changes are having the desired effect and to avoid suboptimization (where improvements in one area lead to new problems in other areas). The ability of the RCA to provide this valuable information makes it an integral component to most needs assessments.

Advantages and Disadvantages

Advantages

- An RCA provides a systematic process for examining performance problems for their root causes rather than relying on unverified assumptions or stakeholder perceptions about causes.

- An RCA ensures that you inspect a performance issue from multiple perspectives to determine the range of causes leading to the less-than-desired performance (as opposed to assuming that the causes of the issues are well known and agreed upon by everyone involved).

- Many times an RCA will identify both the components of the system that are blocking desired performance (for instance, out-of-date-procedures or misunderstood expectations) and the parts of the system that are working well at promoting desired performance (for instance, quality managerial feedback). In the end, improving performance routinely requires both fixing the problems and expanding on the things that are being done right.

Disadvantages

- An RCA will frequently identify more causal factors than you have anticipated or are likely to have the budget to address individually. Therefore, it is important to determine the relative effect of each factor and to address as priorities the effects that are the most critical to success.

- As with other systematic processes, an RCA can include procedures that are not familiar to your organization and thus can require that you build a business case for taking additional time and resources to accurately identify the causal factors leading to the performance issue.

- An RCA focuses on causes and does not tell you which interventions or activities will best address each causal factor. However, possible activities are frequently identified during the process. Only after causes are

A Guide to Assessing Needs

identified is it beneficial to turn to possible interventions or activities to address the causes.

Process Overview

1. Identify a discrepancy in performance (or need) from the information you have collected thus far in the needs assessment. Frequently, you will only want to complete an RCA for the highest-priority needs so that you can save resources.

2. Create a plan for analyzing the identified need (gap in results). In many ways, the steps of the analysis will often look like a miniature needs assessment within the broader needs assessment. For instance, use a variety of techniques—interviews, focus groups, and document or record reviews—to collect information on the causal factors leading to the performance problem. That information will then be used to identify and prioritize the causal factors and their relative attribution to the performance gap.

3. Remember that your analysis may take from a couple of hours to a week or more, depending on the performance issue. Consequently, as you develop your plan, be sure that you take the scope of the analysis into account when developing a budget and schedule.

4. Know that sometimes your RCA will be driven by a need that is directly related to a specific situation or incident (for instance, you find out that a staff member is using your organization's procurement procedures to make fraudulent transactions or to cover up bribes to a local official). In those cases, it is especially important to start by determining exactly what happened and where the processes, procedures, training, policies, or regulations failed to prevent the incident in the first place.

5. Observe that in other cases, however, the need will not be generated by any single event (such as when an agency fails to meet its annual performance targets for two years in a row). In those situations, it is more challenging to determine which events, policies, procedures, or other activities led to the gap in performance. The RCA processes work effectively in both situations, though the tools and techniques for collecting information may differ.

6. Understand that the analogy of peeling an onion is often associated with RCA because causal factors are frequently many layers deep. At the beginning of the analysis, the causes of the need may seem easily identified.

For example, you may initially find through interviews with managers that a procurement problem is caused by younger staff officers who do not have the experience or training to manage procurement matters. But that is only the first layer. Later, when you talk to staff members you might learn that because of time constraints and inadequate staffing, training is offered only twice a year and contains outdated information. Again, however, as you peel away the next layer and talk to the training department about why the course is offered only twice a year, you may discover that the training department only has a budget to offer training twice a year. Additionally, the training department staff members say that they are waiting for the department that sets procurement policies to update the procurement training manual.

7. As is often recommended, ask the question "Why?" at least five times so you can peel away the layers of causal factors. (See the questions and table 3B.8.)

Problem Statement: In rural areas of the country, the number of female students completing primary school education is significantly below the desired results.

1. **Why** are female students in the area not completing primary school?

   – *Because very few of them ever start primary school.*

Table 3B.8   Root Cause Summary Table

Problem: Low education rates for girls in rural areas

Causal factor #1	Path through root cause map	Recommendations
Costs to rural families to send girls to school	• School fees • Girls provide labor in the home (child care, food preparation, water gathering)	• Eliminate or reduce fees • Subsidize parents who send girls to school
Causal factor #2	**Path through root cause map**	**Recommendations**
Cultural norms about girls' education	• Boys regularly favored over girls • Religious or other cultural restrictions	• Advocacy programs • Awareness-raising about longer-term household economic benefits of girls attending school
Causal factor #3	**Path through root cause map**	**Recommendations**
School access	• Schools are not available in all villages	• Education reform to reach rural schools • Visiting seasonal tutors

Source: Adapted from Rooney and Vanden Heuvel (2004).

2. **Why** do they not start primary school?
   - *Because it is a great burden on their family to have them go to school.*
3. **Why** is it a great burden?
   - *Because it is expensive to send a child to school.*
4. **Why** is it so expensive?
   - *Because school fees must be paid for each child.*
5. **Why** are there additional fees for attending school?
   - *Because to get a teacher to come to a rural school, the village must supplement the teacher's salary.*[1]

With each need having many layers of closely related causal factors, plan to analyze at least four or five layers for each causal factor and its root causes. Use fault tree analysis (see page 214), fishbone diagrams (see page 197), concept mapping (see page 220), performance pyramids (see page 236), and many other tools and techniques described in this book to assist you in peeling away the layers of causal factors.

8. Review the information you have collected at each layer of the RCA to identify and prioritize the causal relationships. For instance, using that information, you might determine that the primary causes leading to the performance issue are related to motivation and incentives, with lesser causes being knowledge, skills, and available time to complete required procedures. In the end, you want to have a prioritized list of all the causal factors you identified during your analysis.

   In most circumstances, you will not be able to quantify the contribution of each causal factor to the performance gap—that is, you will not be able to attribute 45 percent of the performance gap to cause A, 30 percent to cause B, and 25 percent to cause C—though it is usually beneficial to prioritize causes from major to minor contributors. You can use a number of collaborative decision-making techniques included in this book to assist in setting the priorities. Often, it is also valuable to create a visual representation of the relationships among causal factors.

   For example, ask several of the participants who provided you with information during your analysis (through interviews, surveys, focus groups, reports that they authored, and so on) to review the prioritized list of causal factors. Each participant should review the list to determine whether (a) all of the causal factors are identified, (b) all of the relationships between the causal factors are taken into account, and (c) the highest-priority factors are those that contribute most significantly to the need.

9. For each high-priority causal factor that is identified (and verified through participant review), find at least two potential interventions or activities that address the causal factor, and ensure that it doesn't continue to negatively affect performance. The activities can then be assessed and compared as possible recommendations coming from the needs assessment.

Tips for Success

- Don't assume that the first causal factor that people tell you about is the root cause of the performance problem. Take time and ask lots of questions as you peel away the layers of causal factors to identify all of the factors leading to less-than-desirable results.

- Focus on what components of the performance system (activities, processes, procedures, equipment, rules, policies, interpersonal relationships, and so on) are limiting the achievement of desired performance.

- Avoid shifting the focus to any solution, intervention, or activity that might be recommended during the analysis. Make note of the recommendation, and maintain your focus on the causal factors. Later, all of the recommended activities for improving performance can be compared and assessed for their potential value (both singularly and in various combinations).

Note

1. Based in part on an example from http://www.isixsigma.com/library/content/c020610a.asp (July 23, 2008).

References and Resources

Altschuld, James W. 2010. *Needs Assessment Phase III: Collecting Data* (Book 3 of *Needs Assessment Kit*). Thousand Oaks, CA: Sage Publications.

Altschuld, James W., and J. N. Eastmond Jr. 2010. *Needs Assessment Phase II: Getting Started* (Book 2 of *Needs Assessment Kit*). Thousand Oaks, CA: Sage Publications.

Paradies, Mark, and Linda Unger. 2000. *Tap Root: The System for Root Cause Analysis, Problem Investigation, and Proactive Improvement*. Knoxville, TN: System Improvements.

Rooney, James, and Lee N. Vanden Heuvel. 2004. "Root Cause Analysis for Beginners." *Quality Basics* (July): 45–53. Milwaukee, WI: American Society for Quality.

Watkins, Ryan. 2007. *Performance by Design: The Systematic Selection, Design, and Development of Performance Technologies That Produce Useful Results.* Amherst, MA: HRD Press, and Silver Spring, MD: International Society for Performance Improvement.

Website

"Root Cause Analysis for Beginners" is available at http://www.nmenv.state.nm. us/aqb/Proposed_Regs/Part_7_Excess_Emissions/NMED_Exhibit_18-Root_ Cause_Analysis_for_Beginners.pdf.

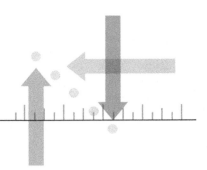

FAULT TREE ANALYSIS

Purpose

A fault tree analysis (FTA) is a step-by-step procedure that is used to logically identify, evaluate, and quantify potential problem causes for a performance gap (failure) in a system and to determine strategies for preventing these causes.

Needs Assessment Applications

In a needs assessment, the typical function of a fault tree analysis is to identify the *causes* of performance gaps in a system (for example, your organization, a division within your organization, or a government unit). FTA is especially useful when specific failures within the system lead to performance gaps. The FTA provides a systematic process for analyzing situations and determining the relevant causes.

An FTA can help you to recognize the interrelationships among causes in the system and to evaluate the potential effects of causes in terms of the failure of the system. By addressing multiple causes, the FTA can also help you identify strategies that can be used to reduce the probability of future problems in the system.

The analysis procedures in an FTA are based on creating a visual representation (a fault tree) that identifies each of the potential causes, the relationships (failure sequences) between the causes, and the prioritized prevention strategies. Fault tree analysis is used widely in many engineering disciplines, but it can also be used in needs assessment as a root cause analysis technique. It can be an effective tool for increasing the chances of success for a specific system. The technical nature of the technique does, however, likely require additional preparation beyond the process overview we provide here.

Advantages and Disadvantages

Advantages

- An FTA can be used with both a large and a small numbers of participants.

- The FTA displays information in a structured, graphic way that makes it easy to interpret and communicate.

- The FTA technique solicits input and insight from a wide number of experts.

- The focus in the FTA technique is on the system being analyzed, rather than on the individual people in the system. Thus, it may be easier to get a buy-in because people are less likely to feel threatened.[1]

- Agreements and diverging views on system inputs are represented in the FTA.[2]

- An FTA can be used effectively for analysis of recurrent and persistent problems, because such problems are likely to have common causes and contributory factors.

Disadvantages

- Because this technique is highly reliant on judgment and insight that are based on subjective opinions, there is a risk of inaccurate information, which compromises the accuracy of the results.

- If the wrong failure sources are identified in an FTA, the subsequent results yielded may experience a ripple effect of this error. Results may, therefore, not be valid or accurate.

- FTAs may fail if the technique is not implemented in a disciplined fashion or if the system problem is so complex that multiple levels of potential causes exist for each problem type.[3]

- When the system of focus for the FTA is very large, quantitative analysis software may be required to analyze the results.

- FTA can be a relatively time-intensive and complex technique; in this book, we provide an overview of the process although additional readings are likely required for a successful application.

Process Overview

1. If the technique is being applied in a formal, scheduled session, take the necessary steps to prepare for conducting the FTA.

   a. If technological methods will be used, acquire concept mapping software, a computer, a projection device (for example, a video projector), and a projection surface or screen.

   b. If nontechnological methods will be used, ensure that you have access to a large surface area (that is, a whiteboard or chalkboard) on which you can create the concept map, as well as thick markers in various colors, tape, and so on.

   c. If you are doing the concept mapping session with a large number of participants, consider identifying a colleague or assistant who is able to create the actual concept map while the facilitator mediates the session.

   d. Identify and invite participants who are experts on the system that will be the focus of the FTA.

   e. Schedule the FTA activity session.

2. Using your list of information required for the needs assessment, define the system that will be the focus of the FTA.

3. Identify the "what should be" for the system either by identifying the system's mission, purpose, or goals, or by defining the criteria for what the "ideal situation" would look like.

4. Working with an expert on the system of focus, begin the process of building the fault tree (see figure 3B.3). Determine, in specific terms, "the top undesired event" for which you want to identify the underlying causes. Write the top undesired event at the top of the tree.

   a. This undesired event will be the foundation on which the FTA will be constructed, so it is important that it be identified in clear terms.

5. Identify the factors (conditions) that are in the immediate vicinity of the top undesired event and that could be causing it. Write those key factors immediately below the top of the tree.

A Guide to Assessing Needs

Figure 3B.3   Example of a Basic Fault Tree Analysis

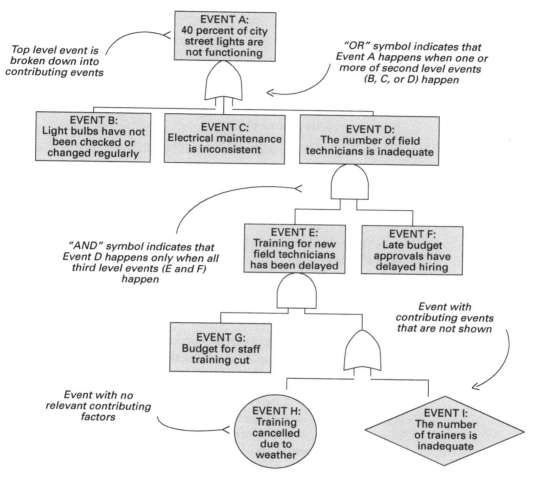

Source: Based on examples from http://syque.com/quality_tools/toolbook/FTA/example.htm and http://syque.com/quality_tools/toolbook/FTA/how.htm.

6. Look at each of the key factors you have identified in the previous step. What subfactors could be causing the key factors? Identify the subfactors, and place them underneath the appropriate factor on the tree.

    a. Do not move on to the next level of analysis until there is consensus that all factors at the current level have been identified.

7. Continue this procedure—building the tree-like graphic—until there is a general consensus that the tree is finished.

8. After the fault tree has been completed, work with experts to carefully and systematically analyze it for accuracy. Compare the fault tree's factors and structure against the actual system being analyzed.

9. Analyze the fault tree. This analysis can be done either statistically or through informal nonstatistical methods (such as brainstorming). To analyze quantitatively, use statistical analysis to determine the probability of all the contributing factors you have listed in the tree.[4] This analysis can be complex, and we recommend doing additional readings before completing the analysis.

10. By drawing on your analysis, you should be able to identify the potential factors, as well as the sequences of factors, that may account for the performance problem that you identified as the top undesired event.

11. Focus particularly on the factors that appear lowest in the tree, because remedying or preventing these root causes is the most effective and efficient way to obstruct or eliminate the critical paths leading to the top undesired event.

Tips for Success

- The FTA technique works best for problems that have a medium level of complexity. For very complex problems, this technique can be difficult to manage or overwhelming for people to interpret.

- Remember that the expert insight that is used to construct the fault tree is generally of a very subjective nature. Take steps to consult as many experts as possible and to externally validate the fault tree and its outcomes. Both of these steps will reduce the subjectivity to some extent.

Notes

1. Based on Jonassen, Hannum, and Tessmer (1989).
2. Ibid.
3. Based on http://www.greatsystems.com/rootcause.htm#FTA.
4. Based on Jonassen, Hannum, and Tessmer (1989).

References and Resources

Jonassen, David H., Wallace H. Hannum, and Martin Tessmer. 1989. *Handbook of Task Analysis Procedures*. Westport, CT: Praeger.

Vesely, William E., F. F. Goldberg, Norman H. Roberts, and David F. Haasi. 1981 *Fault Tree Handbook (NUREG-0492)*. 1981. Washington, DC: U.S. Nuclear Regulatory Commission. http://www.nrc.gov/reading-rm/doc-collections/ nuregs/staff/sr0492/.

Websites

Detailed discussion with description of the meaning of each figure in an FTA graphic is available at http://www.weibull.com/basics/fault-tree/index.htm.

Discussion of fault tree analysis with examples and how-to procedures is available at http://syque.com/quality_tools/toolbook/FTA/how.htm.

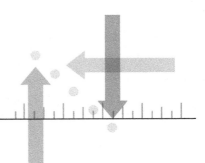

CONCEPT MAPPING

Purpose

Concept mapping is a method used to make a visual representation (that is, a picture or a map) of concepts or ideas and to illustrate their relationships. Terms such as *mind map*, and *idea map* are essentially synonymous with the term *concept map*. A similar method, *cluster mapping*, additionally uses statistics to define clusters of similar items.

Needs Assessment Applications

In the context of needs assessment, concept mapping can be used for various purposes, including data collection, consensus building, and decision making. Specifically, they can be used for the following:

- Facilitate discussion and data collection during interviews or focus groups.

- Support decision making between potential solutions for a given gap.

- Engage in pattern matching for the purpose of consensus building in relation to need identification.

- Identify organizational priorities.

Concept maps can be created by either a single person or a group of people. In the case of a single person creating a concept map, the purpose might be to identify the key ideas relative to a given problem. When concept mapping is used in a group setting, its purpose can be to identify and show the relationship between units within an organization, to brainstorm ideas or solutions, or to systematically identify priorities or plan new approaches.

The key purpose of a concept map is to visually represent key elements and their relationships. This visual representation can be especially useful when complex relationships exist between elements. Concept maps generate qualitative data, but the data can be interpreted using both qualitative and quantitative data analysis.

Advantages and Disadvantages

Advantages

- Concept mapping represents ideas or views from a large group of participants or stakeholders in an easy-to-interpret format.

- It generates data that can be interpreted qualitatively or quantitatively.

- It identifies complex relationships between issues, factors, and so on in a tangible, graphic format.

- Because it is participant focused, everybody can have his or her ideas represented.

- It shows at a glance specific performance areas, their interrelationship, and their strategic priority.

- It is simple to implement and understand for both you and the participant(s).

- Concept mapping uses a structured process that can be replicated easily and reliably.

- It enables the organization to create a shared vision of performance areas and goals.

- It promotes active participation and, therefore, ensures that participant(s) stay on task.

- It can be done using computer software or using paper.

Disadvantages

- In the absence of a structured approach for creating concept maps, this approach can become messy and hard to read.

- Concept mapping includes only a high level representation of the performance area that is the subject of the concept. This method does not easily allow for the inclusion of detailed information.

- In concept mapping, it may be hard to identify all the relationships between the concepts or ideas.

- Interpretation of the concept map data can be involved.

- The use of this method may require an experienced facilitator.

Process Overview

The three main phases of the concept mapping technique are planning, gathering information, and analyzing and interpreting.

Planning

1. Determine the focus of the concept map by using the list of information required for the needs assessment.

2. Identify the data analysis methods to be used after the concept map has been completed.

3. Identify and invite participant(s) to build the concept map.

4. Establish the schedule for the concept mapping session(s).

5. Acquire resources required to conduct the concept mapping session.

   a. If technological methods will be used, acquire concept mapping software, a computer, and a projection device (for example, a video projector) along with a projection surface or screen.

   b. If nontechnological methods will be used, ensure that you have access to a large surface area on which you can create the concept map, as well as thick markers in various colors, tape, and so on.

   c. If you are doing the concept mapping session with a large number of participants, consider identifying a colleague or assistant who is able to create the actual concept map while you (or a hired facilitator) mediate the session.

Gathering Information

1. Start the concept mapping session by introducing the purpose and focus of the concept map to the participant(s).

a. If the concept mapping session is being conducted with a large number of participants, then identify "rules of play" and other information related to the group process.

2. Begin the brainstorming process, encouraging participants to identify as many performance areas as possible related to the focus topic. Emphasize that this is the brainstorming phase of the process and, therefore, that all reasonable contributions are of value.

3. After brainstorming is completed, invite participants to identify redundant information in the list (for example, two contributions that refer to essentially the same thing). Merge and synthesize those instances to create a final list.

4. Begin the structuring process. The process can be started individually, at first, or as a group from the start.

   a. Ask participants to work individually to sort (group or cluster) these performance areas into clusters of their choosing (or use an individual card sorting technique). Beginning the structuring process individually offers individuals a chance to identify relationships among the performance areas before collaborating with the group to come up with a shared sorting of the listed items.

   b. Ask participants to work together to sort (group or cluster) the performance areas into clusters (or use a group card sorting technique). Beginning the structuring process as a group promotes a mediated process of consensus building to identify relationships between performance areas.

5. Items from the list are placed on a "map" (for example, drawn on a big piece of paper, or written on sticky notes that are placed on the wall) to illustrate their relationships. Clusters can be maintained from the previous list, or new clusters may be formed in keeping with the visual map that is developing. More complex maps can be created using statistical techniques and software; in those instances, you should consult the resources that follow.

6. Ask participants to work either collectively or individually to restructure the concept map by hierarchically laying out the concepts or clusters on the basis of one or more dimensions relevant to the focus statement. For example, arrange the items within each cluster by their feasibility within the organizational context. Work to build consensus among the group members on a final map that represents their shared perspectives.

Analyzing and Interpreting

There are different points at which the information captured in the concept map can be analyzed and interpreted. It can be interpreted during the actual concept mapping session (through the active involvement of the participants), after the completion of the concept mapping session (by you or by an external data analysis expert), or at both points. The timing of the analysis and interpretation of the concept map information depends on the purpose and nature of the concept map.

You can interpret data from a concept map in innumerable ways, ranging from "eyeballing" the concept map to determine key trends or priorities, to performing thorough statistical analysis to assess construct validity. For this reason, restrict yourselves to identifying just a few ways you can go about using your concept map data for needs assessment purposes.

Interpreting in-session data

When the concept maps are interpreted during the concept mapping session, consider actively involving the participants in the decision-making process. However, the extent to which in-depth statistical analysis can be done during the concept mapping session is very restricted. Most of the analysis you would do in session will fall into categories such as the following:

- **Coding:** Participants work with the facilitator to set up a simple coding scheme that is related to the focus area of the concept map. The group then works together to code concepts or clusters on the concept map according to the coding scheme. Trends in the concept map data can be analyzed by doing frequency counts on the prevalence of each of the code categories.

- **Rank ordering:** If participants have been asked to use a predetermined scale to rate concepts or clusters of concepts, then you may consider using rank ordering. In this case, you would ask all participants to report the rating they assigned for each cluster or concept. Add up the total rating values per cluster or concept (depending on the unit of analysis), and place the values in rank order according to a dimension relevant to the focus statement for the concept map.

Interpreting post-session data

Multidimensional scaling and hierarchical cluster analysis are two statistical analysis methods that are often used when a thorough understanding of the information in the concept map is required. In addition to those approaches, however, several simple analysis approaches can be used after the concept mapping session has wrapped up.

Here are two examples:

- For decision making between alternate approaches for addressing a performance gap, you might ask participants to rate the cluster on the basis of feasibility or desirability. Then set up your own system—after the concept mapping session—to rate the clusters while using your expertise in the area of need (see figure 3B.4). By comparing the ratings you have given with those given by participants (that is, patterning), you can rank order the various approach clusters to determine the solutions that are most likely to succeed and to match the organization's preferences.

- To compare the views or insights of two different groups of stakeholders, again use an approach to identify patterns. In this case, you would ask the stakeholder groups to separately rate the clusters related to the concept map focus area. You would then analyze the concept maps by comparing how different stakeholder groups rated each of the clusters (see figure 3B.5). Clusters that are generally rated at the same level by each of the cluster groups would indicate a high degree of consensus between stakeholder groups. Clusters where ratings are very different would indicate divergence between stakeholder groups.

Examples

Figure 3B.4 Example of Basic Concept Map to Illustrate Relationships

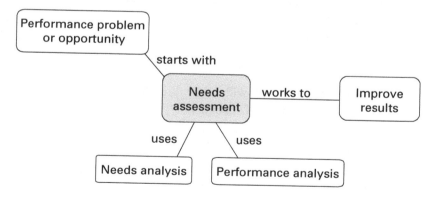

Figure 3B.5 Example of Basic Concept Map with Clusters Overlaid on Individual Statements

Need: only 60% of the country's children graduate from secondary schools in the current year. The target for five years from the current year is 90% secondary school graduation.

Transportation factors

Access to rural schools factors

Family economic condition factors

Migrant employment factors

Number of teachers factors

Community economic condition factors

Gender differences factors

School quality factors

Youth employment opportunity factors

Local culture factors

Tips for Success

- Be sure that you have clearly spelled out the focus area for the concept map prior to the concept mapping session.
- To increase the comfort level of the participants,
  - Explain the concept mapping process to them.
  - Reiterate that their names will not be directly tied to their contributions to the concept map (if applicable).
  - If the participant(s) in the concept mapping session have never worked with concept maps before, consider illustrating the process with a simple example.
- During the initial brainstorming session, include all contributions in the concept map.
- Do not worry about the look or structure of the concept map until the "structuring" phases of the concept map come around.

- Verbally repeat participants' contributions to the concept map as they express them. Doing so will ensure that the concept map is the most accurate reflection possible of the participants' contributions.

- If all participants will collectively work on clustering concepts, use simple strategies to make it visually easy to identify which concepts are being assigned to which clusters. For example, use the same color for all concepts assigned to the same cluster.

References and Resources

Jackson, Kristin M., and William M. K. Trochim. 2002. "Concept Mapping as an Alternative Approach for the Analysis of Open-Ended Survey Responses." *Organizational Research Methods* 5 (October): 307–36. http://www.socialresearchmethods.net/mapping/mapping.htm.

Trochim, William. 1989. "Concept Mapping: Soft Science or Hard Art?" *Evaluation and Program Planning* 12: 87–110. http://www.socialresearchmethods.net/research/epp2/epp2.htm.

Trochim, William, and Mary Kane. 2005. "Concept Mapping: An Introduction to Structured Conceptualization in Health Care." *International Journal for Quality in Health Care* 17 (3): 187–91. http://intqhc.oxfordjournals.org/cgi/reprint/17/3/187.pdf.

Weller, Susan C., and A. Kimball Romney. 1988. *Systematic Data Collection.* Newbury Park, CA: Sage Publications.

Websites

"The Complexity of Concept Mapping for Policy Analysis" by Trochim and Cabrera is available at http://www.isce.edu/ISCE_Group_Site/web-content/ISCE_Events/Cork_2005/Papers/Trochim.pdf.

"Using Concept Mapping to design an indicator framework for addiction treatment centres" is available at http://intqhc.oxfordjournals.org/cgi/content/full/17/3/193.

Additional Tools

Information on statistical analysis of concept maps can also be found in the following sources:

- Free software for creating concept maps is available at http://cmap.ihmc.us/.

- "Q & A: What Is Concept Mapping?" is available at http://www.socialresearchmethods.net/tutorial/Katsumot/conmap.htm.

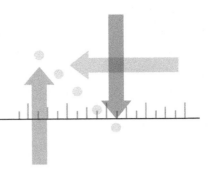

FUTURE WHEEL

Purpose

The future wheel is a future-oriented technique. Future wheel activities are conducted to help participants analyze and explore effects of a trend, event, circumstance, or issue. As such, this technique can be a useful tool for conducting structured brainstorming, determining needs, planning strategically, and building consensus.

Future wheels are laid out as graphic depictions with the future event in a circle in the center, the first-order effects in the first circle out from the event, the second-order effects in the second circle out from the event, and so on. Future wheel activities can potentially be used to explore effects of many different things (issues, trends, and events), so they can be used in virtually any setting (organization, community meeting, school, and so on).

Needs Assessment Applications

The future wheel has a variety of different needs assessment applications, as follows:

- Forecast potential future scenarios.

- Project future trends.

- Systematically explore the possible effects from a current situation or trend.

- Analyze the possible pattern of effects for a potential future event or trend.

- Forecast implications for a variety of alternative circumstances.

- Determine the potential effects of a variety of potential performance solutions.

- Collect data on a group's perspectives on current and future situations and trends.

Advantages and Disadvantages

Advantages

- The future wheel is easy to use and does not require extensive training for the facilitator.

- It is resource lean and, therefore, can be done anywhere, anytime.

- It supports structured brainstorming.

- It is intuitive to the participants.

- It is not time-intensive and can be conducted in one, relatively brief, group session.

- The future wheel can be used at any time in the needs assessment or strategic planning process.

- It can be adapted for use in virtually any context: business and industry, community, personal.

- It promotes systematic thinking about complex relationships between causes and consequences.

- Through the use of concentric circles, it clearly identifies the common bond that all identified effects have to the topic at the center of the future wheel.

Disadvantages

- Because future wheels are laid out in a sequential structure around a central topic, they may be too superficial to identify the complexities of a series of contributing factors that may all have differing levels of influence on the effects identified.

- They may not clarify whether effects are related to each other by causality or by correlation. Indeed, because of the use of the concentric circles, a future wheel may lead individuals to incorrectly believe there is a causal relationship between two effects, when those effects are, in fact, linked only by correlation.

- Future wheels present the potential risk that one or more individuals will believe that effects identified through a future wheel will, in fact, happen when in actuality they are merely "hypotheses" or "best guesses."

- The relatively rudimentary nature of future wheels makes it hard to represent projected time lines associated with the effects added to the future wheel. Such time lines can be an essential ingredient for problem and solution analysis.

- Because participants engage in subjective and projective thinking to create it, a future wheel should be used only as one of many sources of information for more systematic and empirical analysis. It cannot, by itself, be used for coming to conclusive decisions.

Process Overview

The procedure for conducting a future wheel activity is fairly simple and easy to implement. It consists of two key phases: preparation and implementation.

Preparation

1. From the list of information required for the needs assessment, identify a trend, event, or question for the future wheel activity. This trend, event, or question will be the future wheel's main topic. A question might be "What is the result if you continue doing as you are doing?" and an event might be "Effect of talent loss on organizational productivity." The topic should

   a. Focus on current or anticipated future events and their consequences.

   b. Be suited to exploration through a small group interactive session.

2. Invite a small group of people (preferably between 8 and 12 individuals) to participate in the activity. If you intend to use this exercise with more than a dozen or so people, it is recommended that you run the activity multiple times.

3. Determine whether the topic of the future wheel merits the use of outside resources during the actual activity. If so, search for resources that provide key information on the theme or question that you have identi-

fied as being the subject for the future wheel activity. Those resources will be shared with the group of participants during the actual activity. For example, you may want to gather the following:

a. Descriptions of future events or trends from the professional literature

b. Results from future or projection studies

c. Results from other trend analysis or future scenarios

d. Data that provide insight on current or alternative future scenarios

4. Gather the resources required for conducting the activity.

a. Flip charts (or confirm that you will be in a room with a whiteboard)

b. Markers in a variety of colors

Implementation

Preparing participants

1. Begin by warming up the group. Introduce participants to the concept of the future wheel, and explain the process for the activity. Emphasize that all participant contributions are considered valuable and that group members are encouraged to participate actively. Explain that the future wheel is laid out by order of consequences:

a. Primary (or first-order) effects: The most immediate consequences of the future wheel's key topic.

b. Secondary (or second-order) effects: The most immediate consequences following from the first-order consequences. Depending on the topic, you may also opt to include third- or fourth-order effects in the future wheel before continuing.

c. Implications or opportunities: The final wheel of the activities focuses on the implications or opportunities that come from the identified effects.

2. Tell the participants the approach that will be used to add an effect to the future wheel. Some options include the following:

a. Asking participants to brainstorm ideas for effects and adding those effects as they are being identified and without evaluating them first.

b. Discussing each idea and evaluating the plausibility of the idea. If there is a general consensus that the potential effect is plausible, it is added to the concept map.

3. Introduce participants to the key topic for the future wheel activity. Discuss the relevance and importance of understanding the key event. If you are using supplementary resources, provide all the group members with copies of the background resources that you have prepared, and give them time to review the resources.

Creating the future wheel

1. Write the future wheel's key topic (for example, youth unemployment, aging populations) in the center of your drawing space, and place a circle around it.

2. Ask the group to identify the first-order effects. As first-order effects are identified, draw lines out from the center circle (the lines are referred to as "spokes"), and write the first-order effects at the end of the lines. After all key first-order effects have been identified, draw a circle that encloses all the first-order effects.

3. From here, tell participants to shift their focus away from the future wheel's key concept and to instead focus on the first-order effects that were identified. Ask participants to identify the key potential results from the first-order effects. Add those effects to the future wheel by drawing spokes from the circle around the first-order effects and by writing the second-order effects at the end of each of those spokes. After all key second-order effects have been identified, draw a circle around all of them.

4. Continue this process until there is a consensus that the sequence of implications for the key topic is evident.

5. Finally, identify implications or opportunities that emerge from the identified effects, which could include, for example, new programs or policies that will improve performance in relation to the identified issues. The key to this final step is to introduce activities (or solutions) into the discussion.

Discussing and interpreting the future wheel

1. After the future wheel has been completed, give the participants an opportunity to look it over and to synthesize the information in it.

2. Initiate a discussion on the key topic of the future wheel by asking questions targeted to the purpose of the needs assessment. Themes you may want to use to guide the discussion are the following:

   a. Evaluation of the implications of the future wheel's key topic

b. Desirable vs. undesirable primary, secondary, or tertiary effects

c. Effects of the present situation on potential future events

d. Approaches to avoiding negative outcomes

Examining alternative approaches to using future wheels
Future wheel activities can be used in many different ways. Here are some alternative approaches:

1. Invite a panel of experts to participate in the future wheel activity. After the key topic of the future wheel has been identified, the panel should discuss how the key event may affect a variety of themes (for example, recruitment, talent management, profit margins, and so on). Each panel member then should work individually to write down ideas related to the themes raised in the discussion. Use a round-robin approach to ask panel members to contribute their ideas. After a comprehensive list has been created, they should place their ideas in labeled categories. The future wheel can be created by adding the labeled categories as primary, secondary, or tertiary effects.[1]

2. The future wheel activity can also be used as an approach for forecasting the implications of alternative solution scenarios. To use this approach, generate a scenario (for example, the implementation of performance-supporting solutions to improve customer service), and select one aspect from that scenario to explore (for example, an electronic performance support system, or EPSS). Ask participants to identify the specifics of what the selected item can achieve (that is, what functions the EPSS can perform in light of the need), and add those participant contributions as primary effects. Next, ask participants to identify what is required for them to make the items in the "primary effects" section of the future wheel a reality (for example, what resources and applications are required to create and implement the functions of the EPSS). Add this information as the "secondary effects." The future wheel is then elaborated with additional effect levels.[2] (See the example in figure 3B.6.)

Tips for Success

- What key topic you select for the future wheel activity is a critical issue. Make sure that you thoroughly evaluate potential key topics (and how they are formulated) by looking at the information required from the

Figure 3B.6   Sample Future Wheel

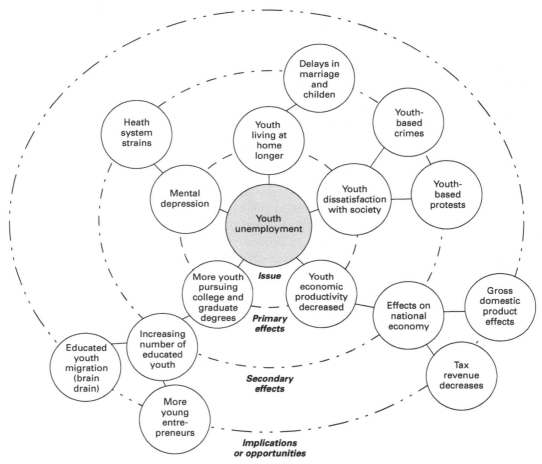

Source: Based on http://www.knoke.org/lectures/futureswheel.htm.

needs assessment, analyzing those requirements, and potentially solicit-ing feedback from outside experts.

• Carefully select participants for the future wheel activity on the basis of the activity's goal. For example, the purpose of the activity is to gather expert insight about the potential implications of a current situation or trend; therefore, select participants who can knowledgably contribute to such an analysis.

- In a clear way, tell participants the approach that will be used for adding information to the future wheel. If the future wheel is being used for anything other than general brainstorming, it is essential to evaluate ideas carefully before they are added to the future wheel.

- Take the time to thoroughly discuss the future wheel after it has been created. At this point, you can stimulate a creative and informed discussion that will be based on a common source of information (the future wheel).

Notes

1. Based on Witkin and Atschuld (1995).
2. Adapted from http://abhijitkohli.googlepages.com/futureswheel.

Reference

Witkin, Belle Ruth, and James W. Altschuld. 1995. *Planning and Conducting Needs Assessments: A Practical Guide*. Thousand Oaks, CA: Sage Publications.

Websites

A four-step example of a future wheel is available at http://www.knoke.org/lectures/futureswheel.htm.

"Future Wheels: Interviews with 44 Global Experts on the Future of Fuel Cells for Transportation and Fuel Cell Infrastructure" is available at http://www.navc.org/Future_Wheels_I.pdf.

A short description and examples of future wheels are available at http://jcflowers1.iweb.bsu.edu/rlo/tarelevance.htm.

Additional Tools

A downloadable template of a future wheel is available at http://www.globaledu cation.edna.edu.au/globaled/go/cache/offonce/pid/1835;jsessionid=050A14CB 101EAF863AE979C80461FCB3.

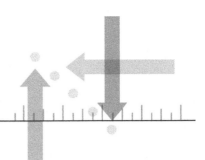

PERFORMANCE PYRAMID

Purpose

The performance pyramid is a framework for ensuring that your needs assessment addresses each component's underlying performance.

Needs Assessment Applications

The performance pyramid (see figure 3B.7 in Process Overview) by John Wedman (2010) is a valuable tool that can be applied throughout a needs assessment to ensure that all aspects of the performance system are considered. Use the performance pyramid to provide structure when you are identifying needs, analyzing needs, and deciding what to do to improve performance.

During your analysis, for example, use the pyramid to determine how each element of the pyramid framework relates to the identified need. Some elements (such as rewards, recognitions, and incentives) may be hindering current performance, whereas others (such as knowledge and skills) may be concurrently supporting the achievement of desired results.

Likewise, use the performance pyramid again when deciding how to create a complete system for improving performance. For example, recommendations coming out of your assessment may include improvement activities related to three elements of the pyramid framework: (a) tools, environment, and processes; (b) rewards, recognition, and incentives; and (c) knowledge and skills. At the same time, you might recommend monitoring the other elements for possible suboptimization (that is, when improvements from your activities have unintended, negative consequences in relation to other elements of the performance system). (For helpful sample templates of improvement activities to use as job aids, see pages 242–244.)

Finally, the pyramid framework can be an effective tool for communicating the results of your assessment with partners and stakeholders. The framework, as a visual, illustrates the relationships among key components in accomplishing desired results; at the same time, it is flexible enough to apply in a variety of contexts.

Advantages and Disadvantages

Advantages

- The performance pyramid provides a valuable framework that ensures that each foundation component of a performance system is addressed in all phases of a needs assessment.

- The performance pyramid offers an easy tool for communicating the systemic characteristics of performance with assessment partners that are internal or external to the organization.

- Relationships between the elements of the pyramid framework (for example, the relationship between the organization's capacity to achieve desired results and the alignment of vision, mission, and objectives required to accomplish results) can provide necessary links for ensuring that improvements in one area don't lead to new performance challenges in others.

Disadvantages

- The pyramid, as a visual, can be misinterpreted as a hierarchy. The six blocks in the inner pyramid image are, in reality, interchangeable. For example, motivation and self-concept can be illustrated as the top component of the pyramid—as could any other elements depending on the context.

- The pyramid does not provide a process for conducting a needs assessment or for improving performance; rather it is just a framework for aligning the elements that support the achievement of results.

Process Overview

Figure 3B.7   Wedman's Performance Pyramid

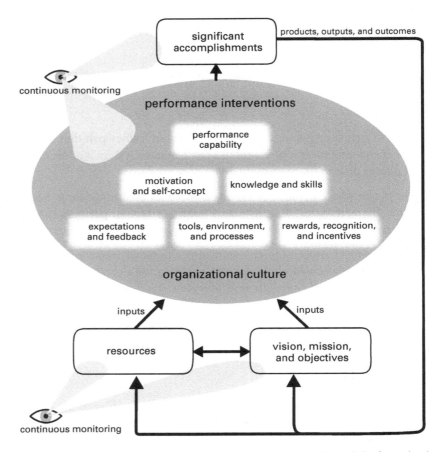

Source: Adapted from Watkins and Leigh (2010). Wedman (2010) has granted permission for use herein.

Needs Analysis Applications

For each identified need, complete an analysis of the need to identify the contributing factors that are leading to the discrepancy between current and desired performance (results). Use the performance pyramid as a framework for planning your analysis, collecting information, and then analyzing the findings so you can make recommendations.

A Guide to Assessing Needs

1. Begin by clearly stating the need in terms of what desired results are not currently being accomplished. Use this precise definition of the need to drive your needs analysis; otherwise, you will typically drift from the performance gap into symptoms of the problem or preferred fixes. Remember, a needs analysis is a systematic process to break apart a need and to determine what components are leading to the performance gap.

2. For each element of the performance pyramid framework, collect information regarding its potential relationship with the identified need. It doesn't matter which element you start with (culture, capacity, feedback, and so on), but by the end of the analysis, you should examine each element for its potential role in relation to the need. Here are some sample questions for each element of the pyramid framework:

- *Motivation and Self-Concept*
  - Are people motivated to achieve the desired results as specified by the need?
  - Are people motivated to accomplish the goals of the organization and its partners?
  - What factors may be reducing motivation?

- *Performance Capability*
  - Are the "right" people available to do the work?
  - Do the best performers stay with the organization or leave?
  - Does the organization have adequate capacity to take on new projects?

- *Expectations and Feedback*
  - Do people know what results are expected?
  - After people have completed a task, are they told what they did well and what they can improve in the future?

- *Rewards, Recognition, and Incentives*
  - Are there incentives for people to accomplish desired results?
  - Are there disincentives for performing well?
  - Are people recognized or rewarded for their performance?

- *Tools, Environment, and Processes*
  - Do people have access to the resources (equipment, time, software, and so on) that are required to meet performance goals?

- Does the organizational environment (or culture) support the achievement of desired results?
- Are there systematic processes in place to guide performance?

- ***Knowledge and Skills***
  - Do people know how to do what is asked of them?
  - Are people given (or do they come with) the necessary skills to achieve desired results?

- ***Organizational Culture***
  - Does the organization's culture support the achievement of desired results?
  - Are there norms within the culture of the organization that hinder any other component of the pyramid framework?

- ***Resources***
  - Do people have the necessary resources (time, money, and so on) to achieve desired results?
  - Have the resources required for achieving desired results been identified?

- ***Vision, Mission, and Objectives***
  - Are people aware of how their work contributes to the team, organization, clients, and larger society?
  - Is there a clear strategic plan that can be used to guide decisions at all levels of the organization?
  - Are people able to be "proactive" because they know where they want to go, or do they always have to be "reactive" to changing events?

- ***Significant Accomplishments***
  - Are the desired results aligned with the vision, mission, and objectives of the organization?
  - What is the return on investment for accomplishing desired results?

- ***Continuous Monitoring***
  - Are there monitoring (or evaluation) systems in place within the organization that can measure performance in relation to each component of the pyramid framework?

- Are performances routinely monitored across the organization?
- Are monitoring results and reports used to improve performance?

3. Ask questions related to each element of the pyramid to both internal and external partners in the needs assessment. Often, external clients and partners can identify contributing factors to performance problems more easily than those on the inside of the organization.

4. Analyze responses to your analysis questions so you identify which elements (or sub-elements) are most closely related to the need; those elements will typically include causal factors contributing to the need as well as other factors that are leading to current successes. You can also use fault tree analysis (see page 214), root cause analysis (see page 207), concept mapping (see page 220), and other tools to support your analysis within the pyramid framework.

5. Move the elements of your pyramid around to illustrate the relationship you have found during your needs analysis. For instance, for the need, you might determine that the expectations and feedback element of the pyramid should really be placed at the top to illustrate its critical role in relation to the need within the organizational context. Then the supporting elements—such as motivation and self-concept or incentives, rewards, and recognition—can be used to illustrate the foundations that must be built to ensure the success of the entire performance system. After all, no single element of the pyramid is more important than the others; for successful performance, you must have all elements working together.

Solution Identification Applications

1. Remember that your needs analysis identifies factors contributing to the performance gap for many of the pyramid's components (for instance, motivation and self-concept or capacity or skills and knowledge). Likewise, you will frequently find several causal factors within a single element of the pyramid (for example, two or three factors with the element of expectations and feedback may be contributing to less-than-desirable performance.

2. Working with your needs assessment's internal and external partners, establish a rough priority of the factors leading to identified needs on the basis of their relationship—positive or negative—with the accomplishment of desired results. Precision is not required, but a rough prioritization can help you focus time, effort, and other resources.

3. For each identified causal factor, pinpoint at least two potential solutions that could help improve the achievement of desired results (for examples, see the Job Aids section that follows). Having choices is important to quality decision making; therefore, it is important to identify at least two options for each factor. One option might seem to be clearly the better choice at first, but that decision is best left until after you have identified a variety of alternatives.

4. Before selecting any of the identified solutions, determine what criteria will be used to weigh your options, thus ensuring that each alternative gets a fair appraisal of its potential.

5. Judge each potential solution for each causal factor on the basis of the criteria established in the prior step. It is frequently useful to apply a systematic process, such as multicriteria analysis (see page 171), to assess each option.

6. When you have selected a variety of activities to address the factors leading to the need (performance gap), use the performance pyramid again to verify that you are addressing all components that (a) support performance and (b) ensure that the complete performance system will benefit from the improvements.

Job Aids: A Sample of Improvement Activities to Consider

Expectation Feedback

Possible improvement activities include clear performance guidelines, reference manuals for processes and procedures, realistic job previews, managerial coaching, quality assurance programs, quality on-boarding or orientation programs, benchmarking, performance appraisals, upward and peer evaluations, identification and documentation of performance indicators, goal setting, routine one-on-ones, and individual improvement plans.

Tools, Environment, and Processes

Possible improvement activities include electronic performance support, job aids, performance aids, process reengineering, knowledge management, process improvement, ergonomics, workstation design, warning systems, labeling and color coding, safety planning, social networking, quality management, team colocation, and six sigma.

Rewards, Incentives, and Recognition

Possible improvement activities include bonus systems, commission systems, profit sharing, merit award systems, annual awards ceremony, employee of the month, job sharing, flex hours, job enrichment, telecommuting, education benefits, personnel in the spotlight, empowerment, and delegation.

Organizational Capacity

Possible improvement activities include recruitment programs, retention programs, early retirement, phased retirement, interviewing, job rotation, mergers, acquisitions, crowd-sourcing, outsourcing, succession planning, affirmative action programs, outplacement centers, cross training, internal recruitment programs, interview standards, and competency models.

Knowledge and Skills

Possible improvement activities include classroom training, e-learning, team learning, mentoring, coaching, quality on-boarding or orientation programs, on-the-job training, brown-bag lunch sessions, webinars, podcasts or vodcasts, and tuition reimbursement.

Motivation and Self-Concept

Possible improvement activities include job crafting, job sharing, flex hours, education benefits, career mentoring, career ladders, job rotation systems, and motivational communications.

Resources

Possible improvement activities include restructuring, supply chain management, cash flow analysis, budgeting and accounting systems, career management programs, career ladders, outplacement, and cost reductions.

Continuous Monitoring

Possible improvement activities include performance monitoring, quality management, six sigma, program evaluations, training evaluations, goal/question/metric programs, financial analysis, client surveys, balanced scorecard, key performance indicators, managerial dashboards, and needs assessments.

Vision, Mission, and Objectives

Possible improvement activities include mega planning, strategic planning, future search, SWOT analysis (see page 127), appreciative inquiry, scenario planning, workforce planning, job forecasting, tabletop analysis (see page 180), values identification, and risk management.

References and Resources

Gilbert, Thomas F. 2007. *Human Competence: Engineering Worthy Performance.* Tribute ed. San Francisco: Pfeiffer.

Watkins, Ryan, and Doug Leigh, eds. 2010. *Handbook for Improving Performance in the Workplace.* Vol. 2: *Selecting and Implementing Performance Interventions.* San Francisco: Wiley/Pfeiffer, and Silver Spring, MD: International Society for Performance Improvement.

Watkins, Ryan, and John F. Wedman. 2003. "A Process for Aligning Performance Improvement Resources and Strategies." *Performance Improvement Journal* 42 (7): 9–17.

Wedman, John F. 2010. "Performance Pyramid Model." In *Handbook of Improving Performance in the Workplace.* Vol. 2: *Selecting and Implementing Performance Interventions*, edited by Ryan Watkins and Doug Leigh, 51–80. San Francisco: Wiley/Pfeiffer, and Silver Spring, MD: International Society for Performance Improvement.

Wedman, John F., and L. Diggs. 2001. "Identifying Barriers to Technology-Enhanced Learning Environments in Teacher Education." *Computers in Human Behavior* 17: 421–30.

Wedman, John F., and S. W. Graham. 1998. "Introducing the Concept of Performance Support Using the Performance Pyramid." *Journal of Continuing Higher Education* 46 (3): 8–20.

Wedman, John F., and M. Tessmer. 1993. "Instructional Designers' Decisions and Priorities: A Survey of Design Practice." *Performance Improvement Quarterly* 6 (2): 43–57.

Websites

Many resources (including podcast interviews) on how to use the performance pyramid in a needs assessment are available at http://www.needsassessment.org.

Website and manual for using the performance pyramid are available at http://needsassessment.missouri.edu/.

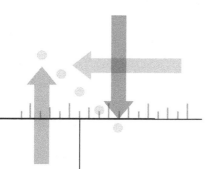

Appendix A

MANAGEMENT AND IMPLEMENTATION GUIDES AND CHECKLISTS

In this appendix, you will find several easy-to-use guides and checklists that can help you complete your needs assessment.

Implementation Plan for a Needs Assessment

This sample planning table provides a general set of tasks for carrying out your needs assessment. Because each needs assessment is unique, this sample can be adjusted to the particular requirements of your specific needs assessment. For instance, a smaller-scale needs assessment may compress several of the activities into a few days of effort, whereas larger-scale assessments may require additional tasks, time, and involvement of partners to be able to appropriately adjust to the complexities of the organization. Nevertheless, the sample planning table can be a guide for you to determine what has to be done, who should be involved, and how long you estimate that it may take to complete a needs assessment.

Completing a needs assessment typically requires a number of people with different roles and levels of expertise. Low-skill tasks, such as scheduling a meeting, can be completed by staff members with minimum qualifications. Medium-skill tasks, such verifying the links between proposed activities and needs, can be completed by staff members with some specialized training. Finally, high-skill tasks, such as data analysis and interpretation, require professionals with task-specific experience and expertise. Depending on your organization, people may have titles that are very different from the ones we have used here.

Recommended Primary Tasks		Sample Activities Within Tasks
Preassessment		
1. Establish the overall scope of the needs assessment.		• Determine who should be the main collaborators in designing the needs assessment. • Schedule a meeting and invite collaborators. • Create an agenda. • Facilitate the meeting. • Sketch out the main goals, tasks, and design of the assessment; decide if external experts should be engaged. • Confirm agreements from the meeting. • Decide how decisions will be made about the implementation of the assessment; for larger needs assessments, create a steering committee (SC) to guide the process.
2. Identify the primary performance issues.		• Identify and create a list of performance problems and opportunities. During the assessment, more or different items could emerge. • Prioritize items from this list that the needs assessment should cover.
3. Define the data requirements.		• Define the type of data required and sources of that information. • Establish what data are *not* readily available, what you might want to collect, and what sources you plan to use. • Gather preliminary data.
4. Create a management plan.		• Define objectives for the assessment. • Prepare a time line and deadlines for tasks. • Identify the assessment team members, roles, and responsibilities. • For more details, see the detailed checklist for needs assessment management activities (see appendix A.2 and www.needsassessment.org/).

5. Validate your management plan.	• Collaborators and SC members should review and critique the management plan. • Gather feedback from others who will have a stake in the success of the assessment: colleagues, peers, clients, partners, sponsors, community members, and so on. • Revise the plan, as required.

Assessment

1. Plan the data collection effort.	• Collect existing data (for example, documents) to be reviewed. • Decide on data collection methods to be used. • Create data collection instruments: surveys, interview protocols, and so on. • Train data collectors (for example, facilitators of focus groups) • Schedule interviews, focus groups, performance observations, or other techniques to be used.
2. Verify that data collection instruments will identify information about gaps.	• Analyze and cross-check all of the instruments. • Ensure that information will be collected on both the current and desired results so you can identify gaps. • Review the data collection techniques with team members so that everyone is aware of the critical information required. • Obtain clearances from individuals or committees (for example, institutional review board) for data collection instruments and plans.
3. Collect data.	• Manage the collection of data to ensure that all critical perspectives are represented. • Check that the instruments, techniques, and sources represent varying perspectives about the primary performance issues. • Determine when the assessment has enough information to move to the next task. • Enter the collected data into a secure database or central location.

(continued on next page)

Recommended Primary Tasks		Sample Activities Within Tasks
4. Determine gaps (needs) by analyzing current and desired results.		• Analyze the information collected to identify gaps between current and desired results. • Verify that information collected from qualitative techniques (for example, interviews) is included in the analysis. • Ensure that comparisons between current and desired results use equivalent information (for example, comparing apples to apples).
5. Prioritize gaps (needs).		• Use information collected to prioritize the identified gaps. • Prioritize gaps according to size, scope, distinguishing characteristics, relative importance, or other criteria. • Review the prioritized list with the assessment team members and SC. • Collect additional information, if required, to refine the prioritization.
6. Determine causes of gaps.		• For the highest-priority needs, create a plan for collecting information on the causal factors that are likely leading to the performance gaps. • Plan for a needs analysis and root cause analysis for each of the highest-priority needs. • Prepare to collect additional information using multiple techniques and tools, if necessary.
7. Collect information about the causal factors (or root causes).		• Identify all significant factors causing the performance gaps. • Use tools (for example, fishbone or fault tree diagrams) to assess the relationships among causal factors.

A Guide to Assessing Needs

8. Analyze and synthesize the information you have collected about both gaps and causes.		• Link together information collected on gaps and causal factors. • Be aware that there are typically multiple relationships among gaps and causal factors (for instance, one causal factor may be related to multiple gaps). • Review the results of the analysis with SC members. • Prioritize needs and related causal factors using one or more decision-making techniques in this book (see Part 3B. Decision-Making Tools and Techniques).
9. Identify possible solutions (activities) to address priority gaps and associated causal factors.		• Identify two or more potential solutions (activities) that can be used to improve the results identified with each priority gap. • Verify that potential activities address one or more causal factors related to priority needs.
10. Evaluate the potential solutions (activities) using agreed-upon criteria so you determine which are most likely to lead to improvements.		• Establish criteria to be used for judging the potential value of each possible solution. • Have the assessment team review the assessment criteria. • Judge each potential activity (that is, intervention, project) using the agreed-upon criteria.

(continued on next page)

Recommended Primary Tasks		Sample Activities Within Tasks
11. Recommend the solutions that will best achieve the desired results.		• Review all of the information collected and the results of the analyses. • Summarize the findings related to priority needs and the causal factors. • Recommend solutions that are likely to achieve success.
Postassessment		
1. Summarize your recommendations in a report or presentation.		• Summarize the assessment of potential activities for each priority gap and causal factor. • Take into account the social, political, technological, cultural, legal, and ethical factors that influence recommendations or decisions. • Review and revise the summary on the basis of feedback from the assessment SC.
2. Communicate your draft findings to your stakeholders.		• Before releasing your needs assessment report, share the findings with stakeholders for review and comment. • If you relied significantly on data from a few individuals, ask them to review the draft report as well.
3. Integrate needs assessment results into activity monitoring and evaluation plans.		• Use the findings of the needs assessment to develop a plan for the monitoring and evaluation of solutions (activities) that occur. • Align assessment, monitoring, and evaluation activities through systematic planning and follow-up.

4. Evaluate your needs assessment process.		• Reflect on the activities of the needs assessment, and note potential steps that could be taken to improve assessments in the future. • For future needs assessments, report on recommendations for improvements to the processes.
5. Document needs assessment efforts.		• Write a summary or full report to communicate the needs assessment steps, decisions, and recommendations (see section 2 under the question "What Should Go in a Needs Assessment Report and Presentation?"). • Create a presentation to communicate the needs assessment recommendations or decisions (see section 2 for further discussion). • Send copies to all stakeholders as well as others who provided assistance during the needs assessment.

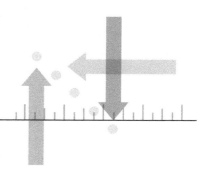

Detailed Checklist for Needs Assessment Management Activities

This detailed checklist provides more specific guidance on the main elements to consider when planning, implementing, and managing a needs assessment. Adapt the checklist to the nature of your needs assessment (that is, according to the assessment scale, purpose, time line, and so on). This particular checklist is developed for teams who are involved with *large-scale* needs assessment projects, programs, or policies.

The checklist should be used as a tool for determining and documenting plans from the preassessment to postassessment stages. Think of it as a living document during the assessment process, and plan to amend it throughout the undertaking so it regularly reflects the current situation.

Focus or title of the needs assessment:	
Name of office or organization managing the needs assessment process:	
Name(s) of checklist preparer(s):	
Date the needs assessment will begin:	
Date of the needs assessment's planned completion:	

For each item that follows, you'll want to indicate who is responsible for each step, plus any deadlines for completion. This is a very long list, and not every step is expected to occur in a given needs assessment. Yet we hope it will provide you with a rather comprehensive list of issues to consider for larger-scale or complex needs assessments.

Overall Purpose of the Needs Assessment

☐ **Issue to be addressed.** Describe the nature of the issue (for example, problem, question, and so on) to be addressed through the needs assessment.

☐ **Purpose or goal.** What is expected to be learned from the needs assessment? Why is the needs assessment to be undertaken?

☐ **Use.** How will the needs assessment findings be used? Who will use them?

Planning and Management

☐ **Requesters.** Who requested that the needs assessment be done? Who will determine if it is successful?

☐ **Sponsor(s).** Who is sponsoring the needs assessment?

☐ **Expected sponsor contributions.** What types of sponsor contributions (for example, money, employee involvement, providing data, and so on) do you expect?

☐ **Authorizations to carry out the needs assessment.** Are there any authorizations required—such as by a government body or an institutional review board—for conducting the needs assessment?

☐ **Budget.** What costs are expected or required for consultants, travel, supplies, rentals, and other items? (Provide details of each cost item for large-scale needs assessments.)

☐ **Time.** How many days or weeks of employee time are expected for involvement with the needs assessment? Include time for all people involved at the different stages (from preassessment to postassessment) and the range of roles (from oversight roles to data collectors).

☐ **Other resources.** Explain other types and amounts of resources required.

☐ **Period for conducting the needs assessment.** Over what period do you expect the needs assessment to occur? When is the final needs assessment report to be submitted?

☐ **Plans for the scope of work or terms of reference.** What is the nature of work to be done? Typically, these features are included in a larger-scope needs assessment:

- Needs assessment purpose and major questions to be addressed
- Overall management plan, time line, and scope of work (including the hiring of any consultants, and so on)
- Data requirements and data sources determination
- Stakeholder or informant determination
- Data collection method and instrument development
- Data collection implementation (for example, focus groups, interviews, and so on)
- Data entry, sorting, and assembly (for example, data entry, data organizing, and so on)
- Data analysis—qualitative and quantitative (for example, content analysis of qualitative data, statistical analysis of quantitative survey data, assembling themes and patterns)
- Ways to assemble the findings (for example, constructing a story about the themes and patterns found, considering missing data and remediation approaches for handling missing information, clarifying the gaps, and so on)
- Written report preparation of the data (for example, writing a report of the analysis, preparing tables with findings, developing graphical displays of information, and so on)
- Reviews and editing of reports (for example, internally, by peer or expert reviewers, and so on)
- Oral reporting of the findings (for example, presentations on findings to internal and external audiences, community, and so on)
- Information dissemination and communication (for example, within team only, to external groups, community announcements in newspapers, and so on)
- Follow-up action planning after completion of the needs assessment

☐ **Responsible individual or team to carry out the needs assessment.** Which individuals or groups will carry out the different steps of the needs assessment? Be sure to differentiate between those who will manage and those who will implement (for example, carry out data collection) the work. Also determine how the work will be divided.

☐ **Internal, external, other.** Will the needs assessment be done by an internal resource (for example, employees of the same agency for whom the needs assessment is being conducted), by an external resource (for example, independent consultants), or through another arrangement (for example, graduate student interns, some internal and some external resources)?

☐ **Skills of the assessors.** Are the skills of the assessors adequate and verified? Is additional training or support required for them? What is the previous experience? Is sample work available?

☐ **Quality assurance.** What are the criteria on which the quality will be judged? How will we ensure that the needs assessment is conducted in a quality manner?

☐ **Conflicts of interest.** What are any potential conflicts of interest related to the planning, implementation, and management?

☐ **Products.** What are the products (for example, a report, a presentation, technical advice, and so on) expected from the needs assessment process? What do the sponsors expect to see at the end of the process? When are the respective products to be delivered?

☐ **Review process.** What are the plans for the needs assessment to be reviewed against different criteria: quality, appropriateness of information, and so on? Who will be the reviewers, and what is the justification for their selection?

☐ **Process monitoring.** What are the key benchmarks or deliverables to be monitored for progress in completing the needs assessment?

☐ **Internal communications.** How will internal communications occur so that all members of the needs assessment team are aware of the important aspects of needs assessment implementation?

☐ **Risks or constraints.** What are known (or possible) risks or constraints to the successful implementation of the needs assessment?

☐ **Credibility of the needs assessment.** How do we ensure that the needs assessment is viewed internally and externally as being valid, free from bias, and so on?

☐ **Costs and benefits of the approach taken in the needs assessment.** What are the provisions to weigh costs and benefits in choosing among different approaches to carry out the needs assessment? How can costs, efficiencies, and benefits be adequately addressed?

Data Requirements and Sources

☐ **Existing logic model review.** Does a logic model (results chain) exist? What are the plans for review and verification that the logic model is properly reflective of the current situation? If it does not exist, could a logic model be constructed, and who will be responsible for doing this?

☐ **Existing data.** What data exist about the issue of inquiry? What do we know about any gaps between current results and possible desired results to be achieved?

☐ **Data quality, credibility, and verification.** What do we know about how data were collected? Are the data sufficiently precise, reliable, relevant, valid, and so on? How will we verify the quality?

☐ **Data sources and access.** What are the data sources (for example, data systems, informants, reports, and so on)? Do we have access to them?

☐ **Useful missing data.** What information would be useful to know but is not available? How might we obtain it?

☐ **Data costs.** What might it cost us to obtain the data?

☐ **Data security.** What are the provisions for securing data and ensuring the protection of the data and the confidentiality (or anonymity) of sources?

☐ **Sufficiency of data and sources.** How will we know if our data are sufficient—appropriate, targeted, comprehensive, and so on? How will we know when we have enough data to guide decisions?

☐ **Sampling.** Will sampling be used? If so, how? Will a sampling expert be engaged?

Stakeholders and Informants

☐ **Stakeholders and informants.** Who (individuals, groups, community, and so on) are possible stakeholders and informants for the needs assessment?

☐ **Primary informants.** Who are primary informants? What information can they provide?

☐ **Secondary informants.** Who are secondary informants? What information can they provide?

☐ **Other informants.** Who are other informants? What information can they provide?

☐ **Outreach and contact information for stakeholders or informants.** How do we reach out to stakeholders or informants? Do we have contact information?

☐ **Communications and protocols for contacting stakeholders or informants.** What are the protocols (for example, obtaining approvals for their participation, sending letters of invitation in advance, and so on) that we must observe in engaging with stakeholders or informants?

☐ **Informed consent and disclosure.** Will letters of informed consent be prepared for informants prior to data collection occurring? Will notifications be prepared and shared with informants about how their information will be safeguarded or disclosed? Will ethics committees be involved in the process of preparing and collecting consent records?

☐ **Coding of informants.** How will codes be assigned to individual informants to track their responses and at the same time protect the confidentiality of the information provided by them?

☐ **Conflicts or biases of stakeholders or informants.** What are any potential conflicts that the different types of stakeholders or informants might have? What are any known biases?

☐ **Updating stakeholders.** Who else should be kept informed on the progress of the needs assessment (for example, groups potentially indirectly affected by the results of the needs assessment)?

Data Collection Method and Instrument Development

☐ **Question development.** What are the main questions and subquestions to be asked? What type of information do we expect to receive from the questions? What are probing questions that data collectors should be prepared to ask following lead questions?

☐ **Data collection methods.** What data collection methods are planned? What are the criteria for selecting the methods (for example, the method is likely to generate a high number of respondents, the method can be implemented within the budget and time constraints, informants usually provide multilayered levels of information with this method, and so on)?

☐ **Data collection phasing and triangulation.** How will the data collection methods be phased? How will the data be triangulated?

☐ **Instrument protocol development.** What topics should the instruments cover? How should the instruments be structured and formatted? Are sample instruments available? Who is to develop the instruments?

☐ **Instrument testing and revisions.** How will the instruments be tested? Who will be responsible for revisions and secondary testing?

☐ **Language requirements.** Are translation or interpretation services required? What will be the review process for translations?

☐ **Incentives and compensation.** Will any incentives or compensation be provided to informants (that is, for their time and effort)? What other arrangements will be made for the convenience of informants (for example, child care for focus group attendees, refreshments, and so on)?

☐ **Administration of data collection.** When will the data collection efforts occur? How will the efforts be divided and coordinated?

☐ **Selection and preparation of data collectors.** Do data collectors have the requisite technical skills? Do data collectors have the appropriate language and cultural or other backgrounds? How will data collectors be trained?

☐ **Approval of data collection plans.** Who or which office (for example, institutional review board) will approve the data collection instruments and plans?

Data Analysis Plans

☐ **Data system management.** What is the system for managing data (for example, a database)?

☐ **Data entry.** How will data be transcribed? How will data be entered into a database?

☐ **Data entry instructions and coding.** Are instructions being prepared for how to enter data? Is a "data dictionary" or explanation about how data are to be coded being prepared?

☐ **Data entry training.** Who is responsible for training data enterers? How and when will training occur?

☐ **Data entry timing.** What are the plans for monitoring the timing of data transcription and entry so as not to lose, in particular, the nuances of qualitative narrative data?

☐ **Data verification.** How will entered data be checked for errors?

☐ **Quantitative data analysis.** How will quantitative data be analyzed (for example, Excel, SPSS, and so on)? What would sample data reports look like?

☐ **Quantitative data analysis reviews.** What is the process for reviewing the correct interpretation and reporting of raw numerical data, statistical analyses, charts, and so on?

☐ **Qualitative data analysis.** (Note multiple items that follow.)
  - *Interpreting qualitative data.* Who is in charge of overseeing the interpretation of qualitative data, providing guidance, and so on?
  - *Content analysis of qualitative data.* How will content be analyzed?
  - *Categorization of qualitative data.* How will categorization of themes occur? Who is responsible?
  - *Coding of qualitative data.* What is the process for coding? Who is responsible?
  - *Data dictionary preparation for qualitative data coding.* What is the process for developing and documenting the data dictionary?
  - *Intercoder reliability for qualitative data analysis.* What are the provisions for multiple raters and for cross-checking of coding or ratings?

☐ **Data transfer.** If consultants or independent groups are conducting the needs assessment, how and in what form will collected data be transferred to the needs assessment manager or team? How will respondent data remain confidential (where appropriate), and at the same time how will certain data be made available to the needs assessment manager or sponsor?

Findings or Results of the Assessment (completed after the assessment is done)

☐ **Current results.** What are the current results being achieved?

☐ **Desired results.** What are the desired results to be achieved? Indicate if there are stages of results (for example, one year out, five years out, and so on) and different levels of results (if any).

☐ **Gaps.** Did the research determine one or more gaps in results? What is it that should be achieved that is currently not being achieved?

☐ **Existing strengths.** What are the identified existing results that are positive or can be considered strengths? What is working well and can possibly be grown or further supported?

☐ **Alignment.** Is there an alignment between gaps identified at the strategic, tactical, and operational levels?

☐ **Prioritization of gaps.** Were the gaps in results prioritized? Based on what criteria?

☐ **Causal analysis.** Were gaps analyzed for primary "causes"?

☐ **Proposed solutions.** Were activities (that is, solutions) identified to address the "causes" of the gaps? How were the solutions prioritized?

☐ **Logic model or results chain development.** Was a logic model developed (or revised) to illustrate the findings? Were indicators and measurements (and any targets and baselines) elaborated in the logic model?

☐ **Capacity building.** How can capacity be built within the organization to achieve desired results?

☐ **Final recommendations.** What were the recommended actions of the needs assessment?

Written Reporting of the Data

☐ **Expected content.** What are the expected contents and sections of the report? In what order will the sections be presented? Are existing reporting templates or tables of contents available?

☐ **Format.** What are the formats indicating how the reports (for example, executive brief, full report, public information brief, and so on) should look?

☐ **Graphics and charts.** What is expected in terms of graphic and chart design? Will specialists in graphics and design be available for this work?

- ☐ **Report timing.** What are the time lines for drafts, revisions, and final versions of the reports?
- ☐ **Audience.** Who are the different audiences for the different reports? Should different audiences get different reports?
- ☐ **Report availability and dissemination.** How will reports be made available—hard copies, posted on websites, copies in public information or community centers?
- ☐ **Language.** In what language(s) will the report(s) be made available? Will report(s) be made available in the language of majority and minority stakeholders? What provisions will be made for those with low literacy skills?
- ☐ **Feedback.** What is the process for giving the supervising authority, stakeholders, consultants, and others an opportunity to provide feedback? Will stakeholders be able to provide feedback prior to the release of the report?

Reviews or Editing of Reports
- ☐ **Reviewers.** Who are the reviewers: internal, external, academic or expert, beneficiaries, and so on?
- ☐ **Reviewer guidelines.** What guidelines are given to reviewers?
- ☐ **Review schedule.** When will reviews occur? What is the expected turnaround time for reviewers?
- ☐ **Reviewer compensation.** Will reviewers be compensated in some way? If so, which reviewers?

Oral Reporting
- ☐ **Expected content.** What will be presented orally?
- ☐ **Format.** What are the formats of oral reporting: community briefings, podcasts, radio, and so on?
- ☐ **Visual tools.** What visual tools (for example, posters, PowerPoint presentations, and so on) will complement oral presentations?
- ☐ **Report timing.** What are the time lines for the oral reporting?
- ☐ **Audience.** Who are the different audiences for the different oral reports?
- ☐ **Communications.** How will stakeholders know what the oral presentation schedule is, who is presenting, and how to participate?
- ☐ **Language.** In what language(s) will the presentation(s) be made available? Will provisions be made available in the language of majority and minority stakeholders?
- ☐ **Feedback.** What is the process for giving stakeholders an opportunity to provide feedback?

Follow-Up Action Planning after Completion of the Needs Assessment

☐ **Decisions.** What will the process be for decision making? Who are the decision makers?

☐ **Communication about decisions.** How will decisions be communicated?

☐ **Documenting decisions.** What is the process for documenting the decision-making process and final decisions?

☐ **Criticisms.** What is the process for documenting or acting on criticisms of stakeholders or doing both?

☐ **Formative evaluation of needs assessment**. What is the process for evaluating and making recommendations for how to improve the needs assessment process?

A Six-Week Needs Assessment Implementation Guide

Completing a comprehensive needs assessment in a short period, for instance six weeks, requires a fair amount of planning and flexibility. To help with quick assessments, we have created a simple guide that illustrates the major considerations and tasks that should be completed during each of the weeks. The guide focuses on four major categories of activities, each defining an important component of the overall assessment. The categories represent activities that distinct subgroups may work on during the assessment or that the whole team may collaborate on in all four categories.

1. **Partner commitment:** Gaining and maintaining the commitment of partners to support your needs assessment is essential, especially when you will be moving quickly to identify and to analyze needs so that you can make decisions.

2. **Planning (desired results):** Defining the desired results at the strategic, tactical, and operational levels provides for the important comparison of current and desired performance. Do not assume that desired results are clear or that adequate indictors and measures are available.

3. **Data collection (current results):** Defining needs (that is, gaps in results) requires data regarding the current achievements with parallel indicators and measures of the desired results. Especially in quick assessments, the data collection process must be efficient to be able to properly identify needs.

4. **Process management:** Organizing and administering your needs assessment is critical to your success.

Use this guide (along with the other tools and techniques included throughout this book) to plan your next assessment, but keep in mind that planning for a successful needs assessment requires both patience and flexibility.

Needs Assessment

	Partner commitment tasks	Planning tasks (desired results)	Data collection tasks (current results)	Process management tasks
Pre-needs assessment	• Plan kickoff meeting. • Identify team. • Identify and meet with sponsor. • Get team members out of other work so that they can participate fully. • Determine initial scope and needs assessment questions to propose to partners. • Identify potential team roles (and subteam roles). • Create a basic project plan for the needs assessment to propose to partners.			
Week 1: Specify requirements.	• Identify and contact partners. • Plan the partners meeting. • Get buy-in for needs assessment scope and process.	• Collect current strategic plans (SP) and related documents (previous needs assessments included). • Identify key partners in defining desired results at multiple levels (strategic, tactical, operational). • Hold kickoff meeting with partners.	• Review currently available data. • Identify needs assessment questions to be answered. • Specify data requirements to complete the needs assessment. • Lay out data collection plan. • Hold kickoff meeting with partners.	• Plan or organize meetings. • Prepare documents required for each subgroup working on the assessment. • Communicate with sponsor and partners. • Establish budget and finalize project plan.
Week 2: Collect initial information.	• Determine desired or required performance. • Determine others who must be involved. • Review data collection protocols. • Bring in others for buy-in (such as other ministries, NGOs, community groups, and so on).	• With partners, conduct a SWOT (strengths, weaknesses, opportunities, and threats) analysis. • Complete balanced scorecard.	• Identify data sources, and inform them of the needs assessment. • Meet with sources, and provide data requirements. • Specify data collection instruments (surveys, interview protocols, and so on).	• Plan and organize meetings. • Prepare documents required for each subgroup. • Communicate with sponsor and partners. • Monitor progress and budget.

Week 3: Complete data collection.	• Ask partners to review work to date.	• Match strategic plan elements with data collection requirements (see current results column).	• Begin data collection. • Specify additional data requirements to match the indicators and measures identified for the desired results. • Complete data collection.	• Plan and organize meetings. • Prepare documents required for each subgroup. • Communicate with sponsor and partners. • Monitor progress and budget. • Assist in data collection and analysis.
Week 4: Analyze data.	• Ask partners to review work to date.	• Add indicators and measures where necessary to the desired results.	• Analyze data. • Match data for current results with that of desired results to identify gaps (that is, needs).	• Plan and organize meetings. • Prepare documents required for each subgroup. • Communicate with sponsor and partners. • Monitor progress and budget. • Assist in data collection and analysis.
Week 5: Analyze needs and identify potential solutions.	• Review data and analysis. • Review draft findings.	• Prepare draft report of desired results (including alignments with current processes, structures, and resources).	• Analyze needs for causal factors. • Complete initial needs analysis to define leading factors contributing to needs.	• Plan and organize meetings. • Prepare documents required for each subgroup. • Communicate with sponsor and partners.

(continued on next page)

	Partner commitment tasks	Planning tasks (desired results)	Data collection tasks (current results)	Process management tasks
			• Identify at least two alternative activities for improving results in relation to each need.	• Monitor progress and budget. • Assist in preparing draft reports.
Week 6: Decide what to do.	• Work with partners to prioritize needs. • Work with partners to identify and prioritize alternative activities for improving performance. • Prepare a draft report of findings—both current results and gaps.			• Plan and organize meetings. • Prepare documents required for each subgroup. • Communicate with sponsor and partners. • Monitor progress and budget.
Post-needs assessment	• Develop required change strategy. • Conduct performance analysis to define the characteristics of the selected activities for improving performance. • Define the performance-improvement process, and establish monitoring and evaluation plans.			• Plan for the dissemination of needs assessment findings. • Assist in writing final reports and creating presentations about the findings. • Evaluate the success of the needs assessment.

A Guide to Assessing Needs

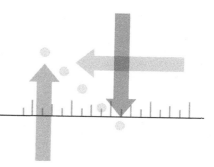

Tools and Techniques to Consider

If you want to collect information about . . .	And if you want to use that information to . . .	Then you might want to consider . . .
Community needs	Identify needs.	✓ Systematic document review ✓ Focus groups ✓ Dual-response surveys ✓ Performance pyramid ✓ Future wheel ✓ Fishbone diagrams ✓ World Café ✓ Nominal group technique
	Prioritize needs.	✓ Root cause analysis ✓ SWOT+ ✓ Scenarios ✓ Concept mapping ✓ Consensus building ✓ Nominal group technique ✓ Pair-wise comparison

(continued on next page)

If you want to collect information about . . .	And if you want to use that information to . . .	Then you might want to consider . . .
Community needs *(continued)*	Select potential solutions.	✓ Multicriteria analysis ✓ Pair-wise comparison ✓ Performance pyramid ✓ Scenarios ✓ Nominal group technique
Needs of specific clients	Identify needs.	✓ Systematic document review ✓ Interviews ✓ Focus groups ✓ Delphi ✓ Dual-response surveys ✓ World Café ✓ Nominal group technique ✓ Performance pyramid ✓ Future wheel
	Prioritize needs.	✓ Interviews ✓ Focus groups ✓ Root cause analysis ✓ SWOT+ ✓ 2 × 2 matrix decision aids ✓ Scenarios ✓ Concept mapping ✓ Nominal group technique ✓ Pair-wise comparison ✓ Tabletop analysis
	Select potential solutions.	✓ Multicriteria analysis ✓ Performance pyramid ✓ Scenarios ✓ Consensus building ✓ Nominal group technique

If you want to collect information about . . .	And if you want to use that information to . . .	Then you might want to consider . . .
Organizational needs	Identify needs.	✓ Survey ✓ Focus groups ✓ Systematic document review ✓ Dual-response surveys ✓ World Café ✓ Nominal group technique ✓ Performance pyramid ✓ Fault tree diagrams ✓ Future wheel
	Prioritize needs.	✓ Root cause analysis ✓ SWOT+ ✓ 2 × 2 matrix decision aids ✓ Scenarios ✓ Concept mapping ✓ Nominal group technique ✓ Tabletop analysis
	Select potential solutions.	✓ Multicriteria analysis ✓ Pair-wise comparison ✓ Nominal group technique ✓ Performance pyramid ✓ Scenarios
Team performance	Identify needs.	✓ Interviews ✓ Focus groups ✓ Guided expert review ✓ Systematic document review ✓ Cognitive task analysis ✓ Task analysis ✓ Case studies ✓ Performance pyramid ✓ Root cause analysis ✓ Fault tree diagrams ✓ Fishbone diagrams

(continued on next page)

If you want to collect information about . . .	And if you want to use that information to . . .	Then you might want to consider . . .
Team performance *(continued)*	Prioritize needs.	✓ Root cause analysis ✓ 2 × 2 matrix decision aids ✓ Scenarios ✓ Concept mapping ✓ Nominal group technique ✓ Tabletop analysis ✓ Pair-wise comparison
	Select potential solutions.	✓ Multicriteria analysis ✓ Pair-wise comparison ✓ Performance pyramid ✓ Scenarios ✓ Consensus building ✓ Nominal group technique
Individual performance	Identify needs.	✓ Interviews ✓ Cognitive task analysis ✓ Performance observations ✓ Guided expert review ✓ Systematic document review ✓ Performance pyramid ✓ Fault tree diagrams ✓ Fishbone diagrams
	Prioritize needs.	✓ Root cause analysis ✓ Scenarios ✓ Concept mapping ✓ Tabletop analysis
	Select potential solutions.	✓ Multicriteria analysis ✓ Pair-wise comparison ✓ Guided expert review ✓ Performance pyramid ✓ Scenarios

A Guide to Assessing Needs

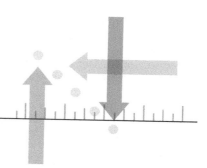

Guide to Selecting Tools and Techniques (Applied Multicriteria Analysis)

Selecting which tools and techniques you should use during your needs assessment will depend on several factors. By rating each of the factors individually, you can attain a quality estimate of which tools and techniques are going to be of the most value. There are, unfortunately, no scientific formulas that guarantee success although assessing each of the factors will help you decide which tools and techniques will be most helpful (see tables A.5.1 and A.5.2).

Appropriateness

The appropriateness of the tool or technique depends on the information you require and the decisions you are hoping to make on the basis of your needs assessment. For instance, ask yourself these questions:

✓ How effective is the tool or technique for collecting the necessary information or making a decision?

Table A.5.1   Tools and Techniques Selection Rating

Instructions: Rate each selection factor on a scale of 1 to 10, with 1 representing the minimum and 10 representing the maximum value for each factor. For example, if using the card sorting tool is highly appropriate for facilitating a decision, it would get a score of 9 or 10; likewise, if you have little experience in conducting a card sort, then it may be rated as a 2 or 3.

Tools and techniques being considered	Selection factor (scored on a scale of 1 to 10)					Total	Rank
	Appropriateness	Costs and benefits	Feasibility	Acceptability	Experience		

Source: Based on Stolovich and Keeps (2009).

Table A.5.2   Example of the Tools and Techniques Selection Rating

Tools and techniques being considered	Selection factor (scored on a scale of 1 to 10)					Total	Rank
	Appropriateness	Costs and benefits	Feasibility	Acceptability	Experience		
World Café	4	7	7	5	4	27	4
Fishbone diagram	6	7	6	5	4	28	3
Focus group	7	5	7	9	5	33	1
Interview	7	4	5	9	6	31	2

Note: Consider applying the techniques of multicriteria analysis to your decisions about which tools and techniques to use in your needs assessment. All you have to do is apply a weight to each selection factor to help you prioritize those that are the most essential to your decisions regarding which tools and techniques to use in your needs assessment. To do so, you simply weight each of the five selection factors (appropriateness, costs and benefits, feasibility, and so on) on a scale of 1 to 10, with 10 being the most critical factors in your decision. Then divide each weighting by 50. For instance, if acceptability to participants is especially important within your organization, then you may wish to weight the factor with an 8 (8 ÷ 50 = .16). Score each of the tools and techniques being considered, and multiply all of the scored items by the factor weighting. For instance, in this example, World Café had an acceptability score of 5, and acceptability had a weight of .16. Thus, the final score of the acceptability of the World Café technique is 4.84.

✓ How efficient is the tool or technique for helping make a decision?

✓ Does the tool or technique complement the other activities you are planning to use to collect information or to make a decision during your needs assessment?

Costs and Benefits

The ratio of costs to benefits can help you determine (a) when simple needs assessment tools or techniques may make more sense than complex processes or (b) when the value of benefits suggest that you should use more sophisticated processes. For instance, ask yourself these questions:

✓ What are the potential costs associated with the tool or technique (for instance, time, money, opportunity costs)?

✓ How do those costs relate to the potential value that the tool or technique can add to your needs assessment (for example, generating buy-in, involving stakeholders, collecting more accurate information)?

Feasibility

Routinely, even the best-suited tools and techniques for your needs assessment may not be feasible in the organizational environment. Be aware of the many factors that can influence the feasibility of choosing one tool or technique over another. For instance, ask yourself these questions:

✓ How likely is it that the tool or technique can be applied successfully?

✓ Will social, political, technological, cultural, or legal factors potentially limit the use of the tool or technique during your needs assessment?

Acceptability

Whichever needs assessment tools and techniques you choose to use in your assessment, they must also be viewed as acceptable by the multiple partners who are part of your assessment effort. For instance, ask yourself these questions:

✓ Will the tool or technique be acceptable to those who will participate in the process?

✓ Will internal and external partners view the use of the tool or technique as an acceptable way to collect valid information or to make informed decisions?

Experience

Successfully using any of the needs assessment tools and techniques gets easier with experience. Although you don't have to be an expert in data collection or decision making to complete a useful needs assessment, the more experience you have, the easier it will be. For instance, ask yourself these questions:

✓ Do you or other members of your needs assessment team have experience in applying the tools or techniques being considered?

✓ Will you feel comfortable facilitating the use of the tool or technique during the needs assessment?

Reference

Stolovich, Harold, and Erica Keeps. 2009. "Selecting Solutions to Improve Workplace Performance." In 2007 *ASTD Handbook for Workplace Learning Professionals,* edited by E. Beich. Alexandria, VA: ASTD Press.

Three-Phase Needs Assessment Process with Additional Details

This process is an expanded version of the three-phase needs assessment process introduced in section 2 (see page 50) as a useful guide for planning larger-scale assessments.[1] Each of the three phases is aligned with identifying, analyzing, and deciding as key tasks in completing any needs assessment, but the three-phase approach adds valuable details for managing an assessment from beginning to end. Use this guide in conjunction with the other implementation guides and tools included in appendix A to lead your next needs assessment.

Phase 1. Preassessment

The purpose of this phase is to determine the overall scope and plan for the assessment and to ensure that implementation goes smoothly and generates justifiable information so you can make decisions.

1. With the sponsors of the assessment, determine the overall scope of the needs assessment.

    a. Determine what questions the needs assessment is intended to help answer.

    b. Or determine what decisions the results of the assessment are intended to inform.

2. Depending on the scope of the assessment, identify the primary performance issues that are leading to the needs assessment.*

   a. Much of the initial information on performance issues will be generated through informal or formal discussions among stakeholders. These discussions may occur in, for example, community assemblies, organizational retreats, or more meetings.

   b. Many documents can be useful in identifying the issues: strategic plans, annual reports, audits, oversight reviews, performance appraisals, and others. Depending on the focus of your organization, issues—such as missed deadlines, low productivity, increasing employee absenteeism, lagging customer satisfaction, a jump in client complaints, new policies, declining market share, increasing poverty, or spread of disease—could be identified.

3. Define what data and information are required from the needs assessment to adequately inform decisions. This step may require that you collect some preliminary information from key stakeholders and partners to be able to define objectives and select methods.*

4. With others, create a management plan for the needs assessment. See the checklist in Appendix A.2 for more details.

   a. Include what the project objectives are for the needs assessment and how those objectives are aligned with other strategic, tactical, and operational goals of the organization.

   b. Include the preliminary scope, context, boundaries, partners, time line, and budget for the needs assessment.

   c. Include the data that are required, the sources of information to be contacted, and the tools and techniques to be used to collect information.

   d. Include which tools and techniques will be used to analyze the data in order to create useful information and to make justifiable decisions.

   e. Include the political, technological, legal, economic, or social factor of the pending assessment that may realistically limit the results that can be accomplished, as well as contingency plans for significant events that may alter your assessment.

5. Validate your management plan for the needs assessment with the assessment's sponsors, colleagues, peers, clients, partners, and others who will have a stake in the success of the assessment.

Phase 2. Assessment

The purpose of this phase is to implement the assessment in a methodologically sound manner that generates justifiable information to make decisions.

1. Make arrangements to collect the necessary information from the various sources; schedule interviews, create surveys, arrange focus groups, collect documents to be reviewed, train group facilitators when necessary, schedule performance observations, and so forth.

2. Review protocols, questionnaires, and other information-collection tools to verify that you capture the necessary information regarding both the current achievements and the desired accomplishments.*

   a. Ensure that data collection provides you with adequate information on both current and desired performance so that gaps in results (or needs) can be measured and prioritized. It is frequently tempting to focus on collecting information about how to solve problems or to implement predefined solutions, but that information is best left out of your needs assessment until needs are adequately identified and compared.

   b. Include in your review a mock analysis of the information that you might collect from sources. This mock analysis, or simulated report of findings, can identify weaknesses in your information-collection techniques that can be addressed before the actual implementation of the assessment.

3. Collect information using a variety of tools and techniques, and include sources that represent varying perspectives on the primary performance issues.

   a. Continue to focus your needs assessment on performance gaps (or needs) rather than on collecting information about potential causes or plausible solutions. If you do identify these items during your information collection, take notes on the good ideas so you can keep them for later. Inevitably, many respondents during your data collection will want to focus on offering plausible solutions, but for your assessment, you should redirect conversations to address all aspects of needs (such as existing performance issues, desired results, current results, and so on).

   b. Because it is easy to fall into the trap of discussing solutions rather than performance results, it is important to have structured (or at least semistructured) instruments or protocols to follow.*

4. Define needs that are based on performance gaps between current and desired results.

   a. Each need should have one or more indicators or performance measures that illustrate the size, scope, distinguishing characteristics, and relative importance of the need. To the extent possible, the comparison of information related to current performance and desired results should be measured on the same scale. For example, a good comparator for current and desired performance would be the number of HIV/AIDS patients receiving medicine versus the organization's objective for the number of patients to receive medicine.

   b. In contrast, if your current performance measurement involves the number of HIV/AIDS patients served, then an example of an imbalanced measurement relationship would be using the percentage of new HIV/AIDS cases in a country or region to determine the desired performance. Both could be useful measurements, but—to the extent possible—you want to have "apples to apples" comparisons. That is, we must measure the same phenomena for the current and desired situations. At the same time, you are not restricted to having a single type of measurement, and it is possible—and often good practice—to have multiple *sets* of measurements for both current and desired performance.*

5. Establish an initial prioritization of needs on the basis of size, scope, distinguishing characteristics, and relative importance.*

   a. Rough estimates of the costs to close each performance gap, in comparison with the costs associated with not closing the performance gap, can be useful in establishing priorities. Costs are not restricted to financial costs; they can also be costs related to time, socioeconomic factors, political desirability, and so on. Rough estimates can be used here. In the next step, you will collect additional information to provide more detailed justification for establishing priorities.

   b. Work with internal and external organizational partners to review the information collected during the needs assessment and to set priorities. Decision-making techniques, such as nominal group or Delphi (see section 3), can be useful in setting priorities.

6. For the highest-priority needs, create a plan for collecting information about the factors that are likely leading to the performance gaps.*

a. Analyze each need for the causal factors (or root causes) that are linked to less-than-desired performance. In addition to seeking out gaps, also take an *appreciative inquiry* perspective about the needs so you can assess what is already working to accomplish desired results. In its simplest terms, appreciative inquiry is an approach that focuses on determining what works instead of the more typical approach of looking for problems. By building on what works and not simply focusing on problems, you can pursue opportunities where success is likely to occur.

b. Categorize potential causal factors to provide structure to your analysis when multiple types of causes exist. Common organizational factors include motivation, self-concept, workforce capacity, knowledge and skills of individuals, clearly defined expectations, appropriate and timely performance feedback, availability of resources, processes, organizational culture, incentives, rewards, recognition, and alignment of individual performance objectives with organizational vision and mission. Besides these factors, consider additional types for your situation, context, and organization.

(1) Use the performance pyramid as a framework, for instance, to identify potential causal factors associated with each need (see page 236 in section 3B).

(2) For each component of the pyramid, collect information to determine if factors within that area are linked to discrepancies in performance.

7. Collect information regarding the causal factors (or root causes) associated with priority needs.

a. For each potential causal factor that you identify, use the appropriate tools and techniques to collect information that illustrates its potential effect on the desired performance. To collect the necessary information for determining the association of the causal factors with the identified needs, use document reviews, task analysis, job analysis, performance observations, dual-response surveys, focus groups, and other techniques.

b. Rarely will a priority need be associated with only a single causal factor. Therefore, to be sure that your assessment includes multiple perspectives, use a variety of techniques to collect information, and don't rely exclusively on either soft data (which are not independently verifiable) or hard data (which are independently verifiable).

8. Analyze and synthesize the useful information you have collected.*

   a. Review the data from multiple perspectives, and also ask partners in the assessment to examine the data so you ensure that the analysis or synthesis does not represent potential biases about the needs, wants, or potential solutions.

   b. Analyze and synthesize the information you have collected using appropriate quantitative (mathematical or statistical) or qualitative (described in terms of words or images rather than numbers) techniques.

   c. Reflect on your findings, and apply your professional judgment.

   d. Include in your analysis the descriptions of possible improvement activities (solutions)—which were identified during the assessment—for each need.

9. For each priority need and its associated causal factors, identify multiple performance-improvement activities that, in combination, could address the complete need.*

   a. Identify at least two improvement activities linked to each recognized causal factor. Many activities will address several causal factors. For instance, a mentoring program may address causal factors associated with motivation, feedback, expectations, and recognition. Likewise, having identified options, you can compare alternatives by effectiveness, efficiency, and cost-benefit ratios.

   b. Verify the alignment of possible improvement activities with the identified causal factors and the performance gap. In the end, not every causal factor will be addressed with a unique improvement activity, but you should explore options for each identified causal factor so that you can find synergies and overlaps that may be useful when evaluating your options.

   c. As a useful starting place for establishing priorities, estimate the costs to close each performance gap in comparison with the costs associated with *not* closing the performance gap. More detailed prioritizations will also require estimating the costs of alternative activities. For example, to address employee motivation issues, estimate the cost of offering a training program versus offering a mentoring program versus offering a bonus program.

10. Evaluate each potential performance-improvement activity to assess its value to your improvement effort.*

A Guide to Assessing Needs

a. Single solutions or improvement activities rarely accomplish sustainable improvements in performance; therefore, you should work to identify an appropriate combination of activities that will accomplish desired results. Evaluate the likely effectiveness and efficiency of each proposed activity as well as of differing combinations of activities.

b. Explore the potential suboptimization of activities—and combinations of activities—to ensure that improvements in one aspect of performance do not come at the cost of decreasing performance in other areas.

11. Use the information to prioritize needs and to make recommendations regarding the improvement efforts that will best achieve desired results within the given context.

a. Consider the long-term goals and objectives of the organization, employees, clients, countries, and others when setting priorities.

b. Take into account the social, political, technological, cultural, legal, and ethical factors that influence setting priorities.

c. With internal and external partners, use decision-making tools and techniques to make decisions and recommendations for what actions should be taken.

Phase 3. Postassessment

The purpose of this phase is to underscore that the assessment does not end once priorities have been set. Information from the assessment must be shared and used to guide decisions. Additionally, situations change, and you should routinely collect and assess information as part of ongoing monitoring and evaluation. This activity supports the implementation of recommendations and offers opportunities to take corrective actions where necessary.

1. Summarize your recommendations in a needs assessment report or presentation.

2. Communicate your findings to your stakeholders. For larger-scale assessments, this step may involve developing a dissemination strategy, communication strategies, and assessment reports and presentations. It is also good practice to share findings with people who provided information and other inputs for your assessment.

3. Integrate postassessment monitoring and evaluation activities into recommended activities that will be undertaken.

4. Evaluate your needs assessment process to determine if changes should be made before you complete your next assessment.

Notes

*Typically, a good number of dependencies are identified in any needs assessment plan. The items noted with asterisks are tasks in a dependent relationship that must be completed before a subsequent task can begin.

1. The three-phase needs assessment process is based on Jim Altschuld's 2010 book series, *The Needs Assessment Kit*, in which he provides guidance for managing an assessment through each of the three phases.

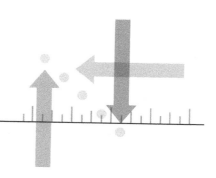

Abbreviations

CTA	cognitive task analysis
EPSS	electronic performance support system
FTA	fault tree analysis
HIV/AIDS	human immunodeficiency virus/acquired immune deficiency syndrome
LDC	least-developed country
M&E	monitoring and evaluation
MDG	Millennium Development Goals
NATO	North Atlantic Treaty Organization
NGO	nongovernmental organization
OECD	Organisation for Economic Co-operation and Development
PERT	Program Evaluation Review Technique
RCA	root cause analysis
SC	steering committee
SMART	Simple Multi-Attribute Ranking Technique
SP	strategic plans
SWOT	strengths, weaknesses, opportunities, and threats
WBI	World Bank Institute
WI	what is
WSB	what should be

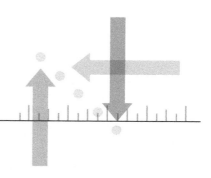

References and Recommended Readings

The following references and related readings are compiled from the references and notes that appear throughout the book.

Altschuld, James W. 2003/2004. "Emerging Dimensions of Needs Assessment." *Performance Improvement* 43 (1): 10–15.

——, ed. 2010. *The Needs Assessment Kit*. Thousand Oaks, CA: Sage Publications. [A 5-volume series with individual titles]

- Altschuld, James W., and David D. Kumar. 2010. *Needs Assessment Phase I: An Overview* (Book 1 of *Needs Assessment Kit*). Thousand Oaks, CA: Sage Publications.

- Altschuld, James W., and J. Nicholls Eastmond Jr. 2010. *Needs Assessment Phase II: Getting Started* (Book 2 of *Needs Assessment Kit*). Thousand Oaks, CA: Sage Publications.

- Altschuld, James W. 2010. *Needs Assessment Phase III: Collecting Data* (Book 3 of *Needs Assessment Kit*). Thousand Oaks, CA: Sage Publications.

- Altschuld, James W., and Jeffry L. White. 2010. *Needs Assessment Phase IV: Analysis and Prioritization* (Book 4 of *Needs Assessment Kit*). Thousand Oaks, CA: Sage Publications.

- Stevahn, Laurel A., and Jean A. King. 2010. *Needs Assessment Phase V: Taking Action for Change* (Book 5 of *Needs Assessment Kit*). Thousand Oaks, CA: Sage Publications.

Altschuld, James W., and David D. Kumar. 2004. "Needs Assessment." In *Encyclopedia of Evaluation*, edited by S. Mathison, 276. Thousand Oaks, CA: Sage Publications.

Altschuld, James W., and T. L. Lepicki. 2009. "Needs Assessment in Human Performance Interventions." In *Handbook of Improving Performance in the Workplace*. Vol. 2: *Selecting and Implementing Performance Interventions*, edited by Ryan Watkins and Doug Leigh, 771–91. San Francisco: Wiley/Pfeiffer, and Silver Spring, MD: International Society for Performance Improvement.

Altschuld, James W., and Belle Ruth Witkin. 2000. *From Needs Assessment to Action: Transforming Needs into Solution Strategies*. Thousand Oaks, CA: Sage Publications.

Beach, E. K. 1982. "Johari's Window as a Framework for Needs Assessment." *Journal of Continuing Education in Nursing* 13 (1): 28–32.

Borcherding, K., T. Eppel, and D. von Winterfeldt. 1991. "Comparison of Weighting Judgments in Multiattribute Utility Measurement." *Management Science* 37 (12): 1603–19.

Brethower, Dale, and Karolyn Smalley. 1998. *Performance-Based Instruction: Linking Training to Business Results*. San Francisco: Jossey-Bass/Pfeiffer.

Brown, Juanita, and David Isaacs. 2005. *The World Café: Shaping Our Futures through Conversations That Matter*. San Francisco, CA: Berrett-Koehler Publishers.

Brown, Juanita, David Isaacs, Nancy Margulies, and Gary Warhaftig. 1999. "The World Café: Catalyzing Large-Scale Collective Learning." *Leverage Magazine* 33: 1–2.

Brown, Juanita, David Isaacs, Eric Vogt, and Nancy Margulies. 2002. "Strategic Questioning: Engaging People's Best Thinking." *The Systems Thinker* 13 (9).

Clark, Richard E., David F. Feldon, Jeroen J. G. van Merriënboer, Kenneth A. Yates, and Sean Early. 2008. "Cognitive Task Analysis." In *Handbook of Research on Educational Communications and Technology*, 3rd ed., edited by J. Michael Spector, M. David Merrill, Jeroen J. G. van Merriënboer, and Marcy P. Driscoll, 577–94. Mahwah, NJ: Lawrence Erlbaum Associates.

Fitz-Enz, Jac. 2009. *The ROI of Human Capital: Measuring the Economic Value of Employee Performance*. 2009. New York: AMACOM.

Gilbert, Thomas F. 2007. *Human Competence: Engineering Worthy Performance*. Tribute ed. San Francisco: Pfeiffer.

Greer, Michael. 1999. "Planning and Managing Human Performance Technology Projects." In *Handbook of Human Performance Technology: Improving Individual Organizational Performance Worldwide*, edited by Harold D. Stolovitch and Erica J. Keeps, 96–121. San Francisco: Pfeiffer.

Gupta, Kavita, Catherine M. Sleezer, and Darlene F. Russ-Eft. 2007. *A Practical Guide to Needs Assessment*. San Francisco: Pfeiffer.

Harless, Joseph H. 1975. "An Ounce of Analysis Is Worth a Pound of Objectives." Newnan, GA: Harless Performance Guild.

Hung, Hsin-Ling, James W. Altschuld, and Y-F. Lee. 2008. "Methodological and Conceptual Issues Confronting a Cross-Country Delphi Study of Educational Program Evaluation." *Evaluation and Program Planning* 31 (2): 191–98.

Jackson, Kristin M., and William M. K. Trochim. 2002. "Concept Mapping as an Alternative Approach for the Analysis of Open-Ended Survey Responses."

Organizational Research Methods 5 (October): 307–36. http://www.social researchmethods.net/mapping/mapping.htm.

Jonassen, David H., Wallace H. Hannum, and Martin Tessmer. 1989. *Handbook of Task Analysis Procedures*. Westport, CT: Praeger Publishers.

Kaufman, Roger. 1992. *Strategic Planning Plus*. Thousand Oaks, CA: Sage Publishing.

———. 1998. *Strategic Thinking: A Guide to Identifying and Solving Problems*. Rev. ed. Washington, DC, and Arlington, VA: The International Society for Performance Improvement and the American Society for Training and Development.

———. 2000. *Mega Planning: Practical Tools for Organizational Success*. Thousand Oaks, CA: Sage Publications.

———. 2006. *Change, Choices, and Consequences: A Guide to Mega Thinking*. Amherst, MA: HRD Press.

Kaufman, Roger, and F. W. English. 1979. *Needs Assessment: Concept and Application*. Englewood Cliffs, NJ: Educational Technology Publications.

Kaufman, Roger, Ingrid Guerra-López, Ryan Watkins, and Doug Leigh. 2008. *The Assessment Book: Applied Strategic Thinking and Performance Improvement Through Self-Assessments*. Amherst, MA: HRD Press.

Kaufman, Roger, Hugh Oakley-Brown, Ryan Watkins, and Doug Leigh. 2003. *Strategic Planning for Success: Aligning People, Performance, and Payoffs*. San Francisco: Jossey-Bass.

Kaufman, Roger, A. Rojas, and H. Mayer. 1993. *Needs Assessment: A User's Guide*. Englewood Cliffs, NJ: Educational Technology Publishers.

Kaufman, Roger, and Ryan Watkins. 1996. "Mega Planning: A Framework for Integrating Strategic Planning, Needs Assessment, Quality Management, Benchmarking, and Reengineering." In *The HR Handbook*, Vol. 1, edited by J. E. Jones and E. Biech. Amherst MA: HRD Press.

Kaufman, Roger, Ryan Watkins, and Doug Leigh. 2001. *Useful Educational Results: Defining, Prioritizing, and Achieving*. Lancaster, PA: Proactive Publishing.

Kellogg Foundation. 2006. "Free Guide for Developing Logic Models." http://www.wkkf.org/knowledge-center/resources/2006/02/WK-Kellogg-Foundation-Logic-Model-Development-Guide.aspx.

Klinder, Bernie. 2005. "Step-by-Step Guide: 12 Steps to Project Management Success." http://search winit.techtarget.com/news/1063152/Step-by-Step-Guide-12-steps-to-project-management-success.

Lee, Y.-F., James W. Altschuld, and J. L. White. 2007a. "Problems in Needs Assessment Data: Discrepancy Analysis." *Evaluation and Program Planning* 30 (3): 258–66.

———. 2007b. "Effects of the Participation of Multiple Stakeholders in Identifying and Interpreting Perceived Needs." *Evaluation and Program Planning* 30 (1): 1–9.

Leigh, Doug. 2003. "Worthy Performance, Redux." http://www.performance xpress.org/0306.

———. 2006. "SWOT Analysis." In *The Handbook of Human Performance Technology*, edited by J. Pershing, 1089–1108. San Francisco, CA: Jossey-Bass/Pfeiffer.

Leigh, Doug, Ryan Watkins, W. Platt, and Roger Kaufman. 2000. "Alternate Models of Needs Assessment: Selecting the Right One for Your Organization." *Human Resource Development Quarterly* 11(1): 87–93.

Lowy, Alex, and Phil Hood. 2004. *The Power of the 2 × 2 Matrix: Using 2 × 2 Thinking to Solve Business Problems and Make Better Decisions*. San Francisco: Jossey-Bass.

Mager, Robert F., and Peter Pipe. 1997. *Analyzing Performance Problems*. 3rd ed. Atlanta, GA: Center for Effective Performance.

McClelland, Samuel B. 1994a. "Training Needs Assessment Data-Gathering Methods: Part 2—Individual Interviews." *Journal of European Industrial Training* 18 (2): 27–31.

——. 1994b. "Training Needs Assessment Data-Gathering Methods: Part 3—Focus Groups." *Journal of European Industrial Training* 18 (3): 29–32.

——. 1994c. "Training Needs Assessment Data-Gathering Methods: Part 4—Onsite Observations." *Journal of European Industrial Training* 18 (5): 4–7.

Mintzberg, Henry. 2000. *The Rise and Fall of Strategic Planning*. New York: Free Press.

——. 2008. *Tracking Strategies: Toward a General Theory of Strategy Formation*. New York: Oxford University Press.

Moore, Shelley. "Difference Between Gantt Charts and PERT Charts." 1999–2011. In *eHow Money*. Demand Media Inc. http://www.ehow.com/facts_4844081_between-gantt-charts-pert-charts.html.

Moseley, J., and M. Heaney. 1994. "Needs Assessments across Disciplines." *Performance Improvement Quarterly* 7 (1): 60–79.

Nutt, Paul. 2008. "Investigating the Success of Decision-Making Processes." *Journal of Management Studies* 45 (2): 425–55.

Organisation for Economic Co-operation and Development (OECD). 2011. *DAC Criteria for Evaluating Development Assistance*. http://www.oecd.org/document/22/0,2340, en_2649_34435_2086550_1_1_1_1,00.html.

Paradies, Mark, and Linda Unger. 2000. *Tap Root: The System for Root Cause Analysis, Problem Investigation, and Proactive Improvement*. Knoxville, TN: System Improvements.

Rooney, James, and Lee N. Vanden Heuvel. 2004. "Root Cause Analysis for Beginners." *Quality Basics* (July): 45–53. Milwaukee, WI: American Society for Quality.

Rossett, Allison. 1987. *Training Needs Assessment*. Englewood Cliffs, NJ: Educational Technology Publishing Co.

——. 1990. "Overcoming Obstacles to Needs Assessment." *Training* 27: 36–41.

——. 1999. *First Things Fast*. San Francisco, CA: Jossey-Bass.

Roth, R., F. Field, and J. Clark. 2011 "Multi-Attribute Utility Analysis." http://msl1.mit.edu/maua_paper.pdf.

Schwartz, Barry. 2003. *The Paradox of Choice: Why More Is Less*. New York: Harper Perennial.

Silberman, Mel. 2003. *2003 Training and Performance Sourcebook*. Princeton, NJ: Active Training.

Sleezer, C. 1992. "Needs Assessment: Perspectives from the Literature." *Performance Improvement Quarterly* 5 (2): 34–46.

Stolovich, Harold, and Erica Keeps. 2009. "Selecting Solutions to Improve Workplace Performance." In 2007 *ASTD Handbook for Workplace Learning Professionals*, edited by E. Beich. Alexandria, VA: ASTD Press.

Triner, Don, Andrew Greenberry, and Ryan Watkins. 1996. "Training Needs Assessment: A Contradiction in Terms." *Educational Technology* 36 (6): 51–55.

Trochim, William. 1989. "Concept Mapping: Soft Science or Hard Art?" In a special issue of *Evaluation and Program Planning* 12 (1): 87–110. http://www.socialresearchmethods.net/research/epp2/epp2.htm.

Trochim, William, and Mary Kane. 2005. "Concept Mapping: An Introduction to Structured Conceptualization in Health Care." *International Journal for Quality in Health Care* 17 (3): 187–91.

Ulschak, Francis L. 1983. *Human Resource Development: The Theory and Practice of Needs Assessment*. Reston, VA: Reston Publishing.

United Nations. 2004. "Needs Assessment Report on the Millennium Development Goals." http://www.unmillenniumproject.org/documents/mp_ccspaper_jan1704.pdf.

Vesely, William E., F. F. Goldberg, Norman H. Roberts, and David F. Haasi. 1981. *Fault Tree Handbook (NUREG-0492)*. Washington, DC: U.S. Nuclear Regulatory Commission. http://www.nrc.gov/reading-rm/doc-collections/nuregs/staff/sr0492/.

Watkins, Ryan. 2005. *75 e-Learning Activities: Making Online Learning Interactive*. Hoboken, NJ: Wiley.

——. 2007. "Designing for Performance: Aligning All of Your HPT Decisions from Top to Bottom" (part 1 of 3). *Performance Improvement Journal* 46 (1): 7–13.

——. 2007. "Designing for Performance: Selecting Your Performance Technologies" (part 2 of 3). *Performance Improvement Journal* 46 (2): 9–15.

——. 2007. "Designing for Performance: Design, Develop, Improve" (part 3 of 3). *Performance Improvement Journal* 46 (3): 42–48.

——. 2007. *Performance by Design: The Systematic Selection, Design, and Development of Performance Technologies That Produce Useful Results*. Amherst, MA: HRD Press, and Silver Spring, MD: International Society for Performance Improvement.

Watkins, Ryan, and Mike Corry. 2010. *e-Learning Companion: A Student's Guide to Online Success*. 3rd ed. Boston: Wadsworth/CENGAGE Learning.

Watkins, Ryan, and Ingrid Guerra. 2003. "Assessing or Evaluation: Determining Which Approach Is Required." In *2003 Training and Performance Sourcebook*, edited by Mel Silberman. Princeton, NJ: Active Training.

Watkins, Ryan, and Roger Kaufman. 2002. "Assessing and Evaluating: Differentiating Perspectives." *Performance Improvement Journal* 41 (2): 22–28.

Watkins, Ryan, and Doug Leigh, eds. 2010. *Handbook for Improving Performance in the Workplace*. Vol. 2: *Selecting and Implementing Performance Interventions*. San Francisco: Wiley/Pfeiffer, and Silver Spring, MD: International Society for Performance Improvement.

Watkins, Ryan, Doug Leigh, W. Platt, and Roger Kaufman. 1998. "Needs Assessment: A Digest, Review, and Comparison of Needs Assessment Literature." *Performance Improvement Journal* 37 (7): 40–53.

Watkins, Ryan, and John F. Wedman. 2003. "A Process for Aligning Performance Improvement Resources and Strategies." *Performance Improvement Journal* 42 (7): 9–17.

Wedman, John F. 2010. "Performance Pyramid Model." In *Handbook of Improving Performance in the Workplace*. Vol. 2: *Selecting and Implementing Performance Interventions*, edited by Ryan Watkins and Doug Leigh, 51–80. San Francisco: Wiley/Pfeiffer, and Silver Spring, MD: International Society for Performance Improvement.

Wedman, John F., and L. Diggs. 2001. "Identifying Barriers to Technology-Enhanced Learning Environments in Teacher Education." *Computers in Human Behavior* 17: 421–30.

Wedman, John F., and S. W. Graham. 1998. "Introducing the Concept of Performance Support Using the Performance Pyramid." *Journal of Continuing Higher Education* 46 (3): 8–20.

Wedman, John F., and M. Tessmer. 1993. "Instructional Designers' Decisions and Priorities: A Survey of Design Practice." *Performance Improvement Quarterly* 6 (2): 43–57.

Weller, Susan C., and A. Kimball Romney. 1988. *Systematic Data Collection*. Newbury Park, CA: Sage Publications.

Williams, Terry, and Knut Samset. 2010. "Issues in Front-End Decision Making on Projects." *Performance Management Journal* 41 (2): 38–49.

Witkin, Belle Ruth, and James W. Altschuld. 1995. *Planning and Conducting Needs Assessments: A Practical Guide*. Thousand Oaks, CA: Sage Publications.

World Café. 2008. "Café to Go." http://www.theworldcafe.com/pdfs/cafetogo.pdf.

Wright, P., and G. Geroy. 1992. "Needs Analysis Theory and the Effectiveness of Large-Scale Government-Sponsored Training Programmes: A Case Study." *Journal of Management Development* 11 (5): 16–27.

Zemke, R., and T. Kramlinger. 1982. *Figuring Things Out: A Trainer's Guide to Needs and Task Analysis*. Boston, MA: Addison-Wesley.

INDEX

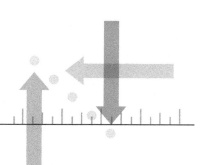

Boxes, figures, notes, and tables are indicated by *b, f, n,* and *t* following page numbers.

needs assessment and, 66
for nominal group technique, 167–69
for tabletop analysis, 182, 183, 185
for World Café, 136
for World Café approach, 133–34
fault tree analysis (FTA), 214–19
advantages and disadvantages of, 215–16
needs assessment applications of, 214–15
performance pyramids and, 241
process overview for, 216–18, 218f
purpose of, 214
root cause analysis and, 211
tips for success, 218
websites for, 219
feasibility in needs assessment, 271
feedback. *See* expectations and feedback
first-order effects, 231, 232, 233
fishbone diagrams, 197–201
advantages and disadvantages of, 197–98
data collection and, 8
needs assessment applications of, 197
process overview for, 198–200, 199f
purpose of, 197
root cause analysis and, 211
tips for success, 200
websites for, 201
focus groups, 95–105
advantages and disadvantages of, 96
needs assessment applications of, 66, 95–96
process overview of, 97–99
purpose of, 95, 95b
qualitative data from, 69
sample outline and protocol, 101–5
closing, 102
introductions, 101–2
leading group, 102
opening remarks, 101
sample protocol, 103–5
tips for success, 99–100
websites for, 100
front-end analysis, 33
FTA. *See* fault tree analysis
future wheels, 228–35
advantages and disadvantages of, 229–30
needs assessment applications of, 228–29
process overview for, 230–33, 234f
alternative approaches, 233
implementation, 231–33
interpretation, 232–33
preparation, 230–31
purpose of, 228
tips for success, 233–35
websites for, 235

G

Gantt charts, 56, 78n9
gap analysis
for dual-response surveys, 119–22, 125–26
fault tree analysis and, 214
for fishbone diagrams, 198
needs, identification of, 30b
needs assessment and, 16–21, 17b, 47, 52, 60–61, 68, 72
performance pyramids and, 239, 241
root cause analysis and, 207, 211
for tabletop analysis, 184–85
for 2 × 2 matrix decision aids, 191, 193–94
Ghana, needs assessment in, 22b
group techniques. *See* focus groups; nominal group techniques
"groupthink," 96
guided expert reviews, 89–94
advantages and disadvantages of, 90–91
data collection and, 8
needs assessment applications of, 89–90
process overview of, 91–94
experts and, 91–93
getting started, 91
planning and conducting review, 93–94
purpose of, 89
tips for success, 94

H

hierarchical (sequential) analysis, 149, 150–51, 151f
hierarchical cluster analysis, 224
hypothetical tradeoffs, 174

I

idea-imposition decision making, 13n2
idea maps. *See* concept mapping
if–then analysis, 149, 151–52, 152f
impacts in logic models, 59, 60
improvement of performance. *See* performance improvements
incentives for participation, 143
individual performance, 23–24
inductive approaches to data analysis, 65
information gathering. *See* data collection methods
inputs in logic models, 60
Internet, 85, 118
interpretation and translation services, 94
interviews, 106–11
advantages and disadvantages of, 106–7
checklist sample, 110–11
cognitive task analysis and, 158–59, 160, 161

tools and techniques for, 11–12, 65–66, 269–76
typology of needs, 73, 74*t*, 78*n*19
Needs Assessment Kit (Altschuld), 5, 284*n*
NGOs (nongovernmental organizations), 47
nominal group techniques, 166–70
  advantages and disadvantages of, 167
  data collection and, 8
  Delphi technique and, 137
  information requirements for, 67
  needs assessment applications of, 166
  process overview for, 167–69
  purpose of, 166
  tips for success, 169
  websites for, 170
nongovernmental organizations (NGOs), 47, 84

O

open-ended questions, 108, 117, 140
Organisation for Economic Co-operation and Development (OECD), 35, 85*b*
organizational capacity, 27, 239, 243
organizational culture, 240
organizational performance, 23
outcomes in logic models, 59–60
outputs in logic models, 60

P

pair-wise comparison techniques, 187–90
  advantages and disadvantages of, 187–88
  needs and solutions, criteria for comparing, 188–89
  needs assessment applications of, 18, 72, 187
  process overview for, 188–90, 189*t*
  purpose of, 187
  sample template for, 190
  websites for, 190
partners, internal and external, 47, 56, 58. *See also* stakeholders
peer reviews, 91
performance analysis, 33. *See also* performance observations; performance pyramids
Performance-Based Instruction (Brethower & Smalley), 24
performance gaps. *See* gap analysis
performance improvements, 6–7, 6–7*f*, 22–25, 37*n*2
performance observations, 144–47. *See also* performance pyramids
  advantages and disadvantages of, 145
  needs assessment applications of, 144
  process overview for, 145–47

  purpose of, 144, 144*b*
  task analysis vs., 148
  tips for success, 147
  websites for, 147
performance pyramids, 236–44
  advantages and disadvantages of, 237
  continuous monitoring and, 240–41, 243
  expectations and feedback and, 239, 241, 242
  improvement activities samples for, 242–44
  knowledge and skills and, 236, 240, 243
  motivation and self-concept and, 237, 239, 241, 243
  needs analysis applications of, 238–41
  needs assessment applications of, 71, 236–37, 238*f*
  organizational capacity and, 239, 243
  organizational culture and, 240
  process overview for, 238
  purpose of, 236
  resources and, 240, 243
  rewards, incentives, and recognition and, 236, 239, 241, 243
  root cause analysis and, 211
  scenarios and, 204
  significant accomplishments and, 240
  solution identification applications for, 241–42
  tools, environment, and processes and, 236, 239–40, 242
  vision, mission, and objectives and, 240, 244
PERT charts, 56, 78*n*9
"positive examples" for document reviews, 87
presentations and reports, 75–77, 76*t*
pricing-out methods, 174
primary effects. *See* first-order effects
process tracing techniques, 163
protocols
  for cognitive task analysis, 161
  for document or data review, 87
  for experts, 92, 93
  for focus groups, 98, 101–5
  for interviews, 107–8, 113–15, 161
  for nominal group technique, 167
  for performance observations, 146
pyramid frameworks. *See* performance pyramids

Q

qualitative analysis techniques, 69
quantitative analysis software, 215

ECO-AUDIT
Environmental Benefits Statement

The World Bank is committed to preserving endangered forests and natural resources. The Office of the Publisher has chosen to print *A Guide to Assessing Needs* on recycled paper with 50 percent postconsumer fiber in accordance with the recommended standards for paper usage set by the Green Press Initiative, a nonprofit program supporting publishers in using fiber that is not sourced from endangered forests. For more information, visit www.greenpressinitiative.org.

Saved:
- 6 trees
- 2 million Btu of total energy
- 541 lb. of net greenhouse gases
- 2,443 gal. of waste water
- 155 lb. of solid waste